Edexcel GCSE
English and English Language
Access Teacher Guide

Written by:
Clare Constant
Janet Beauman
Alan Pearce
Dianne Excell
Simon Murison-Bowie

naldic EAL guidance

A PEARSON COMPANY

Published by Pearson Education Limited, a company incorporated in England and Wales, having its registered office at Edinburgh Gate, Harlow, Essex, CM20 2JE. Registered company number: 872828

Edexcel is a registered trademark of Edexcel Limited

Text © Pearson Education Limited 2010
EAL introduction © NALDIC 2010

The rights of Clare Constant, Janet Beauman and Alan Pearce to be identified as the authors of this work have been asserted by them in accordance with the Copyright, Designs and Patent Act 1988

First published 2010

12 11 10
10 9 8 7 6 5 4 3 2 1

British Library Cataloguing in Publication Data
A catalogue record for this book is available from the British Library

ISBN 978 1 84690 707 4

Typeset by Juice Creative Limited, Hertfordshire
Printed and bound in Great Britain by Ashford Colour Press Ltd, Gosport, Hants

Acknowledgements
We would like to thank Polly Hennessy and NALDIC, the subject association for English as an Additional Language for their invaluable help in the development of this material.

Cover image: *Front*. **iStockphoto:** Krzysztof Kwiatkowski.

All photo and text acknowledgements are in the 'credits' file on the accompanying CD-ROM.

Every effort has been made to contact copyright holders of material reproduced in this book. Any omissions will be rectified in subsequent printings if notice is given to the publishers.

Websites
The websites used in this book were correct and up to date at the time of publication. It is essential for tutors to preview each website before using it in class so as to ensure that the URL is still accurate, relevant and appropriate. We suggest that tutors bookmark useful websites and consider enabling students to access them through the school/college intranet.

Disclaimer
This material has been published on behalf of Edexcel and offers high-quality support for the delivery of Edexcel qualifications.
This does not mean that the material is essential to achieve any Edexcel qualification, nor does it mean that it is the only suitable material available to support any Edexcel qualification. Edexcel material will not be used verbatim in setting any Edexcel examination or assessment. Any resource lists produced by Edexcel shall include this and other appropriate resources.

Copies of official specifications for all Edexcel qualifications may be found on the Edexcel website: www.edexcel.com

Contents

Introduction

Lesson Plans

Controlled Assessment

Introduction

The Edexcel specifications

The new Edexcel GCSE English and English Language specifications have been developed for first teaching from September 2010. The key differences are that the specifications are unitised rather than linear, controlled assessment replaces coursework and there is a spoken language study in GCSE English Language for the first time.

Unit 1 English Today (common unit)

This controlled assessment unit is common to GCSE English and English Language. Section A assesses non-fiction reading, requiring students to respond to two texts they will have had the opportunity to study in advance. There will be a selection of printed and digital texts for you to select from. Section B is a writing task, on the same theme as the reading texts studied in Section A.

What is this unit worth?	20% of the total marks
How is it assessed?	Controlled assessment
What will students be assessed on?	There are two tasks: A – Reading response to non-fiction texts B – Non-fiction writing
How long do students have?	4 hours (2 hours for each task)
What is each task worth?	Each task is worth 10% of the total marks for the course
How are the tasks set?	Edexcel will release a new set of tasks each year before the start of the academic year. There will be two themes available to choose from. Centres may contextualise the task through their choice of texts to study.
What do students have to produce?	Students must produce two responses: A – One reading response, commenting on two on-screen or printed non-fiction texts on the same theme from the selection provided by Edexcel B – One piece of non-fiction writing on the same theme to the reading texts that have been studied

Unit 2 The Writer's Craft (English); The Writer's Voice (English Language)

There is some commonality between these two units, in that the writing task that students must complete in the exam is very similar.

Unit 2 in GCSE English

What is this unit worth?	40% of the total marks
How is it assessed?	Examination
How long is the exam?	2 hours
What is Section A of the exam?	A three-part question based on a Shakespeare play that students have studied
What is Section A worth?	10% of the total marks
What is Section B of the exam?	A three-part question based on a Different Cultures novel that students have studied
What is Section B worth?	10% of the total marks
What is Section C?	One practical writing task
What is Section C worth?	20% of the total marks

Unit 2 in GCSE English Language

What is this unit worth?	40% of the total marks
How is it assessed?	Examination
How long is the exam?	1 hour 45 minutes
What is Section A of the exam?	One question on the language features of a non-fiction text or Different Cultures novel that students have studied
What is Section A worth?	25% of the total marks
What is Section B of the exam?	One practical writing task
What is Section B worth?	15% of the total marks

Unit 3 Creative English (English); Spoken Language (English Language)

Both of these controlled assessment units include the assessment of Speaking and Listening, which remains very similar to that in previous specifications. In GCSE English, students will also be assessed on poetry and creative writing. In GCSE English Language, students complete a spoken language study and writing for the spoken voice task.

Unit 3 in GCSE English

What is this unit worth?	40% of the total marks
How is it assessed?	Controlled assessment
What will students be assessed on?	There are three areas: a) Speaking and Listening b) Poetry Reading c) Creative Writing
How long do students have?	Up to 4 hours for the poetry reading and creative writing tasks (2 hours for each task)
What is each task worth?	Speaking and Listening is worth 20% of the total marks Each of the other two tasks is worth 10% of the total marks
How are the tasks set?	• For Speaking and Listening, Edexcel will provide exemplar tasks which centres can adapt to suit their own students. • For the Poetry Task, Edexcel will set the task, students then respond to the literary heritage poem set in the task and two other poems from one collection in the anthology. • For the Creative Writing task, Edexcel will set the tasks for students to complete.
What do students have to produce?	• For Speaking and Listening there are three equally weighted activities: a) communicating and adapting language b) interacting and responding c) creating and sustaining roles • For Poetry, students will produce one response to a reading task, in which they respond to one literary heritage poem and draw on at least two additional poems from the anthology collection they have studied. Students may produce a written, digital media or multimodal response. • For Creative Writing, students will produce one written response to a writing task and stimulus set by Edexcel.

Unit 3 in GCSE English Language

What is this unit worth?	40% of the total marks
How is it assessed?	Controlled assessment
What will students be assessed on?	There are three areas: a) Speaking and Listening b) Spoken Language Study c) Writing for the Spoken Voice
How long do students have?	Up to 4 hours for the spoken language study and writing for the spoken voice tasks (2 hours for each task)
What is each task worth?	Speaking and Listening is worth 20% of the total marks Each of the other two tasks is worth 10% of the total marks
How are the tasks set?	• For Speaking and Listening, Edexcel will provide exemplar tasks which centres can adapt to suit their own students. • For the Spoken Language Study and Writing for the Spoken Voice tasks, Edexcel will set a choice of tasks for students to complete before the start of the academic year.
What do students have to produce?	• For Speaking and Listening there are three equally weighted activities: a) communicating and adapting language b) interacting and responding c) creating and sustaining roles • For the Spoken Language Study, students must complete one task on two examples of spoken language that they have researched. • For the Writing for the Spoken Voice task, students must complete one task from a choice of three.

Using this Teacher Guide

The Teacher Guide is broken down into two broad sections:

- Visual lesson plans
- Controlled Assessment.

Visual lesson plans (pages 24–121)

With their unique, easy-to-follow layout, the visual lesson plans support the teaching of the Student Book content and show how the print and digital resources can be used together to deliver engaging lessons that help improve students' grades.

Each lesson plan includes the following:

- A starter: to introduce the learning in the lesson.

- Suggestions for how to carry out the Student Book activities, including group, paired and independent work.

- Expert advice on how to make the learning suitable for EAL students, written by NALDIC.

- Plenary activities to round off the lesson and check/consolidate understanding.

- Guidance on how to incorporate any extra assets, such as the videos, worksheets and images found on ActiveTeach, into the lesson.

- Answers to the student book activities, to save you valuable time.

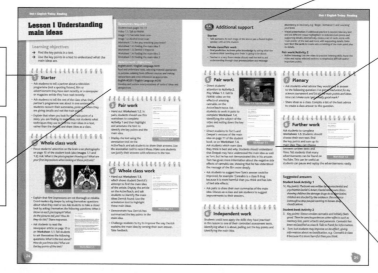

Controlled Assessment (pages 122–135)

The second section of the Teacher Guide provides specific advice on the Unit 1 and 3 Controlled Assessment tasks that you will need to carry out for the new specification. Written by members of the senior examining team, these sections include:

- clear explanation of the requirements of the Controlled Assessments

- a breakdown of the different types of tasks available to you

- advice on choosing, setting and teaching the tasks, tailored to the different ability levels of your students.

Also available: Edexcel GCSE English and English Language Access ActiveTeach (ISBN 978 1 84690 745 6)

ActiveTeach is the on-screen version of the Student Book, together with a range of digital assets including:

- exclusive BBC footage

- video and audio clips

- interactive ResultsPlus grade improvement activities (see pages 8–12 for more detail)

- student worksheets

- additional stimulus photos.

The unique functionality on ActiveTeach enables you to personalise the Student Book content by annotating texts and saving those annotations for next time you deliver the lesson. You can further personalise your teaching by adding your own resources to ActiveTeach via the My Resources tool.

Functional Skills in GCSE English/English Language

Functional skills will be taught for the first time in English, Maths and ICT from September 2010. There are many options available as to when and how you might teach this qualification, for example:

• as a stand-alone qualification with separate functional English teaching, perhaps in Year 9

• integrated into the teaching of GCSE English/English Language

• a mixture of the above: integrated teaching, but with some distinct functional skills assessment practice so students know what to expect in the exam.

Unit 1 of the GCSE English/English Language specifications has been designed to cover the teaching aspects of Functional English in reading and writing. So, in using the Student Book to teach Unit 1, you will also be delivering all of the required teaching and skills that students will need in order to pass the reading and writing elements of functional English qualification at level 2. The chart below illustrates where each functional skill is covered:

Level 2 Reading assessment criteria Select, read, understand and compare texts and use them to gather information, ideas, arguments and opinions.	Coverage in Student Book Unit 1: Reading
Select and use different types of texts to obtain and utilise relevant information.	Lessons 1, 4
Read and summarise succinctly information/ideas from different sources.	Lessons 1, 7, 9, 11, 12, 13
Identify the purposes of texts and comment on how meaning is conveyed.	Lessons 3, 4, 6, 7, 8, 9, 11, 13
Detect point of view, implicit meaning and/or bias.	Lessons 2, 6, 8, 11
Analyse texts in relation to audience needs and consider suitable responses.	Lessons 3, 4, 6, 8, 9, 11, 13

Level 2 Writing assessment criteria Write a range of texts, including extended written documents, communicating information, ideas and opinions effectively and persuasively.	Coverage in Student Book Unit 1: Writing
Present information/ideas concisely, logically and persuasively.	Lessons 6, 7
Present information on complex subjects clearly and concisely.	Lessons 5, 6, 7, 8
Use a range of writing styles for different purposes.	Lessons 1, 3, 9
Use a range of sentence structures, including complex sentences, and paragraphs to organise written communication effectively.	Lessons 6, 8
Punctuate accurately using commas, apostrophes and inverted commas accurately.	Lesson 10
Ensure written work is fit for purpose and audience, with accurate spelling and grammar that support clear meaning in a range of text types.	Lessons 1, 2, 3, 4

ResultsPlus combines expert advice and guidance from examiners to show students how to achieve better results. Many of the ResultsPlus features and activities are based on insight gained from how students have performed in past assessments and are designed to help students improve their responses to controlled assessment tasks and examination questions.

ResultsPlus features are included throughout the Student Book, with extensive examiner guidance and opportunities for students to reflect on and improve their learning. Guidance on how to use the ResultsPlus 'Maximise your marks' features is provided in the lesson plans throughout this Teacher Guide. In addition to the features in the assessment practice pages of the Student Book, interactive ResultsPlus activities can be found on the ActiveTeach. These interactive grade improvement activities build on the ResultsPlus material in the Student Book and are ideal for whole-class teaching.

The main features of the ResultsPlus activities include:

- An examiner who helps you to guide your students through sample answers and mark schemes, and helps them assess their own and their peers' work.

- A highlight feature which encourages students to analyse the questions and identify relevant comments in the sample answers.

- An easy-to-use slider that helps students to understand the mark scheme and the requirements for each band.

- The option to print out each activity and sample answer to aid preparation and to be used as you work through the activities front of class.

The activities have been written specifically to match the grade-bands of each Student Book, with sample answers for the relevant bands and advice on how to improve student answers.

There are four types of interactive ResultsPlus activity:

1 Write a sample answer and self assess

Learning objective:

→ To help students self assess their work against the mark scheme and identify how to achieve better results.

This activity provides an opportunity for students to assess their own work with the examiner's help. Students can time themselves typing an answer to the set question or they can paste in an answer they have prepared in advance. When they have finished writing, students can use the mark scheme to assess what band they think their answer will achieve. The examiner will help the student to check whether they have achieved this band with a series of questions that ask the student to analyse their response in detail. Finally, the student can rework their answer using the feedback as guidance or print their response out for their teacher to check. The answer they have written can also be saved.

1 Students are asked if they want to time themselves answering the question. Alternatively they can skip this and paste in an answer they have already written to this question.

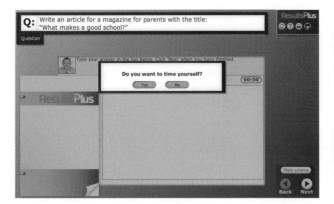

2 Students can analyse the question and highlight relevant details.

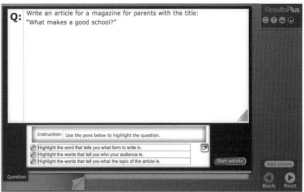

3 Students type/paste their answer in the space provided and select which band they think it has achieved.

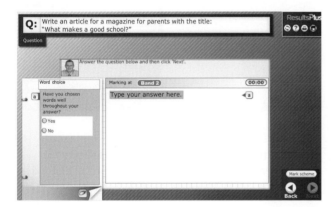

4 Students are prompted to highlight where they have met the mark scheme criteria and/or answer multiple-choice questions about their response.

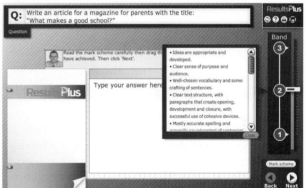

5 Students can then compare their answer with an answer written by the examiner at that band for further self-assessment opportunities.

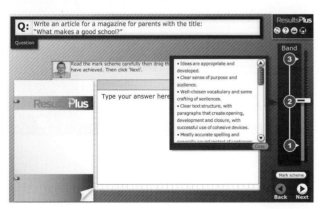

2 Comparing a sample answer

Learning objective:

→ To understand what skills are required at different bands.

→ To understand that there are different ways to achieve the same band.

This activity provides a range of sample student answers for each band. Students analyse and compare answers to the same band and at different bands. Each answer has examiner comments so that students can understand what skills are required at each band and see that there are different ways to achieve the same band.

Students will become familiar with the criteria specific to each band. Students will also be shown the best way to arrive at that band.

1 Initially students can analyse the question and highlight relevant details.

2 A band is chosen to analyse by moving the slider on the right of the screen to show sample answers at that band.

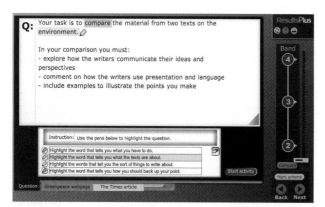 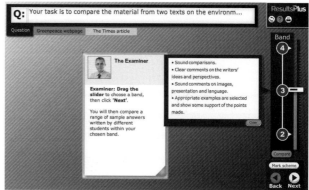

3 The class is presented with different ways of achieving the selected band. They compare the sample answers by highlighting where they think the marks have been awarded in each sample.

4 Finally, the class matches the sample answers to the examiner's comments, to check they have understood where the marks have been allocated or lost.

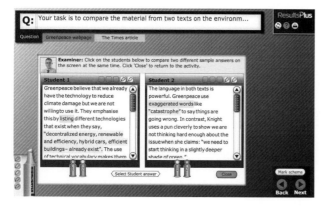 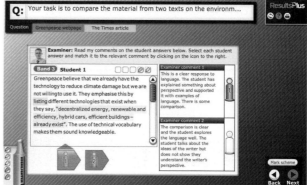

3 Improving a sample answer

Learning objective:

→ To show how to move answers up to the next band.

This activity is an excellent way to show students of all abilities how to improve answers to achieve the next band. The teacher selects a band to aim for. The class will suggest improvements to the sample answer which can be typed into the sample answer on your whiteboard. The printout for this activity allows each student to write down their own improvements in the classroom or at home. You can then see how the examiner would improve the answer and compare the suggestions to those made by the class.

1 Initially students can analyse the question and highlight relevant details.

2 The teacher annotates and discusses how to improve the sample answer with the class. The examiner will then reveal their suggestions and the class can discuss why this improved the band.

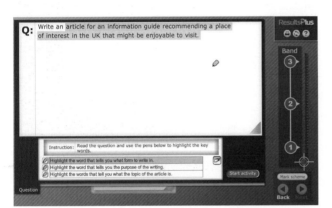

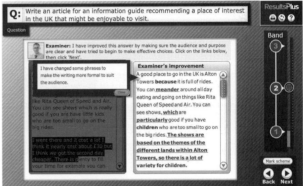

3 The mark scheme can be revealed at any time.

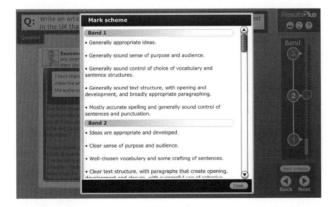

ResultsPlus
(available on the ActiveTeach)

4 Mark a sample answer

Learning objective:

→ To understand the mark scheme.

This activity will help you and your students to pull apart a sample answer with a highlighting tool. Your students will then assess the strengths and weaknesses of each section by answering a series of questions. At the end of their analysis students can suggest the band of the sample answer. This activity gives students a chance to be the examiner and really understand how the questions are marked.

1 Initially students can analyse the question and highlight relevant details.

2 Students highlight parts of the sample answer when prompted by the examiner. Based on this analysis students decide which band the answer deserves, which is checked by the examiner.

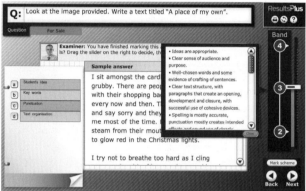

NALDIC guidance for teaching EAL students

Introduction

A growing number of schools and teachers are now supporting students with English as an Additional Language (EAL). More than one in ten secondary students is, or is becoming, bilingual and over 240 languages are spoken by students in UK schools, the most widely used being Panjabi, Urdu, Bengali, Gujarati, Somali, Polish, Arabic, Portuguese, Turkish and Tamil. This Teacher Guide is designed to help your lesson delivery and to give suggestions on how to differentiate materials for your students.

Students learning EAL will vary in their proficiency in their first language and in their proficiency in English. Some, but not all, will be fluent in their first language and have age appropriate academic literacy skills in that language. Some will have age appropriate skills in English similar to their peers. Others will be at very early stages. Others may be fluent in certain uses of English, but have less secure skills in other areas, for example written academic English. Similarly students will use their first language skills for different purposes at different times.

For the purposes of this guide, three terms are used to describe students' English language levels:

- *new* to English language and literacy (likely to be new to the UK and unable to successfully participate in curriculum studies without further assistance and support)

- *exploring* English language and literacy (likely to be able to communicate in everyday and some written English. They may have arrived in the UK during KS3 and their English is likely to show shortfalls in relation to both academic and social activities)

- *consolidating* English language and literacy (likely to be competent in spoken English in the classroom and in informal situations but this fluency may not be reflected in academic reading and writing). (RBKC, 2006)

All these students' attainment is likely to vary significantly between speaking and listening, reading and writing, but they often make faster progress than English-speaking peers assessed at the same levels in National Curriculum English.

Broad principles

When faced with the linguistic challenges of a multilingual classroom, you will need to take a broad view of the language development of EAL students. It's not just about developing students' knowledge of bits of English vocabulary and grammar, nor about teaching these through 'extra' activities. EAL students will be learning about English as a subject at the same time as they are learning about and through English as a language. They will also be at different stages in this process. Learning a new language requires time, exposure and opportunities to understand meanings through interaction and independent reflection.

Context

Language does not occur in a vacuum, but in a context, and this context affects the way things are written and said. First of all, there is the 'context of culture', where users share common assumptions in relation to the way things are done, whether this is buying some bread or delivering a physics lesson. Secondly, language is used within a 'context of situation'. This means the language used varies according to the relationship of those involved, from speaker to speaker, from topic to topic, according to purpose and situation (a second example may be too much).

All speakers are instinctively aware of these differences in their first languages. There are also variations in language according to social class, region and ethnic group. In schools, language also varies from subject to subject. For example, the language used in maths is very distinct to that used in English or history. EAL learners need to become familiar with the variations in written and spoken language that are used in subjects, schools and local communities, as well as understanding the cultural expectations, beliefs and practices associated with the language.

Communication

Language is essentially a means of communication. We use language to interact with one another and to express our feelings or viewpoints, our needs and to learn about the world. The functional nature of language in the classroom means an EAL student cannot focus solely on the mastery of grammar or the understanding of vocabulary. Research indicates that language learning is most effective when learners are involved in meaningful situations. Learners acquire language through social interaction but also through activities that offer an intellectual challenge.

> Aim to give learners the opportunity to engage in social interaction while undertaking activities that offer cognitive challenge. Just as students are marked on the content of their work, EAL students also need to receive feedback on their language use.

Another key principle is the interdependence of speaking, listening, reading and writing. These are often presented as 'four' skills, but in real life contexts they are naturally interdependent. In real life, students acquire the ability to use them simultaneously and interdependently. Their language processes develop as they use multi-modal technologies such as film, video and ICT.

You will need to provide EAL learners with opportunities to develop their language abilities in ways which recognise the interdependence of speaking, listening, reading and writing.

Language learning is not short term. It takes place over time and individual learners acquire language at different rates. There are many contributing factors, such as linguistic or educational backgrounds. Learners thinking and learning styles, motivation and personality also play a role. You may have seen that EAL learners frequently acquire informal conversational skills more quickly than academic language skills (which may take five to seven years to develop). In order to plan appropriately for the linguistically diverse classroom, it is essential to understand the progression of language from spoken (e.g. playground talk) through to written (e.g. exploratory talk).

It is widely acknowledged that bilingualism is an asset and enhances learners' linguistic and cognitive skills. However, in order for students to benefit fully they need to be very proficient in both languages. This implies that the most effective school environment for EAL learners is one in which the development of the first language for both academic and social purposes is promoted alongside the learning of English. EAL learners who are literate in their first language have many advantages. Literacy in another language helps them to make sense of academic texts in English as they have an understanding of how different kinds of texts work. Importantly, learning a new language also offers them insights into their first languages.

Implications for teaching and learning

The principles above have many implications when it comes to planning for and teaching your students. They underpin many aspects of successful teaching in linguistically diverse classrooms, such as:

- making the most of a student's prior knowledge and understanding in their first language and English

- encouraging learners to seek meaning through communicative and independent activities

- helping a student to understand source materials and supporting them to reflect their understanding in their own writing in English

- paying attention to culturally and contextually specific ways of using language

- activities which focus on specific aspects of English at word, sentence and text level which EAL students may find more difficult.

Some detailed practical suggestions are given in the table on the next page.

Rationale for suggested approaches

Reading: structuring texts

The conventional ways of selecting and structuring information, presenting it in specific formats for different purposes and expressing it with specific features of language often seem 'natural' to fluent and experienced first-language users of English. Students have had many years of exposure to these ways of using language at home and at school before they reach your classroom.

EAL students with limited exposure to different types of text in English are at a disadvantage, especially if the practices in their first language are quite different.

Reading: reading for meaning

Many EAL learners will also be at a disadvantage when trying to interpret clues to predict meanings in texts. This may be because the text describes something which is beyond their current experience.

It is important to remember that most bilingual learners will have been exposed to a range of learning and literacy practices before they come into a UK school. The challenge is to build on these experiences pragmatically.

EAL Insights	Practical implications
Different cultures and languages use different ways of expressing meaning not just different vocabulary and grammar.	• Make the socio-cultural assumptions in your talk, tasks and materials explicit. • Give students opportunities to reflect on differences and similarities.
EAL learners need to be able to adapt spoken and written language to suit the context. They also need to use spoken or written language in accepted and predictable ways to perform particular purposes and to communicate meaning.	• Give students a variety of opportunities to engage in understanding in ways which are appropriate to the subject. • Provide feedback on students' language use.
EAL learners may have strengths and weaknesses within the skillset of speaking and listening, reading and writing.	• Be sensitive to the different skills profiles of learners and the interdependence of speaking, listening, reading and writing. • Groupings based on attainment in reading or writing may not always be appropriate. • EAL learners will benefit from an additional focus on speaking and listening activities as a bridge to reading and writing.
EAL learners will not necessarily acquire English skills in the same order as first language speakers.	• Include strategies which build on students' strengths, for example in spoken English or from their first language. • Where more than one student shares a language, opportunities for discussion in that language should be encouraged, as should developing independent translation skills.
EAL learners will be acquiring English language skills across the curriculum and will also be using these skills across the curriculum.	• Work to develop learners' oral language skills alongside their literacy skills. • Build on learners' prior knowledge and the resources they bring. • Make links with students' other languages and work across the curriculum to build their language and literacy capacity.
Bilingualism and bi-culturalism are assets and can enhance learners' linguistic and cognitive skills.	• Build in opportunities to promote the use of first languages for academic and social purposes.

Reading: going beyond the text

Of course, fluent users of English in your classroom do not simply follow a text to recover meaning from the words and sentences: they have to know how to make use of the information for different purposes. This ability to go beyond the text cannot be taught through just the 'nuts and bolts' of language itself: it has to be supported by increasing familiarity with culturally established ways of seeing, knowing and understanding.

EAL learners with a limited experience of dealing with written texts in English may find this aspect of reading an invisible but constant problem. Similarly the task of acquiring new vocabulary is not a simple one to be solved by exposing students to 'key words'. Words have multiple meanings and are used with different emphases in different contexts and students need continued exposure to these meanings.

Writing

Most writing tasks are developed from the curriculum and EAL students may not fully understand the curriculum meanings expressed through spoken English. Words change their meaning according to the context, and the classroom is full of metaphorical and figurative uses of language which are open to misunderstandings. This lack of understanding of content meaning often causes major difficulties in selecting and including appropriate information in writing tasks.

Cameron (2003) identifies some of the following problems that KS4/post 16 EAL students have in writing:

1. even high level (or **consolidating**) EAL learners have difficulty in using ideas from source materials in their own writing.

2. **consolidating** EAL learners may also have difficulty in judging nuances of style, and still experience some of the same problems as their less proficient EAL peers (new and **exploring**) with the use of articles, choice of the correct preposition in fixed phrases, and subject-verb agreement.

3. 'delexical' verbs, i.e. verbs that are 'so frequently used and in so many different contexts that the link between the verb and its meaning become quite weak' (p34), such as 'put', 'do', 'have', 'make' or 'go'. Examples include sentences such as 'make a stop to this', instead of 'put a stop to', and 'they will do more fun' instead of 'they will have more fun'.

4. difficulties with sentence grammar related to length of clause constituents and use of adverbials and sub-ordination to develop more complex sentence structure

Although some of these common areas of difficulty may benefit from specific teaching, Gibbons (2002) likens word and sentence level work to focusing a pair of binoculars. Your first gaze is the whole vista and after a while you use the binoculars to hone in on a detail of the landscape. You know how to locate this detail because you have already seen it as part of the whole. When you have finished focusing on the detail, you will probably return to the whole panorama again but with an enhanced sense of what is there. Additional word and sentence level activities need to be compatible with this 'whole vista' approach and provide further opportunities for 'message abundancy'.

Linking reading, writing, speaking and listening

Learning to write in EAL is inextricably linked to learning English and curriculum content through spoken English at the same time. Given that spoken English is not necessarily the same as the written form, it is important to pay attention to bilingual students' writing in English, even when they seem to understand spoken communication reasonably well.

> This suggests that reading and writing tasks should start with and be supported by teaching and group activities which use spoken English in conjunction with relevant visual materials, realia and hands-on experiential learning tasks. This will go a long way to making meanings comprehensible.

Practical application

Gibbons (2008) describes what this might look like in practical terms.

'If you were a second language learner in that class, you would have had opportunities for participating in an initial shared experience, which is watching the video with everybody else; hearing everyday language alongside academic language in the interactions between teachers and students - the Janus-like talk; seeing the key points written on the board, so you have got a visual representation of what you're hearing;

having the difference between everyday and technical language highlighted through the colour-coding; having access to a chart of definitions; getting practice in putting new concepts into practice; and, finally, using the learning in a new context.'

Gibbons has used the term 'message abundancy' to describe this sort of teaching sequence – 'So that you have more than one bite of the apple, you don't just get told one thing once'.

> 'A lot of EAL students that I've interviewed in secondary say their teachers talk too quickly. I don't think it's actually the speed of the talk that they're responding to, I think it's the speed at which information is given. If you're a second language learner, it helps enormously to have the time to process a new idea. This kind of recycling of the same idea many times over, I think is one of the most important things about a curriculum. I called it message abundancy because it seemed to me that there was an abundancy of messages there and many opportunities to understand something.'

In other words, say less but say it more. For example, rather than aiming for four or five lesson outcomes, accept that two covered thoroughly from several angles with time for independent consolidation and review will be of greater value for an EAL student.

Helping students with exam questions

Examinations require students to be able to read with meaning and answer logically in writing, whatever the subject. You therefore need to teach bilingual students who are still developing their English skills two things:

• how to read the questions

• how to write an answer which follows the cues in the questions (in both reading and writing).

These cues are not always made explicit. It is not always the ideas that bilingual learners need, but the language needed for answering the question.

> Students need a wide variety of experiences and texts and a formula on how to write in different genres so that they can confidently apply what they know to any unfamiliar context.

Experience suggests that EAL learners often encounter difficulties with whole-text genre (which usually gains the highest amount of marks) due to a lack of shared cultural assumptions and experiences. Similarly in reading, inference and deduction, text structure, use of language, and writer's purpose and effect on the reader may continue to cause problems well beyond the new or exploring stages of language learning.

Suggested teaching sequence, sample strategies and activities for EAL development

The teaching sequences suggested within the course materials are supportive of EAL learners' language development as they move through a predictable sequence:

First, developing familiarity with the context and building on the resources students bring	Next, explicitly defining and modelling purpose, function and audience	Then, joint construction which highlights and makes explicit language features and grammar associated with the above	Finally, independent construction and opportunities for assessment and consolidation

This approach is consistent with the principles noted above and is supportive of learners at all stages of acquiring EAL, and is beneficial to all learners and not just those learning EAL. This means the teaching sequence is compatible with teaching a class or set which includes bilingual students at various stages of learning English as well as English-only students. The advantage of this approach is that it is flexible enough to accommodate individual learners' needs at varying stages.

The table on pages 17-18 illustrates the teaching sequence, explains why and how this is helpful and highlights some sample strategies. Throughout the Teacher Guide, activities are provided in various parts of the lesson which exemplify these techniques and help you to make further adaptations to lessons to match your learners' needs.

A glossary of these activities is provided on pages 20-23 which briefly explains how the activity works, why it is useful for bilingual students who are still learning EAL and the EAL language level of learners (new, exploring or consolidating) who would most benefit.

Lesson phase	Why?	How?	Sample Strategies
Introduction Set the context to build field knowledge including concrete experiences, multimedia input, exploratory talk in L1 and L2, reading and note making	• Students have the opportunity to show and build on what they already know about the topic • Develop students' knowledge and understandings of language and content together • Ensure students become familiar with the context, structure of the genre and specific and general vocabulary such as names, objects and actions.	• Develop topic/field knowledge and resources by making links with prior knowledge in first language and English • Consider breaking down topics into more specific sub topics. • Develop opportunities for 'message abundancy.' • Help learners find ways into text and use this to generate their own content. • Use and/or provide personal experiences to add to content. • Consider metaphor, idiom and colloquial language which may be problematic.	Practical experiences Pre-reading oral activities to set up or predict context Brain storming and mind mapping Vocabulary chaining Introduce key visuals, real objects and multimodal introductions Dictogloss Focus on main ideas Presentations, interactive activities, pairing students with first language English speakers Use speech bubbles to show the literal meaning of an idiomatic expression in pictorial form to help students see the difference between the word meaning and the intended message
Modelling Teacher models and defines the task, making audience, purpose, form and expected language features explicit.	• Guide the students in exploring the genre and the language features in genre, field, tenor and mode orally • Language functions/ thinking skills like justify, compare, contrast, analyse, synthesise and explain which are required in GCSE English exam tasks are modelled and scaffolded in context with the appropriate language needed	• Recognize register and genre may be different in L1 and use examples to demonstrate this • Explain and model language functions • Teach how register varies according to social context and involves the language choices made about what is being discussed (field) the relationship between participants (tenor) and how it is communicated (mode) • Make audience, purpose, form and expected language features explicit.	Graphic organisers Key visuals Concept maps Functions Active listening and speaking activities attached to different types of registers Identifying reference items

Lesson phase	Why?	How?	Sample Strategies
Joint construction Moving from informal to formal talk, and scaffolding writing. Teacher guides the discussion by asking questions, making suggestions and re-wording or re-casting. ▼	• Students able to take an increasing role in the joint construction using what they have learnt about the structure and the language features of the genre. • Students develop the oral language skills of pronunciation, intonation, stress and volume.	• Help learners to become meaning seekers and teach strategies to identify, understand and use vocabulary items in source materials including the movement between general and specific vocabulary. • Explain and scaffold sequencing and structuring conventions • May need help with prepositions in formulaic phrases and delexical verbs	Identify key words from sources and use to generate content Using connectives Sequencing activities Grouping strategies which require students to communicate with their peers Organizing ideas into a logical sequence Collaborative activities
Independent construction Students supported in the task of independent construction by breaking down into sub tasks, by grouping strategies and by supporting independent learning ▼	• EAL students will need to have several practices and opportunities to peer assess, edit, and rewrite before they become competent. • Independent construction should be scaffolded by a range of grouping strategies, frames and aids	• Meaning-making activities • Activities which develop and scaffold independent meaning making skills • Tasks may be broken down into smaller tasks such as: • planning a number of paragraphs in a logical sequence;; • a good introduction for one or several pieces of work in different genres; • a good conclusion which links to the introduction; tasks which build skills in integrating evidence to justify opinions.	Pair and group work Key visuals Graphic organizers. Using English and bilingual dictionaries ICT based tools
Assessment and consolidation Provide ongoing assessment and consolidation on both language and content.	• Making assessment criteria explicit.may help students to realize what they have to do to reach higher levels in examinations and progress in their language learning • Need to assess language and content holistically and separately	• Provide individual feedback on errors/development points unless these apply to large numbers of students. • Sentence level difficulties for EAL learners may include: subject/verb noun/pronoun agreements and some plurals; articles; endings for tense/person; and modal verbs • Provide examples of a learning sequences followed by a test and an exemplar answer which shows how the marks awarded increase if certain features are included in the answer • Take account of examples from recent exam questions and the both KS3 and 4 marking schemes	Assessment strategies which require students to communicate with their peers and provide further opportunities to recycle and consolidate language Oral and written feedback on both content and language Visual approaches to identifying how well assessment criteria have been met Peer and self assessment strategies

Further resources and reading

Cameron, L. (2003). *Writing in English as an additional language at Key Stage 4 and post-16.* London: OfSTED

Cummins, J. (1984) *Bilingualism and Special Education: Issues in assessment and pedagogy.* Clevedon, England: Multilingual Matters.

Cummins, J. (2001) *Negotiating Identities; Education for Empowerment in a Diverse Society* (2nd Ed.). Los Angeles: CABE

DfEE (2001) Literacy across the curriculum (DfEE Ref 0235/2001)

Excell, D. (2006) Key Stage 3: Observations on Baseline Reading Tests and Formal Assessments for EAL Learners in *NALDIC Quarterly 4.2* Reading: NALDIC

Gibbons, P. (2002) *Scaffolding Language, Scaffolding Learning: Teaching Second Language Learners in the Mainstream Classroom.* Portsmouth, NH: Heinemann

Gibbons, P (2008) *'Challenging Pedagogies: More than just good practice' in NALDIC Quarterly 6.2* Reading: NALDIC

Halliday, M.A.K. (1975) *Learning how to mean.* London: Edward Arnold

Leung, C. (2004) *English as an additional language - Language and Literacy Development.* Royston: UKLA McWilliam, N. (1998) *What's in a Word: vocabulary development in multilingual classrooms.* Stoke-on–Trent: Trentham

Mohan, B. (1986) *Language and Content.* Reading, MA: Addison-Wesley

OFSTED (2005) *Could they do even better? The writing of advanced bilingual learners of English at Key Stage 2: HMI survey of good practice.* London: Office for Standards in Education.

RBKC (2006) *English Language and Literacy in Curriculum Learning* London: RBKC

Glossary of EAL teaching and learning techniques

Mainly oral

What is the technique?	How to do it?	Why do it?
Visual presentation	Teacher uses an oral, visual and animated presentation to key learners into the topic matter.	EAL learners can quickly learn new vocabulary when they can associate it with a picture or artifact.
Talk partners An organised form of pair work.	Learners are carefully matched in pairs in order to discuss their responses to teacher questions when asked.	EAL beginners can be placed with more able, fluent speakers of English who can model appropriate language use.
Hot seating	Learners are given a character, often with a role play card to support. A learner who has read and understood their character sits in the middle of a circle of learners. Other pupils take it in turns to ask questions of the character who responds in role.	EAL learners hear real language in context. They are able to listen to other fluent speakers. Oral rehearsal develops the exploratory talk of more advanced learners and is good preparation for writing.
Discussion in first language	EAL learners are given time to talk about new subject content in their first language with another speaker of the same language.	EAL pupils are able to use subject knowledge learnt in their first language and key into a topic. Sometimes vocabulary is similar, especially in science subjects with Latinate vocabulary.
Oral prediction	Before reading the teacher asks learners to predict from title, pictures or sub- headings what the text will contain.	This technique requires learners to build on their prior knowledge including how texts work. It helps information retrieval.
Brainstorming or Spider diagram	A group of pupils are asked to generate ideas and words related to a (new) topic. These are usually recorded visually by the teacher or another student.	Gives EAL learners a chance to learn key topic vocabulary. Several pupils working together can extend each others' repertoire.
Mind mapping or concept mapping	This is a systematic type of brainstorm. Pupils link key topic words or concepts into sentences or sentences into paragraphs. The teacher may initially give key words to pupils to find links. These may be colour coded.	Allows EAL learners to build on prior knowledge and transfer learning from their first language.
Envoys Pupils carry information from one group to another	A group of 3 or 4 learners complete an oral or reading task on topic. For example describing a character from a book and choosing quotations to illustrate their points. Other groups work on different characters in the same way. After a period of time an envoy from each group is sent to the next group in a clockwise direction and reports to the new group. Then a second envoy goes to the next group and so on until all groups have heard each others' work.	EAL learners hear real language in context. They are able to listen to other fluent speakers.
Washing line A type of evaluative or ranking activity	Pupils are given adjectives or other evaluative statements. They have to arrange the words (or themselves) from strongest to weakest (e.g. *fantastic-excellent-good- OK*)	This is a good vocabulary expansion activity for more advanced EAL learners. It develops understanding of shades of meaning.

What is the technique?	How to do it?	Why do it?
Active listening (e.g. cloze)	Students have a prepared text with words deleted. The teacher reads the complete text and learners listen in order to insert the missing words.	EAL learners get a chance to hear a model text. Depending on which words are omitted they can concentrate on key grammatical or vocabulary items.
Information gap activities or barrier games	There are many types of barrier game. Each learner has a different piece of information (e.g. diagram, picture or text.) They both have to complete a single task by asking for and using information from the other. So one learner might have a map and draw a route while listening to their partner's set of directions.	The barrier or information gap requires real language to be used to complete a task. EAL learner can be paired with supportive, fluent speakers who can help scaffold the task through careful wording or questioning.
Message Abundancy The repetition of key words or concepts	The teacher presents the same information in two or more different ways in a lesson; for example, on a DVD, through text highlighting and while speaking.	EAL learners have several opportunities to pick up and absorb new words, phrases and concepts.

Mainly reading

What is the technique?	How to do it?	Why do it?
Jigsaw reading Groups read different texts and then regroup to feedback.	The class is divided into groups of 4 or 5. Each group is given a different text to read and questions or task about a topic. After the task has been completed, one person from each group comes together to form a new group with information from each text. They can then share their expertise about the topic.	The texts and tasks can be designed for different levels of EAL learner at appropriate reading levels. Emerging EAL learners will be supported by working collaboratively.
Underlining/Highlighting Learners use highlighters to mark different aspects of a text	Learners are given a complete text with instructions to highlight key aspects. These can be grammatical, such as underlining past tense verbs in blue, time connectives (conjunctions) in red; semantic e.g. all the nouns relating to time; or content based. For example all the sentences describing a character.	The technique draws learners' attention to the form and structure of texts at sentence or paragraph level.
Identifying reference items	Teacher highlights reference words in a non fiction text (for example pronouns: it, this, these, theirs) learners have to identify and highlight the nouns to which they refer.	This helps more advanced EAL learners focus on the difficult process of cohesion and back referencing. It draws attention to how texts work.
Matching activities Learners have to match words and definitions or two parts of a sentence.	Words and definitions are printed on card which is then cut up. Learners work in pairs to match them up.	Through working together learners can practise using new vocabulary. Being able to move and manipulate text helps identify key language patterns.
Sequencing Learners have to re assemble or sequence a cut up text.	A complete text printed on card is cut up. Learners work in pairs to reassemble the original text in the correct sequence.	Learners understand how a text works and begin to use their knowledge of key grammatical items such as conjunctions and pronouns which link sentences and paragraphs.

What is the technique?	How to do it?	Why do it?
Relevance sorting Learners have a set of cards with key points about a particular question. *E.g. What were the causes of the first world war?*	The key question is written in the centre of concentric circles. Pupils place their supporting evidence cards around the centre with the most relevant points nearer to the centre.	This is a useful planning strategy for essay writing in English or Humanities subjects. It enables learners to prioritise and organise the writing of longer texts.
Ranking and justifying activities (e.g. Diamond Nine)	Learners are given a set of cards to evaluate in some way. For example, deciding which character is most to blame for an event in a narrative. They must arrange the cards in order from best to worst. In a Diamond Nine there are always nine cards which must be ordered into a diamond pattern.	EAL learners hear the language of justification and evaluation. It supports EAL learners in bridging talk and writing.
Joint construction Various activities that involve the teacher guiding learners in how texts work.	Teacher or other students model how to read a text, such as skimming and scanning or how to write a paragraph with topic sentence and supporting evidence.	Helps EAL learners to become meaning seekers and teaches strategies to identify, understand and use vocabulary items in source materials They can take an increasing role in the joint construction using what they have learnt about the language features of a new genre.

Mainly writing

What is the technique?	How to do it?	Why do it?
Cloze A specialised form of gap filling	A text is prepared with **one type** of word omitted, e.g. all nouns, all verbs. It can also be used for learning new subject vocabulary.	Supports EAL learners in looking at semantic patterns or sentence structures such as past tenses, prepositions.
Selective cloze	A text is prepared with every 7th or 8th word deleted (or every 10th if it is for beginners) Learners collaborate in pairs to find suitable replacements for the omitted words	Helpful for teachers to assess learners' comprehension of more complex texts. If they cannot get about 80% correct the text is too difficult.
Dictogloss A supported dictation	This is a listening and writing activity. The teacher chooses a short text on a topic that is familiar to the learners. (about 100 words for EAL beginners and intermediates) She/he reads the text aloud whilst learners listen. On the second and third readings learners may write notes. Next, pupils work in pairs and then fours to try to reconstruct the original text.	Learners hear a model text on a familiar topic. They collaborate to reconstruct complex sentences and scaffold each other's learning.
Sentence starters	The teacher prepares a topic-specific list of key sentence patterns for learners to use. An extended version of this technique, covering a complete text, would be a writing frame (see below)	This is best for beginner and developing EAL learners who are unsure of how to start writing.
Writing frames	The writing frame is best used as genre –specific scaffold. The teacher usually provides key connectives and linking phrases.	Emerging EAL learners are supported to link together short simple sentences into complex sentences and paragraphs.

What is the technique?	How to do it?	Why do it?
Key visuals or Graphic organisers	Key visuals are a type of graphic organiser. They are used to show the underlying structure of a text, for example a flow chart signifies a sequential text; a two way table can illustrate an argument for and against; or a tree diagram can classify scientific information. Teachers can either use the visual to help students make notes whilst reading about a topic or use the visual and notes as a plan and preparation for writing.	The use of visual organisers helps EAL learners see the underlying structure, form and purpose of key genres of English writing.
ICT based tools (e.g. bilingual dictionaries and thesauruses)	Apart from use of book – based thesauruses and dictionaries, Microsoft Word can be used to great effect. Learners highlight and then right- click on a word and select 'synonyms' or definitions. A dialogue box will appear with other suggested words with a similar meaning.	Emerging and consolidating EAL pupils need to expand their vocabulary as fast as possible. Using a bilingual dictionary supports the transfer of learning from first language into English.
Substitution tables	Teacher provides model sentences with various choices in a tabular form. Learners generate their own sentence following the set patterns. 	Today	is	sunny
Yesterday	will be	cloudy
Tomorrow	was	snowing		The technique enables EAL pupils to focus on form and write accurate grammatical sentences whilst also having some vocabulary and content choice.
Peer Assessment strategies	When a first draft of a text has been written, learners swap their writing and read and comment on its effectiveness or mark work according to agreed success criteria.	It provides further opportunities to recycle and consolidate language and encourages real life communication with peers.
Oral and written feedback on both content and language.	Teachers mark work with specific grammatical or linguistic foci. For example in a narrative text, requiring learners to have consistent use of the past tense, or in an argumentative text, to use a range of modal verbs.	The technique draws attention to the form and structure of texts. Can help EAL learners to realize what they have to do to reach higher levels in examinations and progress in their language learning.
Visual approaches to identify how well assessment criteria have been met.	During class work, especially during the listening phase at the start of a lesson, the teacher asks learners to display coloured cards to show whether they have understood. Green signifies the student is confident, Amber, not sure and Red no understanding. (Also known as traffic light system)	EAL learners may be initially reluctant to ask for help. This gives them a less threatening way of signaling (in) comprehension.
Self assessment checklists	Students mark a self assessment check sheet with • , X or O to show whether they have understood.	EAL learners may be initially reluctant to ask for help. This gives them a less threatening way of signaling comprehension.

Strategies listed in the glossary and other key EAL-friendly approaches are highlighted in bold in the EAL support panels.

Lesson 1 Understanding main ideas

Learning objectives

→ Find the key points in a text.

→ Use the key points in a text to understand what the main ideas are.

1 Starter

- Ask students to tell a partner about a television programme (not a sporting fixture), film or advertisement they have seen recently, or a newspaper or magazine article they have read recently.

- Ask students to tell the rest of the class what their partner's programme was about in one sentence. As students recount their summaries, point out when they are giving details and not the main points.

- Explain that when you look for the main point of a story, you are finding its main ideas. Ask students what techniques they use to find the main ideas in a text, rather than the details, and share ideas as a class.

2 Whole class work

- Focus students' attention on the brain scan photographs on page 10 of the student book (also **Images 1.1** and **1.2**). Ask: *What is the photographer showing us? What are your first impressions when looking at these pictures?*

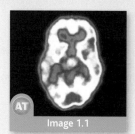
Image 1.1

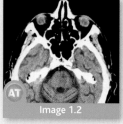
Image 1.2

- Explain that first impressions are not thorough or reliable. Good readers dig deeper by asking themselves questions about what they read or see. Ask students to take a closer look by asking themselves the following questions: *What is shown in each photograph? What do the pictures tell you? How do they do this?* Share responses.

- Ask students to read the newspaper article on page 10 or on **Worksheet 1.1**. Tell students to ask themselves the following questions: *What is the text about? How do you know this? What are the key points of the text?*

Worksheet 1.1

Resources required

Student book pages 10–11
Video 1.1: *Talk to FRANK*
Image 1.1: Cannabis brain scan
Image 1.2: Alcohol brain scan
Worksheet 1.1: Are you wrecking your brain?
Worksheet 1.2: Finding the main idea 1
Worksheet 1.3: Derrick's response
Worksheet 1.4: Finding the main idea 2
Worksheet 1.5: Finding the main idea 3

Assessment objectives

English AO2i / English Language AO3i
Read and understand texts, selecting material appropriate to purpose, collating from different sources and making comparisons and cross references as appropriate.

English AO2ii / English Language AO3ii
Develop and sustain interpretations of writers' ideas and perspectives.

3 Pair work

- Hand out **Worksheet 1.2**. In pairs, students should use this worksheet to complete **Activity 1** and then highlight and annotate the text to identify the key points and the main idea.

- Display the text using the annotation tool on the ActiveTeach, and ask students to share their answers. Use the annotation tool to record these. Make sure students can justify their answers with reference to the text.

Worksheet 1.2

4 Whole class work

- Hand out **Worksheet 1.3**, which shows student Derrick's attempt to find the main idea of the article. Display the article on the ActiveTeach, and ask students to identify the main ideas Derrick found. Use the annotation tool to highlight these main ideas.

- Demonstrate how Derrick has summarised the key points in the main idea.

- Challenge students to try to improve the way Derrick explains the main idea by writing their own answer. Take feedback.

Worksheet 1.3

Additional support

Starter
- **Talk partners:** At each stage of the lesson pair a fluent English speaker with an EAL student.

Whole class/Pair work
- **Oral prediction: Activate prior knowledge** by asking what the students think 'wrecking your brain' is going to be about.
- Teacher or a very fluent reader should read the text to aid understanding through clear **pronunciation** and **message**

abundancy as necessary, e.g. 'illegal', 'Alzheimer's' and 'wrecking' your brain.
- **Visual presentation:** If additional practice is needed, take any text and use different colour highlighters to indicate main points and supporting details. Alternatively, create a set of cards, some with 'main points' of the text and more with supporting details. Extra task: **Sort the cards** to create sets consisting of the main point plus its details.

Pair work/Activity 2
- **Active listening:** Use the video to practise listening skills. Pause the video and replay selected sections to emphasise difficult and/or important points.

5 Pair work

Video 1.1: *Talk to FRANK*

- Direct students' attention to **Activity 2**. Play **Video 1.1:** *Talk to FRANK* video on the effects of smoking cannabis, on the ActiveTeach twice. Ask students to work in pairs to complete **Worksheet 1.4**, identifying the subject of the video and noting down the key points.

- Direct students to Tom's and Deepak's versions of the main idea on page 11 of the student book, or on **Worksheet 1.4**. Ask students which main idea they think is best and why. Students should understand that Deepak may have understood the main idea as well as Tom, but he has not demonstrated this in his answer. Tom has given more information about the negative side effects of cannabis use, showing that he has understood the message of the film more deeply.

- Ask students to suggest how Tom's answer could be improved, for example: 'Cannabis is a class B drug because it is more harmful than you think and has lots of bad side effects.'

- Ask pairs to share their own summaries of the main idea. Discuss as a class and ask students to suggest improvements to their answers.

Worksheet 1.4

6 Independent work

Students could now apply the skills they have practised in this lesson to one of their controlled assessment texts, identifying what it is about, making notes on the key points and identifying the main idea.

7 Plenary

- Ask students what advice they would give in answer to the following question: *I've got to read a text for my science coursework and list all the main points and ideas. How can I make sure I get a really good mark?*

- Share ideas as a class. Compile a list of the best advice to create a class answer to the question.

8 Further work

Ask students to complete **Worksheet 1.5**. Students should choose their own text, find the key points and sum up its main idea. They can choose between written texts and films. Tell students that many advertisements can be found on YouTube. This can be useful as students can pause and replay the advertisements easily.

Worksheet 1.5

Suggested answers

Student book Activity 1

1c. *Key points: The book was written by neuroscientist and psychiatrist Daniel G Amen; Daniel Amen runs clinics showing children the damage drugs do to their brains; children are shocked by the evidence; the evidence is enough to stop people wanting to loosen drug classifications.*

Student book Activity 2

3. *Key points: Simon smokes cannabis and initially feels good. Then he sees/experiences other effects such as memory loss, panic attacks and paranoia. Cannabis has been reclassified as class B. Talk to FRANK for information.*

4. *Tom; but students may improve on his effort, giving information about reclassification, e.g. Cannabis is class B because it is more harmful than you think.*

Lesson 2 Understanding the writer's perspective

Learning objectives

→ Work out what the writer's perspective is.

Resources required

Student book pages 12–13
BBC Video: *The One Show*
Image 2.1: Bullying poster
Image 2.2: Why do people bully? poster
Worksheet 2.1: The writer's perspective
Worksheet 2.2: *Quantum of Solace* review
Worksheet 2.3: Perspective table
Answer sheets 2.1–2.2: Suggested answers

Assessment objectives

English AO2i / English Language AO3i
Read and understand texts, selecting material appropriate to purpose, collating from different sources and making comparisons and cross references as appropriate.

English AO2ii / English Language AO3ii
Develop and sustain interpretations of writers' ideas and perspectives.

1 Starter

- Choose a current topical issue that students are aware of to discuss in class, for example: which football players should be bought/transferred, which is the best/worst act on *The X Factor*, should under 14s be allowed on *Britain's Got Talent*.

- Ask different students to share their opinions on this issue. Ensure that different perspectives are heard.

- Discuss students' contributions, and draw their attention to two students who did not agree. Explain that they had different 'perspectives' on the issue. Ask other students to summarise what those perspectives were.

- Watch the **BBC Video: The One Show**, available on the ActiveTeach. Ask students to point out different perspectives in the video.

BBC Video: *The One Show*

- Explain what a perspective is and that students need to learn to work out writers' perspectives.

2 Pair work

- Write a list of other topical issues on the board and encourage students to come up with some issues of their own. Each student should pick an issue and tell a partner their thoughts and feelings about it. The other student should repeat the exercise with an issue of their choice.

- Either working as a whole class or in groups, ask students to share their partner's perspective on the topic. They should explain how they recognised their partner's perspective. Partners should give each other feedback about how well they have listened and understood their perspective.

3 Whole class work

- Display the bullying poster, **Image 2.1**, or direct students to page 12 of the student book. Take students through the worked example on page 12 to demonstrate how to work out a writer's perspective. Encourage students to answer the points in the student book in their own words.

Image 2.1

- Display the second bullying poster, **Image 2.2**, or page 12 of the student book. Ask students the same questions to work out the main ideas in this poster.

Image 2.2

- Ask students to complete questions 1 and 2 in **Activity 1** in pairs using **Worksheet 2.1**. Students should find the main ideas in the text then comment on the writer's perspective.

- Discuss the writer's perspective as a class, encouraging students to share their sentences. Ask students to justify their ideas about the writer's perspective by drawing on evidence in the text.

Worksheet 2.1

- Ask students to comment on the differences between the perspectives of the writers of the two bullying posters. Record ideas on the board.

EAL Additional support

Starter
- **Talk partners**: Pair EAL learners with the same first language or with a fluent English speaker to work together to understand the concept of different 'perspectives'. Use **message abundancy** to clarify perspective through its root as a 'point of view'.
- **Activate prior knowledge** to find examples from students' own backgrounds to present to the whole class.

Pair work/Activity 2
- **Active listening**: Read the film review to the class, using expression, pauses, gestures and facial expression to aid understanding.

- **Clarify** words as necessary such as: 'charisma', 'punch-ups', 'earlier vintage' and 'franchise production line'.
- **Collaborative activities: Activate prior knowledge** by asking all students what they know about Bond, Bourne and Daniel Craig, who may be unfamiliar to EAL students.
- When completing **Activity 2** question 3, it may help to use **joint construction**, to **model** or **scaffold** students, explanations of which summary they most agreed with. Alternatively, create **gapped sentences** to practise or test the use of 'both', 'similarly', 'however', 'whereas'.

Independent work
- Use **sentence starters** and **writing frames** to support EAL students when they talk or write about a writer's perspective.

---

4 Pair work

- Ask students to look at the film review on page 13 of the student book, or use **Worksheet 2.2**. Students should work in pairs to complete **Activity 2**, recording their answers on the worksheet. Emphasise the need to find evidence to prove their ideas are valid.

  Worksheet 2.2

- Explain to students that when they comment on the writer's perspective, they need to think about the main ideas rather than details. To demonstrate this, write the following sentences on the board:
  - *The writer is pleased with the action sequences and Bourne-type scenes even though earlier Bonds wouldn't have acted in that way.*
  - *The writer thinks the storyline isn't great, but Daniel Craig's Bond makes up for it.*

- Explain that the second sentence is a better summary of the writer's perspective as it gives a more general sense of what the writer felt about the film rather than focusing on details. For example, the writer may have loved the action scenes but hated everything else; we cannot tell from the first sentence.

- As a class, read the two explanations of the writer's perspective on page 13 of the student book or on **Worksheet 2.2**. Ask students to say which they agreed with most and to justify their opinion.

- Ask pairs to share their own explanation of the writer's perspective. Write some examples on the board and ask students to suggest improvements, ensuring that students focus on the writer's overall feelings about the film.

5 Independent work

Students should complete the first part of **Activity 3**. They could look at the reading task they have been given for their controlled assessment to complete the first column in the table on **Worksheet 2.3**, which asks them to summarise the writer's perspective and explain how they worked this out.

Worksheet 2.3

---

6 Plenary

Ask students to come up with a list of top tips for working out and summarising the writer's perspective.

---

7 Further work

Ask students to complete the remainder of **Activity 3** and record their answers on **Worksheet 2.3**. The texts they choose should not all be of the same type and at least one should be a campaign poster, leaflet or advertisement, which they should bring to the next lesson.

Suggested answers

Student book Activity 1 – see Answer sheet 2.1

Student book Activity 2 – see Answer sheet 2.2

Lesson 3
Audience and purpose

Resources required

Student book pages 14–15
Audio 3.1: Road Safety podcast
Image 3.1: *Freshwater Fishing* cover
Image 3.2: *Girl Talk* cover
Worksheet 3.1: Best car seat yet
Worksheet 3.2: Identifying the audience
Worksheet 3.3: Purposes
Worksheet 3.4: Identifying purposes 1
Worksheet 3.5: Identifying purposes 2

Assessment objectives

English AO2i / English Language AO3i
Read and understand texts, selecting material appropriate to purpose, collating from different sources and making comparisons and cross references as appropriate.

English AO2ii / English Language AO3ii
Develop and sustain interpretations of writers' ideas and perspectives.

Learning objectives

→ Work out who a text is written for – the audience.
→ Recognise what the writer's aim is – the purpose.

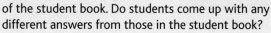

1 Starter

Ask students to work in groups. Working against the clock, each group must decide on an ideal Saturday night's viewing for one of these different audiences: teenage boys; young women; families with children of mixed ages; retired people; teenagers and young adults who enjoy going clubbing. Discuss students' reasons for their choices, drawing out their current understanding of audience.

2 Whole class work

- Display **Image 3.1**, the *Freshwater Fishing* magazine cover, on page 14 of the ActiveTeach.

Image 3.1

- To demonstrate how to work out at whom a text is aimed, go through each question and sample answer on page 14 of the student book. Do students come up with any different answers from those in the student book?

3 Pair work

- Using Texts A – C (**Worksheet 3.1, Image 3.2** and **Audio 3.1**), ask students to work in pairs to complete **Activity 1**, available on **Worksheet 3.2**. Students should begin by working out the audience for each text, then identify what features make it suitable for that audience.

Image 3.2

- Students should then consider how the writer wants the audience to respond to the text. They may find it helpful to consider the following questions: *Does the writer want the reader to take some sort of action? Does the writer want to pass on information? What does the writer want the reader to feel – entertained, curious, scared, alarmed?* Explain that this is the purpose of a text.

Worksheet 3.1

Worksheet 3.2

4 Whole class work

- Display the box of purposes on page 15 of the student book using the zoom feature on the ActiveTeach. Ask students if they can think of any television programmes which have these purposes, for example: cookery programmes to teach, comedy to entertain, natural history programmes to inform, documentaries to analyse, argue or persuade, car programmes to review, etc.

- Ask students to describe how these programmes achieve their purposes, for example: cookery programmes include demonstrations, documentaries include interviews with experts who give their opinion or make an argument. If students have suggested magazine-style programmes such as *Top Gear,* ask them to comment on the purpose of different sections and how they achieve these purposes.

- Make sure students understand that some texts have mixed purposes, for example: cookery programmes inform/teach and also entertain.

Additional support

Starter
- Use shared **first languages** of EAL learners to explore the meanings of 'purpose' and 'audience'. A **bilingual dictionary** could be useful.

Pair work/Activity 1
- **Talk partners:** Pair fluent English speakers with EAL students to discuss colloquial language used in the web article (e.g. 'rear-facing', 'hassle', 'it's a breeze').

- **Word wall** or **washing line:** The verbs (purposes) in the box on page 15 could be stuck on a display with sticky tack so the students could physically take them from the display to use in a whole class modelling activity or in a substitution table for more practice.

5 Pair work

- Direct students to **Activity 2**. Introduce the idea that some texts do something *for* their audience whereas others want a response *from* their audience.

- Ask students to complete **Activity 2** in pairs, recording their ideas on **Worksheet 3.3**. Set a time limit and discuss answers as a class.

Worksheet 3.3

6 Independent work

- Ask the class to list six programmes they enjoy watching. Students should then work independently to complete **Worksheet 3.4**. They should pick four of the programmes selected by the class. For each programme they should a) identify its purpose; b) decide whether the programme either wants a response from viewers or wants to do something for them; c) decide what features the programme contains that help it achieve its purpose.

- Afterwards students should swap lists with a partner and assess each other's answers.

Worksheet 3.4

7 Plenary

Ask students to explain to a partner how to identify a text's audience and identify a text's purpose.

8 Further work

Ask students to collect three other texts, such as newspaper articles, leaflets from the library, doctors or charity shops, etc. Students should complete **Worksheet 3.5**, deciding for each text who its audience is and what the purpose is. They should give reasons for their answers.

Worksheet 3.5

Suggested answers

Student book Activity 1

Text A *Audience: parents with small children. Features: information about car seat, safety, usability, etc.*

Text B *Audience: young teenage girls. Features: pink colour, girly fonts, hearts and cartoons, photos of young girls and Miley Cyrus.*

Text C *Audience: pedestrians, particularly teenagers. Features: interviewers are teenagers, most interviewees are teenagers, statistics given relate to teenagers.*

Student book Activity 2

Get a response from audience: persuade, argue, advise
Do something for audience: explain, review, comment, inform, analyse, entertain

Lesson 4 Purpose

Learning objectives

→ Work out what a text's purpose is.

1 Starter

BBC Video: Audience and purpose

- Show the **BBC Video: Audience and purpose**, available on the ActiveTeach, and ask students to pinpoint four points of advice the speakers give about how to work out a text's purpose.

- Afterwards ask students in pairs to decide whether they agree or disagree with the speakers' advice and what advice they can add.

- Point out that the lesson's objective is to identify purposes.

2 Whole class work

- Ask students to close their books. Display the Toyota Prius review on page 16 of the student book, or on **Worksheet 4.1**. Model how to work out a text's purpose using the steps on page 16 of the student book.

Worksheet 4.1

- Highlight the main points and ask students to comment on the writer's perspective. Refer back to the table of purposes in Lesson 3 on page 15 of the student book. Ask whether the writer of the advertisement wants the audience to do something, or whether they want to do something for the audience. Lead students to the conclusion that the purpose is to inform.

Resources required

Student book pages 16–17
BBC Video: Audience and purpose
Video 4.1: Be Humankind
Weblink 4.1: Food Standards Agency interactive
Worksheet 4.1: Toyota Prius
Worksheet 4.2: How to be the life of the party
Worksheet 4.3: LG Cookie
Worksheet 4.4: Should Rafa be sacked?
Worksheet 4.5: Identifying purpose
Worksheet 4.6: Audience and purpose

Assessment objectives

English AO2i / English Language AO3i
Read and understand texts, selecting material appropriate to purpose, collating from different sources and making comparisons and cross references as appropriate.

English AO2ii / English Language AO3ii
Develop and sustain interpretations of writers' ideas and perspectives.

3 Pair work

- Using **Weblink 4.1**, **Video 4.1** and **Worksheets 4.2, 4.3** and **4.4**, ask pairs to use these strategies to complete **Activity 1**, available on **Worksheet 4.5**. Remind students that texts can have mixed purposes. Tell them that texts that are meant to persuade or inform are often also designed to entertain as this helps them get their message across.

Weblink 4.1

Video 4.1: Be Humankind

Worksheet 4.2

Worksheet 4.3

Worksheet 4.4

Worksheet 4.5

Additional support

Pair work
• Ensure pairs are a **mixture** of EAL and fluent speakers of English to aid understanding of idioms (e.g. 'dress to kill', 'flashy', 'fake it', 'hard pressed') and technical vocabulary (e.g. 'compact', 'megapixel').

• Share responses as a class. Take feedback on any texts whose purposes were more difficult to find. Determine if these difficulties were related to form, purpose or content, and provide additional support as needed.

4 **Independent work**

• Students should complete **Worksheet 4.6** independently, identifying the audience and purpose of their controlled assessment task or the sample controlled assessment task on pages 50–53 of the student book.

Worksheet 4.6

5 **Plenary**

Discuss students' answers to **Activity 1,** and ask them to explain their decisions.

6 **Further work**

• Ask students to complete **Worksheet 4.6** again, but this time they should find their own text and be prepared to explain its audience and purpose and to justify their decisions.

• Alternatively, provide students with a text of your choice, for example: a poster in school, a leaflet, or an advertisement on a board near school.

Suggested answers

Student book Activity 1

Text A inform and entertain

Text B persuade

Text C advise and entertain

Text D review

Text E comment and persuade

Lesson 5 Understanding presentation

Resources required

Student book pages 18–19
Image 5.1: Hop Farm Festival poster
Image 5.2: Colours Fest '09 poster
Worksheet 5.1: Presentational features 1
Worksheet 5.2: Presentational features 2
Worksheet 5.3: Effects of presentational features

Learning objectives

→ Recognise different presentational features.
→ Understand the effect of presentational features.

Assessment objectives

English AO2i / English Language AO3i
Read and understand texts, selecting material appropriate to purpose, collating from different sources and making comparisons and cross references as appropriate.

English AO2ii / English Language AO3ii
Develop and sustain interpretations of writers' ideas and perspectives.

1 Starter

- If possible show students a word-processing page and ask them to demonstrate different ways of presenting the word 'Fantastic', for example: bold, italics, different font, size, colour and so on. Explain that these different ways of *presenting* something are called presentational features.

- Now brainstorm a list of presentational features that can be used when creating a poster, for example: large headings, smaller text for detail, images. Write your class list on the board.

- Ask students whether they think it is important to think about audience and purpose when designing presentational features. Ask: *Would it be appropriate to use a bright pink fun-looking font to ask for a donation to a charity helping victims of an earthquake? What sort of font would you use in a poster for young children? Would you do something different for posters aimed at adults?*

- Read through the learning objectives with students and explain what they will need to know about perspective.

2 Whole class work

- Display **Image 5.1**, using this poster to model recognising presentational features. Point out the size and font of the main heading. Ask students to comment on its position and style.

Image 5.1

- Point out the other text (list of bands, contact details, etc.) and ask students to comment on their size, colour and position.

Image 5.2

- Now display **Image 5.2** and ask students to complete **Activity 1** using **Worksheet 5.1**, identifying and discussing the presentational features in each text.

3 Group work

- Explain that writers design their presentational features carefully so they will both appeal to the reader and also tell them something about the subject. Point out that the font in **Image 5.1** is brown, like the earth and trees, which gives it a natural feel. Ask students what the font colours in **Image 5.2** remind them of.

- Ask students to work in groups of four to complete **Activity 2**, noting down all their details about how the presentational features are used in the texts. They should record their ideas in a mind map.

- Divide each group into two and ask the pairs to note down what ideas the details suggest to the reader.

- Pairs should come together again to discuss their ideas and add them to the mind map.

- Ask each group to find five differences in the way presentational features are used in the posters and come up with ideas about why these differences are there. Share ideas as a class.

Additional support

Group/Pair work

- Before starting these activities, **remind** students of the meaning of audience, purpose and form.

- **Remind** students that in exam questions words such as 'explain', 'comment', 'discuss' all require students to use appropriate words to explain. Display a set of **cards with words and phrases** such as: 'because', 'so that', 'which shows that', 'which suggests', 'gives the impression', 'making the reader...' and model their use when making a point, giving evidence and explaining. Invite student participation and repeat or rephrase correct usage to give **message abundancy.**

Starter
- **Talk partners**: Pair strong English speakers with EAL learners, to establish the meaning of the technical vocabulary on page 18 of the student book.

- List these technical terms on the **word wall** for ready reference during discussions.

Whole class work
- Students may need to be **reminded** of synonyms for 'identify'.

4 Pair work

- Ask pairs to comment on the different use of colour in the two texts. Model how to capture those thoughts in appropriate sentences. Write key vocabulary on the board, for example: *suggests, creates the impression that..., hints..., makes readers notice...*

- Students should work in pairs to complete questions 1 and 2 of **Activity 3**. They should list and make notes on five differences in the way presentational features are used in the posters. They can record their answers in the table on **Worksheet 5.2**.

Worksheet 5.2

- Next, ask pairs to complete question 3 of **Activity 3**, writing sentences comparing the presentational features.

- Finally, students should work individually to answer questions 4 and 5, composing their final two sentences about the overall impression of presentational features.

- Share responses as a class.

5 Plenary

- As a class, brainstorm the presentational features you might use to create a poster advertising a family fair at a local park. Ask students to suggest specific details such as font colour, size and style and background images.

- Now ask the class to brainstorm the presentational features they might use to create a poster advertising a Hallowe'en party at the local youth club for 14–17 year olds. Encourage students to be as specific as possible.

6 Further work

- Ask students to find a text that makes use of presentational features, such as a CD, DVD or videogame cover, an advertisement, a newspaper or a magazine cover. They should stick a copy of their chosen text to **Worksheet 5.3** and comment on the effect of the presentational devices.

Worksheet 5.3

- Alternatively, provide them with a colour photocopy of an image of your choice.

Suggested answers

Student book Activity 1

2. *Text A heading; different fonts, font sizes and colours; image; background.*

3. *Text B heading; different fonts, font sizes and colours; image; backgrounds; frame; shapes; boxes.*

Student book Activity 3

2. *Colour – A Natural muted brown and soft crayon colours; country feel in background and font: may suggest folk or indie music? Gives the impression that the festival will have a rural, hippy feel. B Bright colours; impression of energy, energetic music; variety of colours might suggest variety of music.*

   Images – A Hot air balloon and pennants suggest slightly old-fashioned, country fair feel. However, balloon suggests adventure. B Rainbow and flowers contrast with modern building – could suggest variety or up-to-date music; image and rainbow seem to burst out of venue – suggest energy.

   Text – A Main heading font has flowers on it, suggest nature; body text font has old-fashioned feel. Hand-drawn font on pennants – adds to mellow, country feel. B Heading is modern, chunky, funky: suggests music will be current and lively.

   Background – A Earthy brown patches give slightly muddy feel – adds to natural feel and suggests music and event have their feet on the ground. B Bright and dark blue suggest night sky or 'touch the sky' feeling.

Lesson 6 Exploring the effects of presentation

Learning objectives

→ Understand the effect of different presentational features.

→ Work out how presentational features support the text's main ideas.

Resources required

Student book pages 20–21
Weblink 6.1: NSPCC webpage
Image 6.1: Odeon voucher
Image 6.2: Computer game cover
Worksheet 6.1: Plain text
Worksheet 6.2: Presentational features 1
Worksheet 6.3: Presentational features 2
Worksheet 6.4: Assessing presentational features
Answer sheet 6.1: Suggested answers

Assessment objectives

English AO2i / English Language AO3i
Read and understand texts, selecting material appropriate to purpose, collating from different sources and making comparisons and cross references as appropriate.

English AO2ii / English Language AO3ii
Develop and sustain interpretations of writers' ideas and perspectives.

English AO2iii / English Language AO3iii
Explain and evaluate how writers use linguistic, grammatical, structural and presentational features to achieve effects and engage and influence the reader.

1 Starter

- As a class, brainstorm a list of presentational features a writer can use in a text.

- Now display the text on **Worksheet 6.1** about a fireworks festival in Rugby. Ask students how they would use presentational features to grab the reader's attention and encourage them to attend the event.

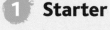

Access Unit 1 English Today: Reading

Lesson 6: Worksheet 6.1
Plain text

Fawkesmead Rugby Fireworks and funfair
Gates open 6pm. Display 7.30pm
Advance tickets from www.fawkesmeadrugby.com
Advance tickets Adults £6 U16's £4 U5's FREE Family £15
On the night Adults £7 U16's £5 U5's FREE Family £20
[Family 2 adults + 2 children or 1 adult +3 children]
Fawkesmead Rugby Ground, Ash Way, Sparksdon

Worksheet 6.1

- Display **Worksheet 6.1** and ask students to amend it. Students should justify their 'improvements' before making them. Ask the rest of the class to evaluate the effect.

- Explain that presentational features are used for effect and contribute to the text's main ideas.

2 Whole class work

- Display the Odeon voucher, **Image 6.1**, on the ActiveTeach or focus students' attention on page 20 of the student book.

25% OFF
ANY FILM AT ODEON
Image 6.1

- Model how to work out the writer's main ideas and perspective of the image, pick out the presentational features used, discuss their impact and then work out how they add to the writer's ideas and perspective (see suggested answers).

3 Group work

- Using **Weblink 6.1**, launch the NSPCC home page. Students should practise the skills modelled earlier as they study the NSPCC home page. Hand out **Worksheet 6.2** and have students complete question 1 of **Activity 1** individually. Share responses as a class.

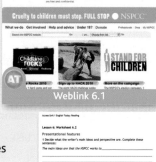

Weblink 6.1

Worksheet 6.2

- Students should then work in small groups to complete **Activity 1**, listing five presentational features and commenting on what they suggest. They should record their ideas on **Worksheet 6.2**.

- Have groups share their ideas with the class. Annotate the text with students' ideas using the annotation tool on the ActiveTeach.

- Work together to develop sentences on the NSPCC's presentation. Make a note of some key vocabulary on the board, for example: *suggests, creates the impression that…, hints…, makes readers notice….*

Additional support

Starter

- As you brainstorm, use **message abundancy**, to **review** the 'presentational features' in the table on page 18 of the student book.
- **Remind** students about audience, purpose and text form and **clarify** the cultural/idiomatic vocabulary in Worksheet 6.1.
- The **modelling** text on page 20 is very helpful – extend this to **highlight** words and phrases which are useful for commenting: 'Using blue links...with...', 'All this strengthens...'
- Create a **spider diagram** as a visual analysis of the voucher to show the hierarchy of information and presentation used to convey the message.

Group work

- The **sentence starters** in Activity 1 are helpful – highlight the use of 'should'.
- **Talk partners: Ensure** groups include fluent English speakers and EAL students, to aid understanding.
- **Clarify** 'NSPCC' and 'ChildLine'.

Independent work

- Before starting Worksheet 6.3, re-introduce the idea of forming sentences using 'because' to comment by using simple known contexts. For example, 'I know he attends this school because he is wearing our uniform'. Explain that these sentence starters are a **writing frame** for answering question 3.

---

4 Independent work

- Ask students to read the text they have been given for their controlled assessment or read a sample controlled assessment text on pages 50–53 and note down the text's main ideas and perspective.

- Share responses and check that all students have understood correctly.

- Now ask students to attempt **Worksheet 6.3** individually, using the skills developed in this lesson to study the texts used in their controlled assessment task.

- You could give each student a second copy of **Worksheet 6.3** and ask them to complete it for their second controlled assessment text.

Worksheet 6.3

5 Plenary

Ask students to share some of their answers to **Worksheet 6.3** and to verbally compare two controlled assessment reading task texts. Encourage students to use words like *but, however, also, similarly*.

6 Further work

Hand out **Worksheet 6.4** and display **Image 6.2**, a computer game cover. Students should analyse the cover and label the presentational features. They should then write five sentences to explain how the presentational features support the writer's main ideas and perspectives.

Worksheet 6.4

Suggested answers

2 Whole class work

- *Main ideas: 25% off weekday films of all kinds.*
- *Perspective: The writer wants the reader to take advantage of the offer and go to an Odeon cinema.*
- *Presentational features: Colour blue looks cool and sophisticated – also reflects the light of the screen. A variety of people in the image – shows the offer is open to everyone and that everyone will enjoy the cinema. People look interested and excited, reinforcing the idea that cinema is fun.*

Student book Activity 1 – see Answer sheet 6.1

Lesson 7 Commenting effectively on presentation

Learning objectives

→ Compare the way presentational features are used in texts.

→ Comment on presentation effectively.

Resources required

Student book pages 22–27
Weblink 7.1: Eurotrip
Image 7.1: Hop Farm Festival poster
Image 7.2: Colours Fest '09 poster
Image 7.3: Caravan fire safety brochure
Image 7.4: Frances the Firefly fire safety brochure
Worksheet 7.1: Comparison table
Worksheet 7.2: Connectives
Worksheet 7.3: Using connectives
Worksheet 7.4: Connective challenge
Answer sheet 7.1: Suggested answers

Assessment objectives

English AO2i / English Language AO3i
Read and understand texts, selecting material appropriate to purpose, collating from different sources and making comparisons and cross references as appropriate.

English AO2ii / English Language AO3ii
Develop and sustain interpretations of writers' ideas and perspectives.

English AO2iii / English Language AO3iii
Explain and evaluate how writers use linguistic, grammatical, structural and presentational features to achieve effects and engage and influence the reader.

1 Starter

- Display the Hop Farm and Colour Fest posters students studied in Lesson 5 (**Images 7.1** and **7.2**) on the ActiveTeach.

- As a class, draw up a checklist of presentational features to use to make comparisons, for example: images, font colour, font size, background, headings and so on.

- Brainstorm a list of comparison vocabulary on the board, for example: *similar, different, compare, same, unlike, however, in contrast, similarly, however, but*. Challenge students to make quick comparisons between the posters using this vocabulary. Check students' understanding of these words.

- Explain that students will need to compare presentational features.

Image 7.1

Image 7.2

2 Whole class work

- Introduce the strategy for making comparisons given on page 22 of the student book.

- Model this process using the caravan fire safety brochure. Display **Image 7.3**. Read the text as a class and briefly demonstrate how to pick out the main ideas, highlighting or annotating the text using the annotation tool on the ActiveTeach. Include the main ideas on how to get out of a fire, as well as the causes.

- Now discuss the writer's perspective, explaining that the writer wants people to be aware of the dangers of candles and cigarettes in causing fires in caravans.

Did you know?
- On average 1,400 fires per year occur in caravans.
- More than five fires a day are started by candles.
- Every three days someone dies from a fire caused by a cigarette.

These tips will help keep you and your family safe from fire.

Image 7.3

- Now display the Frances the Firely brochure, **Image 7.4**. Ask students to work out the text's main ideas and the writer's perspective. Share ideas as a class.

Image 7.4

- Ask students to close their books. Briefly ask them to comment on how the coloured background, images and font help communicate the ideas and perspectives in Text A, the caravan brochure. Encourage students to ask themselves why each feature has been included. Make sure they link each feature back to the main ideas and perspectives of the text.

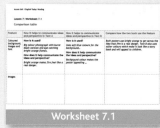
Worksheet 7.1

- Display the table on page 23 by opening **Worksheet 7.1** on the ActiveTeach. Do students agree with these ideas?

3 Pair work

- Ask students to work in pairs to complete the middle two columns of the table on **Worksheet 7.1**, making notes on the effects of background images and fonts as set out in **Activity 1**.

Additional support

Starter
- Re-introduce the **word wall** from Lesson 5 and extend it as the lesson progresses.
- The focus on language for comparison, connectives and modelling in this lesson is very helpful for EAL learners.

Pair work
- **Active listening**: Hearing the exemplar text read aloud by a fluent English reader could aid understanding for EAL learners.

- **Talk partners**: Pair EAL learners and English speakers to discuss the idea of 'perspective', both literally and as a synonym for point of view or opinion.

Whole class/Independent work
- **Extend** the exemplar sentences on page 23 to include sentences using the remaining connectives to show what is different ('but', 'on the one hand', 'on the other hand') and what is similar ('and', 'also', 'in the same way').

- In pairs, students should write a sentence comparing how the features are used in Text A and Text B. If students find this difficult, draw their attention to the sample text on the use of background colour, images and font found in the chart. Ensure students understand that they need to draw evidence from both texts when making comparisons.

4 Whole class work

- Hand out **Worksheet 7.2** and ask students individually to group the connectives into a) ones they know and use b) ones they recognise but don't use c) ones they do not know at all.

- Share responses. Now introduce connectives that help explain what is different. Read the example on page 24 to students and challenge them to come up with examples of their own, focusing in particular on those connectives that students did not use or did not recognise.

- Repeat the exercise with connectives that are used to explain similarities.

- Challenge students to use the connectives they don't normally use or did not previously know for the rest of this lesson.

Worksheet 7.2

5 Independent work

Ask students to work through **Activity 2** on **Worksheet 7.3**, using their completed tables and their 'challenge' connectives to write complex sentences and paragraphs comparing the presentational features in the texts.

Worksheet 7.3

6 Pair work

- Ask students to look at **Weblink 7.1** and complete **Activity 3** on page 25. Students should then assess their own work using the criteria given in the ResultsPlus Maximise your marks section.

Weblink 7.1

- Students should work in pairs to complete the **Putting it into practice** activity on page 27.

7 Plenary/Peer assessment

Check that all students are now familiar with all the connectives; have students model sentences using their 'challenge' connectives. You may like to start with sentences comparing the texts in the student book, then move on to more general sentences.

8 Further work

Ask students to use their 'challenge' connectives. They should record five opportunities they have taken to use their connectives while writing in other subjects. Students can record their sentences on **Worksheet 7.4**.

Worksheet 7.4

Suggested answers

Student book Activity 1 – see Answer sheet 7.1

Lesson 8 Understanding why images are used

Learning objectives

→ Understand why images are used in texts.
→ Explore the content of images.

Resources required

Student book pages 28–29
Image 8.1: Spooky house
Image 8.2: Beach house
Image 8.3: House with solar panels
Image 8.4: Pirate Pete illustration
Image 8.5: Anatomy illustration
Resource 8.1: Young Carers leaflet
Worksheet 8.1: Why images are used 1
Worksheet 8.2: Why images are used 2
Worksheet 8.3: Why images are used 3
Answer sheet 8.1: Suggested answers

Assessment objectives

English AO2i / English Language AO3i
Read and understand texts, selecting material appropriate to purpose, collating from different sources and making comparisons and cross references as appropriate.

English AO2ii / English Language AO3ii
Develop and sustain interpretations of writers' ideas and perspectives.

1 Starter

- Show students the three photographs of houses (**Images 8.1–8.3**). Ask them to decide which image they would use for each of the following purposes:
  - the front cover of a ghost story novel
  - an advertisement for holiday homes on a website
  - a leaflet about home improvements.

- Students should give reasons for their choices.

Image 8.1

Image 8.2

Image 8.3

2 Whole class work

- Display **Image 8.4**, an illustration from a children's book, on the ActiveTeach or page 28 of the student book. Explain that an image can be used to show the writer's perspective, make the audience want to read the text and/or help the text achieve its purpose.

Image 8.4

- Take students through the worked example on page 28. First, ask students what they think the writer's perspective is. If they find this difficult, explain that in this example finding the writer's perspective means finding what the writer thinks about the characters in the story. Ask students: *Who do you think the audience is for this book? How do you know? Do you think the pictures will make the audience want to read the text? What is the purpose of the text? Does the illustration help the text achieve its purpose?*

- Tell students to ask themselves the following questions to determine why an image is in a text: *What is the image showing? What is the image making readers notice and think?* Model using these questions to analyse one of the house images used in the starter activity.

3 Pair/Whole class work

- Using **Image 8.5**, an anatomy book illustration, ask students to work in pairs on **Activity 1** to investigate how the image works with the text's main ideas. Students can record their answers on **Worksheet 8.1**.

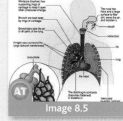
Image 8.5

- Discuss students' answers as a class. Encourage students to comment on why they think the image has been used and how it helps support the writer's purpose.

- Ask students to suggest other texts that use images and comment on how they support the writer's purpose, for example: instruction manuals (to clarify instructions); cookery books (to show the reader what the food should look like and to make the reader want to cook the food). Encourage students to be as specific as they can and cite any examples they have seen recently.

Worksheet 8.1

EAL Additional support

Starter
- Revise audience and purpose. Ensure students understand that all the uses given for the images are designed to persuade someone to do something (to read a book, to buy a holiday, to carry out home improvements).
- **Talk partners**: Pair fluent English speakers with EAL learners to enable EAL learners to learn the vocabulary necessary to discuss the images, their effect and their part in persuading the reader to do something.
- **Word wall**: Use individual cards in a movable display on the wall. Each card will have a **language technique** which can be used to talk about the effect on the reader such as '**suggests** that...', '**encourages** the idea that...', '**involves** the reader in...', '**creates** the impression...', '**adds** emphasis...', '**makes** the reader **feel**...', '**implies**...' etc.
- You might like to make multiple copies of the cards so that students can physically take them from the display to use. This will help to give them confidence in the discussion and to remind them of the phrases used to 'talk about' or 'write about' (comment on) in future work.

Pair/Whole class work
- Start a **washing line** with reasons for using images (e.g. 'to show', 'to clarify') and then during class add other reasons as the class suggests them. A **card sort** could then be used to develop responses in later activities.
- Ask students to consider the negative and positive consequences of not including any images in different kinds of text.

Pair work
- **Activate prior knowledge**: Providing opportunities for EAL students to **predict** what the text on page 29 might be about, using clues provided by the images and other presentational features.
- The **sentence starters** and **writing frames** could be extended to include 'explaining' connectives such as 'because', 'therefore', 'however'.
- It may be appropriate for EAL students who speak the **same first language** to discuss 'suggest', 'imply' and other words on the **word wall** and **writing frames** to ensure understanding. **Bilingual dictionaries** could be useful.

4 Pair work

- Display **Resource 8.1**. Ask students to work in pairs to complete parts 1–4 of **Activity 2**. Students can record their ideas on **Worksheet 8.2**. Students should work out the purpose of the text and the writer's perspective using the strategies they have learned in previous lessons. Briefly check answers as a class.

Resource 8.1

Worksheet 8.2

- Ask students to look carefully at the image and think about what it adds to the leaflet. Ask students to role-play a discussion between the writer and the Young Carers charity, in which the writer has to justify the choice of image and how it supports the ideas and perspective of the leaflet. Ask volunteers to share their role-plays with the class.
- Answer parts 5–7 of **Activity 2** as a class, recording students' ideas on the board. Support students in constructing sophisticated sentences that explain what the image adds to the leaflet.

5 Plenary

Discuss the following texts and ask students to suggest an image that would support each text's main ideas and purpose. They should comment on what qualities the image would need to have in order to be effective (e.g. whether it should be eye-catching, accurate, life-like, etc.).
- poster for a charity that helps the homeless
- webpage giving directions to a theatre
- leaflet advertising a zoo
- poster for a disaster movie
- textbook that explains how a car engine works
- instruction manual for a television

6 Further work

Ask students to choose an image from a newspaper, magazine, textbook, CD, DVD or game cover, or website. Students should complete **Worksheet 8.3** to explain what the image adds to the text it belongs to.

Worksheet 8.3

Suggested answers

Student book Activity 1
1. *The organs in the human body and their location.*
2. *Informs readers about what is inside the human body. Image gives much of the information in the text. The label information is not enough to understand where organs are. The image allows the reader to visualise the positions of the organs.*

Student book Activity 2 – see Answer sheet 8.1

Lesson 9 Commenting on images

Learning objectives

→ Explore the way an image is presented.

→ Comment on the effect of an image.

Resources required

Student book pages 30–31
Image 9.1: Knife crime poster
Image 9.2: Stop The Traffik poster
Image 9.3: Man with snake
Image 9.4: Girl and snake
Worksheet 9.1: Colours
Worksheet 9.2: Knife crime poster
Worksheet 9.3: Freeze-frames
Worksheet 9.4: Effects of images 1
Worksheet 9.5: Effects of images 2
Answer sheets 9.1–9.3: Suggested answers

Assessment objectives

English AO2i / English Language AO3i
Read and understand texts, selecting material appropriate to purpose, collating from different sources and making comparisons and cross references as appropriate.

English AO2ii / English Language AO3ii
Develop and sustain interpretations of writers' ideas and perspectives.

English AO2iii / English Language AO3iii
Explain and evaluate how writers use linguistic, grammatical, structural and presentational features to achieve effects and engage and influence the reader.

1 Starter

- Display **Worksheet 9.1**. Ask students to tell you what words or ideas they associate with each colour (for example, red – danger, hot; white – purity, cold; black – night, evil, death; green – nature, fresh; purple – royal; blue – peace, water, cool). Accept one-word or short phrase associations. Be aware that students from different cultural backgrounds may have different associations.

- This is an opportunity to develop students' vocabulary in describing and discussing colour, for example: deep, dark, bright. Write up a word bank on the board or as a poster so students can use the words in later activities.

Worksheet 9.1

2 Whole class work

- Ask students to choose different colours to decorate a) a room for a teenage party; b) a formal meeting room for MPs; c) a toddler crèche, and d) their ideal classroom.

- Share ideas as a class, then model how to use the phrases on page 30 of the student book to express your ideas about the colours in sentences, for example: 'I would use simple strong colours in a crèche to suggest that it is a fun and lively place to be.'

3 Pair work

- Students should work in pairs to complete **Activity 1**. They should comment on what red and green imply or suggest in different contexts.

Image 9.1

- Display **Image 9.1**, the Crimestoppers poster. Ask students to look at the image and complete **Activity 2**, recording their ideas on **Worksheet 9.2**. Students should work out the main ideas before commenting on the colour.

- Share ideas as a class.

Worksheet 9.2

4 Whole class work

- Display **Image 9.2**. Ask students to tell you their first impressions and reactions. Discuss the idea that 'a picture is worth a thousand words'. Ask students what story they think the picture tells. Explain what human trafficking is, and that Stop The Traffik is a charity working to stop it (more information is available on the Stop The Traffik website).

Image 9.2

- Explain how angle and position of an image can change the effect. For example, if the angle looks up at something it might make it look powerful or 'edgy'. Looking down on something may make you feel superior, or it might encourage feelings of pity. Discuss how the angle in **Image 9.2** adds to the sense that the baby has been discarded.

Additional support

Starter
- **Visual presentation**: Use the starter to refresh the use of 'suggest' and 'imply'.
- **EAL first language discussion**: In pairs, learners can discuss any cultural significance of the colours in their language or background and share it with the whole class.

Whole class work
- Use **writing frames** and the **movable word wall** to remind students to use 'suggests' and 'implies' when explaining or describing colour choices.

Pair work
- **Talk partners**: Pair an EAL student with a fluent English speaker to discuss Activities 1 and 2.

Whole class work
- Make a **washing line** with key words such as 'content', 'colour', 'angle' and 'composition'. It will also be useful to discuss prepositions (which EAL learners find difficult) such as 'beside', 'at the front'.
- **Clarify** words as necessary, e.g. 'edgy', 'pity'.

Group work
- Ensure a good **mixture** of EAL and fluent English speakers in each group.
- **Envoys** activity could be used for sharing ideas about the scenarios.
- It could be appropriate to use **joint construction** as a class to **model** how to write a paragraph about composition whilst using the **word wall** to find phrases and words for suggesting and implying.

- Explain composition. Point out that the things shown at the front of an image are usually the most important and those at the back less important, but that sometimes key details can be hidden elsewhere for the reader to notice.

- Model how to work out and explain the choice of composition and angle. Tell students that they should ask themselves the following questions: *What can I see? What is the main focus of the image? What does the angle tell me? How do I feel about the composition of this image?* Discuss each question with reference to the Stop The Traffik poster.

angle to comment on the effect of each text. They can record their answers on **Worksheet 9.4.**

Image 9.4

Worksheet 9.4

---

5 Group work

- Divide the class into groups of four. Hand out one of the scenarios from **Worksheet 9.3** to each group, and ask students to create a freeze-frame to show the scenario on their card. Tell students to try to picture the image in their mind, then reproduce it as best they can. They can specify the angle from which the photo is taken.

- Have each group present their freeze-frames to the class, explaining the angle of the photograph and the basic information about the freeze-frame, for example: that it is of a pop group or a group of friends. Ask the rest of the class what the composition of each image tells them about the scenario of the freeze-frame.

Worksheet 9.3

6 Pair work

Image 9.3

Display **Images 9.3** and **9.4** on the ActiveTeach or page 31 of the student book. Ask students to complete **Activity 3** in pairs. Students should use their understanding of composition and

7 Plenary

Students should work in groups and form a publisher's meeting to decide whether they would use Image A (**Image 9.3**) or Image B (**Image 9.4**) as part of a tourism advertising campaign encouraging people to visit India. Ask them to justify their choices by commenting on the content, composition, angle, colours, etc. of the pictures.

8 Further work

Ask students to find an advertisement or newspaper story that includes a strong image. They should then complete **Worksheet 9.5**, which asks them to comment on the angle and composition of the image and what each suggests. Remind students to bring their image to class with them.

Worksheet 9.5

Suggested answers

Student book Activities 1–3 – See Answer sheets 9.1–9.3

Lesson 10 Understanding moving images

Learning objectives

→ Explore the features of moving image text.

→ Comment on the effect of features in a moving image text.

Resources required

Student book pages 32–34
Video 10.1: War on Want campaign
Video 10.2: Prince's Trust campaign
Weblink 10.1: Eurotrip
Images 10.1–10.10: Images A–J
Worksheet 10.1: Sorting images
Worksheet 10.2: Soundtrack
Worksheet 10.3: Film transcript
Worksheet 10.4: Filming techniques
Worksheet 10.5: Writing a paragraph
Answer sheets 10.1–10.2: Suggested answers

Assessment objectives

English AO2i / English Language AO3i
Read and understand texts, selecting material appropriate to purpose, collating from different sources and making comparisons and cross references as appropriate.

English AO2ii / English Language AO3ii
Develop and sustain interpretations of writers' ideas and perspectives.

English AO2iii / English Language AO3iii
Explain and evaluate how writers use linguistic, grammatical, structural and presentational features to achieve effects and engage and influence the reader.

1 Starter

- Ask students to work in role: they are working for a charity called War on Want, and they want to make a film persuading people that buying clothes that have been produced in sweatshops is wrong. Ask them to suggest what kind of images they would include in their film, for example: shots of the factory, interviews with workers, images of workers' living conditions contrasted with images of shoppers and so on.

- Show students the whole of **Video 10.1**, the War on Want campaign film, available on the ActiveTeach. Ask students to identify the writer's main ideas and perspective.

Video 10.1: War on Want

- Brainstorm a list of similarities and differences between reading film and reading texts or images. For example, when reading film you need to consider words, images and sound; when reading a written text you only need to consider the words.

- As a class, devise a list of strategies you could use when studying a film rather than a paper text, for example: replay, pause frame by frame/scene by scene, use of mute, use of transcript.

2 Whole class work

- Working through page 32 of the student book, model how to read a scene in a film using the questions and a still from the War on Want film. Ask students: *What is this scene showing you? What does the soundtrack add to the scene?*

- Ask students to consider how this builds towards the writer's main ideas and perspective. Ask: *How does the writer feel about the situation? What does he or she want us to feel?*

3 Group work

- Show the whole class the Prince's Trust video available on the ActiveTeach (**Video 10.2**) once. Briefly discuss what the film's main ideas are and what the writer's perspective is.

- Then ask students to work in groups to complete question 1 of **Activity 1** and sort the images on page 33 of the student book (**Images 10.1 to 10.10**) into the order they appear in the film. Students can cut out the images and paste them in the correct order on **Worksheet 10.1**.

Worksheet 10.1

Video 10.2: Prince's Trust

4 Whole class work

- Ask students to work in pairs to complete question 2 of **Activity 1**. Play **Video 10.2** without sound. Discuss the effect of having no soundtrack.

- Then show the film again with the soundtrack on and stop at the end of each scene to discuss and note down the effects of the soundtrack in the chart on **Worksheet 10.2**. You may want

Worksheet 10.2

Additional support

Starter
- After the brainstorm activity draw a **Venn diagram** to indicate the similarities and differences between reading film and reading images.
- Add new words such as 'soundtrack', 'voiceover', 'close-up' and 'camera shots' to the **washing line/word wall** as a ready reference during discussions.

- Make the suggested answers into a short **dictogloss** as a **model**.

Whole class work
- **Active listening**: In addition to the activities given, repeated viewing of both videos may be necessary for EAL students to understand the soundtracks.

Pair work
- Before Activity 2, read the exemplar questions to ask about the video on page 34 and **clarify** words as necessary such as 'suspicious', 'anonymous', 'effect'.

---

to use the film transcript on **Worksheet 10.3** to support this activity. For scene breaks, see suggested answers.

- As scenes progress, gradually move from whole class work to pair responses, and end with students working to individually record their responses on **Worksheet 10.2**.

Worksheet 10.3

5 Whole class work

- Explain that different camera shots can give different effects in a film. Check students' understanding of vocabulary needed to discuss this, for example: close up, distance shot, foreground, background, angle, focus, above (looking down), eye level, below (looking up), composition.
- Display **Image 10.7** and show students that section of **Video 10.2**. Model how to look at the way the scene is shot and what effect this may have. Tell students to ask themselves lots of questions about the shot. Discuss ideas as a class and make notes on **Image 10.7** using the annotation tool on the ActiveTeach.

6 Pair work

- Students can practise their skills as they work through the first part of **Activity 2**. They should work in pairs to choose five images from page 33 and discuss the effect of the way each shot has been filmed, asking themselves questions about the each image. Students can record their ideas on **Worksheet 10.4**.

Worksheet 10.4

- For part 2 of **Activity 2**, pairs should comment on the effect of angles, composition, soundtrack and filming, making specific references to the film. Students may like to comment on which of these aspects they found particularly effective. In part 3, they should identify the writer's perspective.

- Take feedback from pairs on their answers to **Activity 2** and go over any areas in which they struggled.

7 Independent work

- Ask students to look at **Weblink 10.1** and complete the example controlled assessment task in **Activity 3** on page 35. Students should then assess their own work using the criteria given in the ResultsPlus Maximise your marks section.

Weblink 10.1

- Students should work in pairs to complete the **Putting it into practice** activity on page 37.

8 Plenary

A dog rescue charity is looking for advice on how to make sure their film really moves viewers and makes them want to donate. Students should agree a list of five top tips on how a film-maker can use features such as angle, composition and soundtrack to achieve this.

9 Further work

Give students a copy of **Worksheet 10.5**. They should study an image and write a paragraph about the effect of the way it has been filmed.

Worksheet 10.5

Suggested answers

Starter – see Answer sheet 10.1

Student book Activities 1–2 – see Answer sheets 10.1-10.2

Lesson 11 Understanding language choices

Learning objectives

→ Recognise what language choices the writer made.

→ Recognise how language choices suit the writer's audience, purpose, main ideas and perspective.

Resources required

Student book pages 38–39
Video Weblink 11.1: Love Film
Worksheet 11.1: Mizz
Worksheet 11.2: Language choices 1
Worksheet 11.3: Ferrari
Worksheet 11.4: Rehoming
Worksheet 11.5: Language feature bingo
Worksheet 11.6: Language choices 2
Worksheet 11.7: Language choices 3
Worksheet 11.8: Examples of language features
Answer sheet 11.1: Suggested answers

Assessment objectives

English AO2i / English Language AO3i

Read and understand texts, selecting material appropriate to purpose, collating from different sources and making comparisons and cross references as appropriate.

English AO2iii / English Language AO3iii

Explain and evaluate how writers use linguistic, grammatical, structural and presentational features to achieve effects and engage and influence the reader.

1 Starter

- Ask students to explain the meaning and give their own examples of the following key vocabulary: *slang, formal, informal, standard English, describing words (adjectives, adverbs), verbs, fact, opinion, alliteration, technical words* and *direct address*.

- Collate a list on the whiteboard or create a class poster of examples of each of the terms above that can be displayed and referred to during the lesson.

2 Whole class work

Focus students' attention on question 1 of **Activity 1**, available on **Worksheet 11.2**. Display Text A, the Mizz website, on page 39 of the student book or **Worksheet 11.1**. Using Text A, model identifying different types of vocabulary or language feature, and record them in the table on **Worksheet 11.2**, for example, direct address: 'Probably not a good idea though guys.' You may wish to extend the list of types of vocabulary to include features such as imagery and jargon.

Worksheet 11.1

Worksheet 11.2

3 Pair work

Ask students to work in pairs to use the terms in the box in **Activity 1** to identify the language features highlighted in Texts A, B and C (**Worksheets 11.1, 11.3** and **11.4**). You may want to review the language fetures glossary on page 38 first. Challenge them to find any further examples of their own. They should record their ideas on **Worksheet 11.2**. Although they are working in pairs, each student should complete their own copy of this worksheet.

Worksheet 11.3

Worksheet 11.4

Additional support

Starter

- Add the key vocabulary to the **word wall** as an easy reference if there is no whiteboard available (and for future P.E.E. work).
- **Bilingual dictionaries** may be useful.
- A **card sort** matching feature and meaning would be a useful kinaesthetic reinforcement.

Whole class/Pair work

- **Active listening:** Read out Texts A, B and C to the class using expression, pauses, gesture and facial expression to aid understanding. Students should note down any words they do not understand. Watch the film clip twice.
- **Clarify** words as appropriate, asking L1 English students (possibly girls) to explain vocabulary in Text A such as 'quirky cute', 'delish', 'yummy' and 'pout'. Explain 'balmy' as a play on words. Ask other L1 students to explain vocabulary in Text C, e.g. 'Dinos', 'F1'.
- **Talk partners:** Pair fluent English speakers with EAL students to aid individual completion of the tables in Activity 1.
- Create a short **dictogloss** from the Text A exemplar in question 3 as a model for future independent commenting.

4 Whole class work

- Launch **Video Weblink 11.1**, the Love Film video. Hand out bingo cards from **Worksheet 11.5** and play the video again. This time as students watch the video, they should try to identify the types of language on their card and note the examples they find. The first student to complete their bingo card calls out 'Bingo!' and is the winner.
- Check answers as a class.

Access Unit 1 English Today: Reading

Lesson 11: Worksheet 11.5

Language feature bingo

| Describing words | Informal English | Verbs |
| Fact | Opinion | Alliteration |

| Opinion | Fact | Verbs |
| Alliteration | Direct address | Informal English |

| Verbs | Informal English | Slang |
| Alliteration | Technical words | Opinion |

Worksheet 11.5

5 Pair work

- Ask students to close their books. Display Text A (**Worksheet 11.1**) on the ActiveTeach. Ask students what they think are the main idea, perspective, purpose and audience for the text. If students find this difficult, model this process for them. Compare students' ideas with those in the student book (page 38, **Activity 1**, question 2 chart).
- Ask students to work in pairs to complete question 2 of **Activity 1**, identifying the main idea, perspective, purpose and audience for each text. They should record their ideas on **Worksheet 11.6**. Each student should complete their own copy of the worksheet.

Access Unit 1 English Today: Reading

Lesson 11: Worksheet 11.6

Language choices 2

Fill in the table below to list each text's:
a) main ideas b) perspective c) purpose d) audience.

Text	Main idea	Perspective	Purpose	Audience
A	There's a free lip gloss with the fortnight's edition of Mizz.	It's an exciting flavour and smells great so don't miss out.	To persuade people to buy the magazine.	Teenage girls
B				
C				
D				
E				

Worksheet 11.6

- Ask students to swap partners. This may be useful as students can share fresh insights. Now ask students to complete question 3 of **Activity 1**, writing two sentences to explain how the vocabulary suits the main ideas, perspective, purpose and audience of each text. They should record their answers on **Worksheet 11.7**.

Access Unit 1 English Today: Reading

Lesson 11: Worksheet 11.7

Language choices 3

Write two sentences about each text to explain how the type of vocabulary suits the text's:

a) main ideas   b) perspective   c) purpose   d) audience.

Text A is for teenage girls and it's meant to persuade them to buy Mizz magazine, which has a free lip gloss on it. Using slang like 'cute' and 'so delish' shows teenagers the magazine will speak their language which helps persuade them to buy it too.

Text B

Text C

Worksheet 11.7

6 Plenary

Divide students into teams and hold a quick-fire quiz using the terms on **Worksheet 11.5**. Shout out a term and ask each team to buzz to give an example. If they give a correct example, challenge them to suggest where they might hear or read this kind of language, for example: in a magazine, junk mail, newspaper, leaflet, formal letters, *EastEnders*, the news, *Top Gear*, etc. Award a bonus point for a correct answer.

7 Further work

Hand out copies of **Worksheet 11.8**. Challenge students to collect examples of each type of language and record them in the table.

Access Unit 1 English Today: Reading

Lesson 11: Worksheet 11.8

Examples of language features

Type of vocabulary or language feature	Name of the text where you read or heard this type of vocabulary or language feature	Example
slang		
formal		
informal		
Standard English		
describing words		
verb		
fact		
opinion		

Worksheet 11.8

Suggested answers

Student book Activity 1 – See Answer sheet 11.1

45

Lesson 12 Commenting on sentences

Learning objectives

→ Understand how a writer uses different types of sentence to communicate their ideas and perspectives.

→ Explain what effect the writer's choices have.

1 Starter

- Before opening the student book, hand out **Worksheet 12.1** and ask students to match the sentence types to the examples. Take feedback to check that students are familiar with how these different types of sentence are constructed: command, question, list, exclamation, short simple sentence. Ask students to suggest further examples of each type of sentence.

- Extend to cover compound sentences and complex sentences. Compound sentences contain two or more clauses joined by the connectives 'and', 'or' or 'but' and can be used to add a point: *Bournemouth is on the coast, and it has a sandy beach*. Each clause or part of the sentence can make sense on its own. Complex sentences contain a main clause and one or more dependent clauses (clauses that do not make sense on their own). The clauses can be linked by a connective such as 'after', 'because', 'who', 'although' or 'when': *We went to the beach because it was a sunny day*.

Worksheet 12.1

2 Whole class work

- Display the text on **Worksheet 12.2**, which contains the sentences on page 40 of the student book in the correct order. Read the text and ask students what the writer's ideas and perspective are.

- Ask students to identify the different sentence types, then model how each sentence type helps the writer express their ideas and perspective and what effect each type of sentence can have on the reader. For example, a question engages the reader and makes them think about the answer; an exclamation adds some energy and makes the opinion sound stronger; a short sentence, after longer sentences or at the end of a paragraph, has more impact and makes the reader notice that final point more.

Worksheet 12.2

Resources required

Student book pages 40–41
Video 12.1: Giving blood
Worksheet 12.1: Types of sentence
Worksheet 12.2: Sentences in order
Worksheet 12.3: Sentence purposes
Worksheet 12.4: Identifying sentence types
Worksheet 12.5: Giving blood
Worksheet 12.6: 'Celebrity'
Worksheet 12.7: Talent Quest
Answer sheet 12.1: Suggested answers

Assessment objectives

English AO2i / English Language AO3i
Read and understand texts, selecting material appropriate to purpose, collating from different sources and making comparisons and cross references as appropriate.

English AO2iii / English Language AO3iii
Explain and evaluate how writers use linguistic, grammatical, structural and presentational features to achieve effects and engage and influence the reader.

- Refer students to **Activity 1** and ask them to use **Worksheet 12.3** to complete it in pairs, answering questions about how to use different types of sentences.

Worksheet 12.3

3 Pair work

- Zoom in on the Janet Street-Porter text on page 41 of the ActiveTeach. Students should check their understanding of the effect of the sentences as they attempt **Activity 2** on **Worksheet 12.4**. They should highlight and label the different sentence types before answering question 2.

Worksheet 12.4

- Share responses as a class, and ask students to justify their opinions.

4 Independent work

- Watch **Video 12.1**, the Giving blood video, on the ActiveTeach. Ask students to identify the main ideas, purpose and perspective of the video. They should give reasons for their answers, with reference to the images, sound and script of the video.

Video 12.1: Giving blood

Additional support

Starter
- For students in the early stages of English acquisition, it may be useful to pair EAL learners who share a **first language** to establish the concept of the different sentence types and find comparable examples in their own language.
- **Substitution tables** for each sentence type will help EAL students to appreciate the different sentence structures.
- Put the sentence types on a **word wall** for ready reference in the lesson. The extension to cover compound and complex sentences (bullet 2) would be a logical progression towards better commenting. You might like to use **writing frames** or **tables** to reinforce this.

Whole class work
- Use **message abundancy** as you read the text to **clarify** words and phrases such as 'nicked', 'cheap', 'trendy', 'out of fashion'.

Pair work
- **Talk partners:** Pair EAL learners with fluent English speakers to complete Activity 2.
- Create a **card sort/matching activity** of different sentence types from the text in Activity 2.
- It may be appropriate to discuss the concept of 'rhetorical questions' as an extension.
- When taking feedback, you could ask students to discuss their own experiences and opinions of social networking sites.

Independent work
- Use a good student response to Activity 3, which includes a variety of sentence types, to construct a short **dictogloss**.

- Now ask students to complete **Activity 3**, recording their answers on **Worksheet 12.5**. They should identify different sentence types in the transcript before explaining why the writer chose these sentences and what the effect is of each one.
- Ask students to share their sentences with a partner and to check each other's ideas and clarity of expression.

Worksheet 12.5

- Ask students to work with a partner and discuss their notes. Students should give each other feedback on both their ideas and how clearly they expressed them.
- Students can make further notes after feedback.

---

7 Plenary

- Hold a quick-fire quiz, reading out different sentence types and asking students to shout out examples.
- Alternatively, build a class paragraph on the board using different sentence types. Start the paragraph as follows: *Why do we wear a school uniform?* Suggest sentence types that could follow and why they might be used, then ask students to come up with suggestions. For example, you could follow the question with a list of reasons, or an exclamation to show the writer's strong opinion: *Because we have to!*

---

5 Whole class work

- Ask students how they could use what they have learned so far when looking at the texts they have been given for the controlled assessment tasks. Encourage students to suggest the strategies they would use and discuss the skills they have learned.
- **Worksheet 12.6** contains a text called 'Celebrity'. Play Buzz! with this text. Split the class into teams of four or five and give each member a different feature to recognise, for example: questions, exclamations, simple sentences, commands. Read the text aloud. When students hear their feature, they stand up and say 'Buzz'. The first person to buzz wins the point for their team. Award another point if their team can explain what effect it has in the text.

Worksheet 12.6

---

8 Further work

Hand out **Worksheet 12.7**. Students should view the webpage and then answer the questions explaining how the writer's choice of sentences helps the text achieve its purpose.

Worksheet 12.7

---

6 Independent work

- Ask students to work independently to identify and label the types of sentence that are used in the texts they have been given for their controlled assessment tasks then make notes about the effects they have.

Suggested answers

Student book Activity 1
1. a) exclamation b) command c) list d) short sentence

Student book Activity 2
1. question, list
2. a

Student book Activity 3 – See Answer sheet 12.1

Lesson 13 Commenting on a writer's language

Learning objectives

→ Understand how writers use different language features and sentence types.

→ Explain what effect the writer's choices have.

1 Starter

BBC Video: Exploring language

- Watch the **BBC Video: Exploring language**. Discuss as a class how Fry uses language to communicate ideas and perspective. Ask students to identify how he uses describing words to show his feelings.

- As a class, compile a class reference page or poster. Students need to give definitions and examples of the following types of sentence: list, command, exclamation, short sentence and question. They should also give examples of vocabulary that is formal, informal, technical, descriptive or humorous (for example, puns and superlatives).

2 Whole class work

- Explain that there is no point in spotting that a writer has used a feature unless you go on to explain what its effect is. Writers choose their words and sentences to achieve a specific purpose and express their ideas and perspective.

- Zoom in on the Trek's New TT Bike article on the ActiveTeach or on **Worksheet 13.1**. As a class, work through the first four questions of **Activity 1**, asking students to identify the audience and main ideas and perspective before focusing on the effect of the specific sentences and vocabulary.

- If students find it difficult to comment on the sentence types, draw out the idea that the writer has used fairly long sentences to make the text sound flowing and conversational. Students can record their answers on **Worksheet 13.2**.

Worksheet 13.1

Worksheet 13.2

Resources required

Student book pages 42–45
BBC Video: Exploring language
Weblink 13.1: Eurotrip
Weblink 13.2: Blog
Worksheet 13.1: Trek's new TT bike
Worksheet 13.2: Commenting on language 1
Worksheet 13.3: Dancing is rubbish article
Worksheet 13.4: Commenting on language 2
Worksheet 13.5: Commenting on language 3
Answer sheet 13.1: Suggested answers

Assessment objectives

English AO2i / English Language AO3i
Read and understand texts, selecting material appropriate to purpose, collating from different sources and making comparisons and cross references as appropriate.

English AO2ii / English Language AO3ii
Develop and sustain interpretations of writers' ideas and perspectives.

English AO2iii / English Language AO3iii
Explain and evaluate how writers use linguistic, grammatical, structural and presentational features to achieve effects and engage and influence the reader.

3 Independent/Pair work

- Ask students to complete question 5 of **Activity 1**, filling in the gaps with words from the box or the text. Students can use **Worksheet 13.2** to record their answers.

- Take feedback, reading the paragraph and having students call out the appropriate words to fill in the blanks. Revise any words they got wrong.

4 Independent/Pair work

- Introduce students to the list of words they can use when explaining the effect of a language feature. Model a couple of examples, e.g. *The fact that the writer has included his own opinions makes you feel that he is an expert on bikes. The use of technical language suits the audience, who are already interested in bikes.*

- Students should work in pairs or individually to craft their sentence for **Activity 2** about why the writer has used a list. Share responses.

Additional support

Starter
- Select words from the **word wall** as a reminder when compiling the poster.

Whole class work/Activities 1 and 3
- **Remind** students of the work on perspective in Lesson 2.
- **Active listening:** Read to the class using expression, pauses, gestures and facial expression to aid understanding. Students should **highlight** any unknown words.

- Use this opportunity to explain cultural references such as: 'TT', 'needless to say', 'snapper', 'comeback', 'very low profile', 'fork blades' (page 43) and 'overrated', 'jerk' and 'polka' as well as celebrity names (page 44).
- **Talk partners:** Always ensure that EAL students are well supported by fluent English speakers in group or pair work.

Independent/Pair work Activity 2
- Link the words in the box on page 43 with the **word wall** for techniques.
- Give alternative commenting phrases to 'suggests' (e.g. 'reminds the audience', 'makes us think'). This will enable students to comment more effectively on the effects of language.

5 Whole class / Pair work

- Play Buzz! with the Dancing is rubbish article on page 44 of the student book or on **Worksheet 13.3**. Write the following features on the board and ask students to listen out for them in the text:
  - sentences: lists, commands, short sentences, questions
  - vocabulary: superlatives, descriptive, or humorous, e.g. puns.

Worksheet 13.3

- Read the text once all the way through.
- Put students into teams. Read the text to the class again and ask students to buzz when they hear one of the features. A correct buzz wins a point for the team. Any team can win another point if, within 30 seconds, they can explain what effect that feature has in the text.
- In pairs, students should work through **Activity 3** using **Worksheet 13.4**. Students should read the text to pick out words that show the writer's attitude. They should then write sentences to analyse the language used in the text. Encourage students to use the words listed in the box on page 43 of the student book when explaining the language features.

Worksheet 13.4

6 Independent work

- Ask students to look at **Weblink 13.1** and complete the example controlled assessment task in **Activity 4** on page 45. Students should then assess their own work using the criteria given in the ResultsPlus Maximise your marks section.
- Students should then work in pairs to complete the **Putting it into practice** activity on page 47.

7 Plenary

Ask students to consider how successfully they have achieved the lesson's objectives. Ask them to say which aspects they found most difficult. Ask others to offer advice on how to tackle this aspect. Encourage all students to note down a target for improvement.

8 Further work

Give students a printout from a current blog which gives a strong opinion, and ask them to answer the questions on **Worksheet 13.5**, which requires them to analyse sentence and vocabulary choices. You may wish to use the blog on **Weblink 13.2**. Alternatively, ask students to complete the exercise using their own example of a blog or magazine article that gives an opinion.

Worksheet 13.5

Suggested answers

Student book Activity 1 – See Answer sheet 13.1

Student book Activity 2

1. *The writer lists the names in the sentence so that he can impress readers with his expert knowledge, and to prove that his perspective that the new bike was needed is right.*

Student book Activity 3

1. *'overrated'; 'sweaty'; 'rubbish'; 'it's not right and it's not ok'; 'humiliation of a village forced to polka'.*

Lesson 14 Comparing texts

Learning objectives

→ Compare writers' use of presentation and language to communicate their ideas and perspectives.

→ Explain the differences and similarities that you notice.

Resources required

Student book pages 48–49
Image 14.1: Spooky house
Image 14.2: Beacon house
Weblink 14.1: Mazuma mobile
Resource 14.1: Texts A and B
Worksheet 14.1: Mazuma mobile
Worksheet 14.2: Nokia 3510
Worksheet 14.3: Comparison chart
Worksheet 14.4: Identifying reasons
Worksheet 14.5: Comparing texts
Answer sheet 14.1: Suggested answers

Assessment objectives

English AO2i / English Language AO3i
Read and understand texts, selecting material appropriate to purpose, collating from different sources and making comparisons and cross references as appropriate.

English AO2ii / English Language AO3ii
Develop and sustain interpretations of writers' ideas and perspectives.

English AO2iii / English Language AO3iii
Explain and evaluate how writers use linguistic, grammatical, structural and presentational features to achieve effects and engage and influence the reader.

1 Starter

- Show students the two contrasting images (**Images 14.1** and **14.2**) and ask them to list five differences and five similarities as quickly as possible. Afterwards discuss how they worked to identify them.

- Explain that they are using similar skills and processes when comparing texts: that is, looking for similarities and differences in the way writers use presentation, images and language.

- Remind students that to do well in their assessment they have to go beyond just spotting a difference, to explain what effect the differences have on the text's purpose, ideas and perspective.

Image 14.1

Image 14.2

- Using **Worksheet 14.3**, make a class chart to compare the texts. Ask students to compare the presentation and language in each text. Encourage students to express their ideas in full sentences, using the connectives they have learned.

Worksheet 14.3

2 Whole class work

- Display **Resource 14.1**, a slide of both Texts A and B, and hand out **Worksheets 14.1** and **14.2**. Begin **Activity 1** as a class. Ask students to identify the main ideas and perspectives in each text.

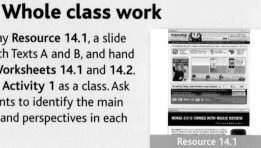
Resource 14.1

Worksheet 14.1   Worksheet 14.2

3 Group/Pair work

- Divide the class into groups and ask them to discuss the reasons for the differences in images, presentation and language in the texts and to fill in this information in the table on **Worksheet 14.4**. Set a time limit.

Worksheet 14.4

- Brainstorm a list of phrases that might be useful when talking about images, presentation and language features of a text, for example: *suggests, hints at, gives the impression*. Compile a list on the board.

Additional support

Whole class work Activity 1
- **Active listening**: Read both texts aloud using expression, pauses, gestures and facial expression to aid understanding. Ask students to note down words they find difficult.
- **Clarify** cultural and idiomatic language using **message abundancy**, for example: 'ultraslim', 'hot looks', 'moved up a gear', 'had better watch out', 'bevelled', 'over the top', 'funky'.
- Encourage the use of **highlighting** to identify points of similarity and difference.

Group/Pair work
- **Jigsaw reading**: Divide the class into groups including EAL students and fluent English speakers. Give the two texts to different groups to discuss and analyse main ideas and perspectives, images, language and presentation. Send envoys to share findings with groups analysing the other text.
- **Share** analyses with the whole class using good sentences as exemplars.
- Provide clear **sentence starters** for comparing two texts – refer to the **word wall** and find comparative connectives. A kinaesthetic activity could be powerful support: place sentence starters and connectives from the word wall on a **washing line** and encourage students to make sentences using evidence from the text and their own comments.

- Students should now work in pairs or individually to compose sentences explaining how the writers of Texts A and B have used images, presentation and language to express their perspectives. Remind students to use connectives to help them make comparisons.
- Share sentences as a class.

4 Whole class work

- Challenge students to be agony aunts to a letter writer called 'Worried', who has this problem:
I've got to compare these texts for my assessment. How can I work efficiently in the two hours we have got so that I can get it all done? Please help!
- As a class, identify each stage of the process, from identifying the main ideas of each text to writing the comparison. This is an opportunity for students to revisit and consolidate the strategies they have learned in the whole unit.
- Break the controlled assessment task down into sections, and draw up a list of tips, reminders, questions to ask, or useful words for each section. Include sections on looking at still and moving images as well as text. Make sure you discuss timing so that students understand that they cannot spend too long planning.

5 Plenary

Discuss the advice you have compiled as a class. Ask students to identify which aspects they have found most difficult as they worked through this unit. Ask each student to set a target area for improvement.

6 Further work

Ask students to find an advertisement and a review for the same film. If they find this online (for example, on LoveFilm) they should provide a URL or screenshot. If they find printed texts, they should bring them to class. Students should complete **Worksheet 14.5**, which asks them to compare two texts.

Worksheet 14.5

7 Controlled assessment practice

- On pages 50–53 of the student book, a practice controlled assessment reading task is provided. You could work through this with students as they practice before they sit their assessment.
- On the ActiveTeach there are accompanying ResultsPlus grade improvement activities which help students understand how to improve their answer.

ResultsPlus interactive

Suggested answers
Student book Activity 1 – See Answer sheet 14.1

Lesson 1 Purpose

Learning objectives

→ Identify and understand a range of purposes.

→ Know what language features to use in your writing to achieve your purpose.

Resources required

Student book pages 56–59

BBC Video: *The Culture Show*

Worksheet 1.1: Purposes

Worksheet 1.2: Capital punishment

Worksheet 1.3: Purpose and features chart

Worksheet 1.4: Naked desire

Worksheet 1.5: End factory farming

Worksheet 1.6: 3000 miles. Two guys in a boat.

Worksheet 1.7: Controlled assessment

Answer sheet 1.1: Suggested answers

Assessment objectives

English AO3i / English Language AO4i

Write clearly, effectively and imaginatively, using and adapting forms and selecting vocabulary appropriate to task and purpose in ways that engage the reader.

1 Starter

- Display **Worksheet 1.1**, which shows a range of different purposes (persuade, comment, inform, argue, explain, advise) to link to the correct definitions. Students may find it difficult to distinguish between writing to persuade and writing to argue. Persuasive writing usually wants to provoke an action by the reader and may involve practical suggestions. An argument is less likely to do this.

Worksheet 1.1

- Show the **BBC Video: *The Culture Show*** reviewing the film *Casino Royale* (available on the ActiveTeach). Ask students to comment on what they think the purpose of the clip is, explaining why.

BBC Video: *The Culture Show*

2 Whole class work

- Model how to identify the purpose of a text using this example:

  Write an article for a magazine in which you persuade readers to take a specific point of view about an environmental issue.

- Underline the key words in the task and ask students which word tells them the purpose (*persuade*).

- Discuss the two questions 'What do I want my writing to achieve?' and 'What do I have to communicate to the audience to achieve this purpose?' Then model making notes on what to include when writing the text.

3 Group work

- Ask students to attempt **Activity 1** in small groups, using the two questions again to identify the text's purpose, how to achieve it and what to include. Set a time limit.

- Work with a group of lower achievers to ensure they have understood how to use the questions to work out the text's purpose. Model how they can ask themselves questions such as: 'Will listing smoking dangers inform readers about the dangers of smoking?' to check whether each idea will help achieve the text's purpose.

- Ask students to share their decisions, giving reasons.

4 Whole class work

- Zoom in on the capital punishment text on page 57 of the ActiveTeach, or on **Worksheet 1.2**. Model how to identify the key features that enable a text to achieve its purpose. Read the text aloud and ask students to sum up what it is about.

Worksheet 1.2

- Now read through the text sentence by sentence, using the annotation tool on the ActiveTeach to pick out and annotate the following examples, one at a time:

  The text starts with a strong opinion, then gives facts and evidence to support the writer's viewpoint. The writer ends the first paragraph with an opinion stated as fact, followed by a question 'In the 21st century…' The question uses the emotive word 'murder' to draw readers into agreeing. In the second paragraph, the writer states reasons that are given for capital punishment (the opposite point of view) and then argues against them.

- Ask the class what sort of a text they think it is. Challenge them to explain why, drawing on the features you have pinpointed to support their ideas.

EAL Additional support

Starter
- **Talk partners:** Pair EAL students with fluent English speakers to ensure the meaning of 'purpose' is understood. Pairs should work together on Worksheet 1.1. Alternatively, pair EAL students who share a first language to **discuss** 'purpose' **in their L1** and find synonyms and contexts.
- Add the verbs from the worksheet to the **word wall**.

Whole class work Activity 1
- **Remind** students about the podcast genre.
- Ensure the groups include EAL and fluent English speakers.
- A **cloze text** may help to emphasise the link between purpose and language choice. For example, you could create a short persuasive text and focus on emotive language in the cloze.
- Make a **dictogloss** of the text on page 57 to draw attention to the features used to support writer's purpose.

Group work Activity 2
- **Writing frames, sentence starters** or **a substitution table** could be useful for some EAL learners to tackle the questions about their controlled assessment in Activity 2.

Group work Activity 3
- **Active listening:** Read Texts A, B and C on pages 58 and 59 to the class, or ask a fluent reader to do so. Encourage the whole class to clarify new or unusual vocabulary. Discuss the similarities and differences between the texts.
- Note: Encourage EAL students to read a wide variety of non-fiction and fiction texts (or listen to audio versions) as models for improving their own general knowledge, vocabulary and style.

---

5 Group work

- Students should read through Texts A, B and C, available on **Worksheets 1.4, 1.5** and **1.6**. Ask students to complete parts 1 and 2 of **Activity 2**, writing their answers on **Worksheet 1.3**. They could work in groups of three, with each student focusing on one text. They should then explain to their group how the features contribute to the purpose of their text. Encourage the other members of the group to ask questions. Make sure all students complete **Worksheet 1.3** and have read all the texts.
- Students should complete the remainder of **Activity 2** in their groups.

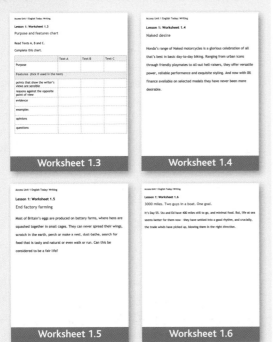

Worksheet 1.3

Worksheet 1.4

Worksheet 1.5

Worksheet 1.6

6 Independent work

- Ask students to complete **Activity 3**. Students should identify the features to include in a response to the task and write two paragraphs of their response.

7 Plenary

- Ask students to close their books and to recall the two questions that helped them pinpoint the purpose of the text they need to write.
- Compile a class list of 'top tips' on how to work out what to include in a particular text type and how to write it.

8 Further work

Ask students to find another text with the same purpose as the one they have to write for the controlled assessment. They should study the text and annotate the features that enable it to achieve its purpose. They can then note down which features they might include in their own text to achieve a similar purpose. Students should complete **Worksheet 1.7** as they work through this text.

Worksheet 1.7

Suggested answers

Student book Activity 1

2. *List of smoking dangers; Facts and statistics on the number of underage smokers; Evidence of the damage smoking does to young lungs*

Student book Activity 2 – See Answer sheet 1.1

Lesson 2 Audience

Learning objectives

→ Work out what to write for a specific audience.

→ Begin to understand how to write for your audience.

Resources required
Student book pages 60–61
BBC Video: *News Special* and *Newsround*
Weblink 2.1: Cbeebies advertisement
Weblink 2.2: Heart foundation advertisement
Weblink 2.3: Clearasil advertisement
Weblink 2.4: Abbey advertisement
Worksheet 2.1: Audience chart
Worksheet 2.2: Jo's response
Worksheet 2.3: Audience interests

Assessment objectives
English AO3i / English Language AO4i
Write clearly, effectively and imaginatively, using and adapting forms and selecting vocabulary appropriate to task and purpose in ways that engage the reader.

1 Starter

- Display the four advertisement images (**Weblink 2.1–2.4**) using the ActiveTeach. For each advertisement ask students: *What is the advert selling? How is the advertiser making it a 'must have'? Who do you think the advertiser is trying to sell the product to, and why?*

- Drawing on the selling techniques the advertiser has used, ask students to suggest an ideal audience for each advertisement. Ask students to suggest what the needs of this audience might be and how the content of the advertisement is meant to appeal specifically to that audience.

- Show students the **BBC Video: *News Special* and *Newsround*.** Ask them to identify the audience for each clip. Discuss the differences between the clips as a class and how effective these are for the audience.

BBC Video:
News Special and *Newsround*

2 Whole class work

- Using the example on page 60 of the student book, model how to read a brief and discover the audience and the content that should be written about.

- Write some other briefs on the board and ask students to identify the audience and make suggestions about what they could include to appeal to that audience. For example: *Write a podcast giving teenagers advice on how to make their money go further.* Students should consider what options are practical for the audience, for example: selling unwanted goods on eBay, buying in sales.

3 Pair/Independent work

- Focus students' attention on **Activity 1.** Ask students to suggest what factors they might need to consider when thinking about what kind of exercise the target audience would be interested in, for example: their age, likely interests and abilities, how close they are to sports facilities, how much money/ time they might have. Students should record their answers on **Worksheet 2.1.**

Worksheet 2.1

- Now tell students to imagine that they are writing a leaflet about a new leisure centre. Ask students to consider what information they might include to appeal to the different audiences in the table. For example, they might emphasise the fun aspects of the leisure centre for the 12-year-old boy. For the overweight 40-year-old they might focus on classes that are suitable for beginners, or classes that are held at the weekend to suit his schedule.

4 Pair work

- Ask students to work on **Activity 2** in pairs. Set a time limit and ask each pair to write a paragraph that could be included in the advice leaflet, using one of the suggestions given. Ensure that all the bullet points are covered by different pairs.

- Share responses as a class and discuss how well they suited the audience.

Additional support

Starter
- Teachers should be prepared to **clarify** cultural, technical and idiomatic language at any stage, although students need to know that lack of understanding could happen in an assessment – they must learn **transferable strategies** for **selecting relevant detail** about text features, regardless of whether they have prior knowledge of the subject or not.

Whole class work
- **Oral prediction** will enhance the **whole class modelling** activity:

ask students to predict the kind of content and language appropriate to two different audiences, e.g. teenagers and pensioners.

Pair/Independent work
- As an alternative to Activity 1, you could create a simpler **matching activity** with suggested topics of interest for each audience.

Whole class work
- **Active listening:** The teacher or fluent readers should read Jo's response and clarify words as appropriate (e.g. 'nagging', 'row').
- Construct one rewritten sample text as a **model** and use it as a **dictogloss** which will help EAL students (and others) to rewrite the other text independently as preparation for the later **peer-assessment** activity.

---

5 Whole class work

Ask students to read Jo's work on page 61 of the student book, or on **Worksheet 2.2**. Ask them to comment on the features that Jo has included in her writing and whether or not they will suit her audience. They should also suggest how Jo could improve her work. For example, Jo talks about her own situation – not the general one facing her readers. Jo needs to give her readers ideas about how to work through the issues she raises; Jo says what her mum should <u>not</u> do, not what all parents should. At the end of the second paragraph, Jo needs to give solutions to the kinds of problem she raises; Jo does not say how parents can help teenagers make good choices.

Worksheet 2.2

6 Independent work

- Ask students to complete **Activity 3** independently.
- Share some responses as a class and encourage students to comment on whether these responses are now more suitable than Jo's response for the audience.

7 Independent work/Peer assessment

- Ask students to complete **Activity 4** independently, using what they have learned about audience to identify what the audience for the controlled assessment task will be interested in. Students should record their ideas on **Worksheet 2.3**.

Worksheet 2.3

- Ask students to swap their chart with a partner who is doing the same controlled assessment task. Ask students to give each other feedback on how well they have worked out the audience's needs.

8 Plenary

As a class, discuss 'dos and don'ts' for writing for a specific audience. For example, do consider what the audience wants to know, do remember that the audience might not share your interest, etc. You may want to use Jo's example work as a stimulus.

9 Further work

Ask students to collect information leaflets. You could suggest that they look for these in libraries, doctors' surgeries or youth centres. Ask students to identify the audience for the information leaflet and make notes on how the writer has tried to make the leaflet suitable for the audience. Remind students to consider images as well as text.

Suggested answers
Student book Activity 1
- *12-year-old boy: cheap form of exercise; something he can do with his friends; might include activities at a leisure centre as he lives near lots of facilities.*
- *40-year-old man: needs to be suitable for all abilities as he is not physically fit; needs to be something he can do early in the morning/late at night or on weekends; he might be able to afford exercise classes or even a personal trainer.*
- *Older couple: would need to be something they can do anywhere, e.g. walking, as they might not be near a leisure centre or swimming pool; possibly not too strenuous as they are older.*

Lesson 3 Formal and informal language

Resources required

Student book pages 62–63

Worksheet 3.1: Formal/informal writing bingo

Worksheet 3.2: Formal/informal emails

Worksheet 3.3: Matching situations

Worksheet 3.4: Sunita's response

Assessment objectives

English AO3i / English Language AO4i

Write clearly, effectively and imaginatively, using and adapting forms and selecting vocabulary appropriate to task and purpose in ways that engage the reader.

Learning objectives

→ Understand how to write for the audience and purpose of your task.

1 Starter

- Ask students to generate a list of features which they associate with formal writing and those which they associate with informal writing. For example, formal: no contractions, higher level vocabulary; informal: contractions, slang, expressive punctuation, lower level vocabulary.

- Hand out a bingo card from **Worksheet 3.1** to each student. Then display and read out the emails provided in Texts A and B from page 62 of the ActiveTeach, or from **Worksheet 3.2**. Ask students to spot the different features on their bingo card and cross through that square, writing down what example goes with the feature. The first student to cross through all the features on their card calls out 'Bingo!' The student then has to justify all their crosses to win.

Worksheet 3.1

Worksheet 3.2

2 Whole class work

- Discuss with the class a range of different situations that would require formal and informal writing. For example, formal: asking a local councillor to improve facilities in your area, asking a local business person for work experience (even if you know him or her personally), writing to complain about service in a shop; informal: emailing a friend, writing to a relative to give them news or chatting on MSN or Facebook.

- Ask students to jot down further examples on slips of paper. Encourage them to be quite specific, for example, 'an email to your friend arranging to meet at the weekend', rather than 'an email'. Fold all the slips of paper and put them in a box.

- Split the class into two teams. Students from each team take turns to pull out a slip and decide whether it would be a formal or informal situation. If the other team thinks the answer is wrong they can challenge the answer and earn the point. The team with the highest score wins.

3 Independent work

Ask students to complete **Activity 1** independently, recording the answers on **Worksheet 3.3**. They should match the snippets from texts to the correct audience and situation and identify the language features that enabled them to make that choice. Ask students to explain their choice to a partner and refer to you if they disagree.

Student book page 62

Worksheet 3.3

Additional support

Starter

- Add to the **word wall** throughout the lesson to accumulate a list of language features to use as an *aide memoire*.
- **Talk partners:** Pair fluent English speakers with EAL students to ensure understanding.
- It may be appropriate to pair EAL students who share the same **first language** to **discuss in L1** when they would need to write formally and what conventions are important in their first language.
- **Clarify** any words in the bingo cards as necessary (e.g. 'expressive punctuation', 'contractions', 'slang', 'higher/lower level').

Whole class work

- Create a **washing line** of language items to arrange from the most informal to the most formal as a kinaesthetic activity.
- **Jigsaw reading:** Find two additional texts, one formal, one very colloquial, and cut them up into sentences. Put students into groups and give out one of the texts to each group to reassemble. Students should identify the text as formal or informal. Students can then exchange texts to compare differences.
- **Active listening:** Read **aloud** the two emails on page 62 and the letter on page 63 with expression and pauses to aid understanding and **clarify** unknown words as appropriate (e.g. 'resubmit', 'gonna', 'mardy', 'guzzling', 'footie', 'aerobics'.)

4 Pair work/Peer assessment

- Now ask students to work in pairs to complete questions 1 and 2a) of **Activity 2** on page 63 of the student book. Sunita's response is also available on **Worksheet 3.4**.

  > Access Unit 1 English Today: Writing
  >
  > Lesson 3: Worksheet 3.4
  > Sunita's response
  >
  > Some students just get mardy at the thought of taking any exercise. But if you don't do any exercise when you're at school and spend all your time guzzling and studying (or not) then you won't do any different when you leave school.
  >
  > Perhaps you'll have a longer and happier life if you get into some good habits while you're younger. Thirty minutes each day isn't long. Schools could just set up games of footie, or take kids for a run or set up an aerobics or dance class. It doesn't have to cost a lot.

  Worksheet 3.4

- Ask pairs to join up to make groups of four to discuss their ideas and come up with the best five suggestions for question 2a).

- Ask students to complete question 2b), rewriting Sunita's letter, independently.

- Students should swap their work with a partner and assess how well they have rewritten the paragraph. Students should comment on the level of formality. You may want to write the following criteria on the board:
  - standard English
  - correct grammar
  - correct punctuation
  - no slang
  - no contractions.

5 Plenary

Write the following text on the board and ask students to suggest ways to make the tone more appropriate for the audience.

Open evening for prospective parents

Come and see our school – it's gr8! We've got great sports teams, a wicked school band and our teachers are ace. You'll definitely want to send your kid here – our school rulez!

7pm, Friday, be there!

6 Further work

Ask students to write their own letter in formal English to the editor of a newspaper, arguing for or against making students do some exercise for 30 minutes each day. Prepare for this by discussing points for and against so that students complete their plans prior to writing their text independently.

Suggested answers

Student book Activity 1

1. Sentence A (b); Sentence B (a); Sentence C (c)

Student book Activity 2

1. a) parents b) formal

2. a) avoid slang; avoid colloquialisms; avoid contractions – use full words; use higher level vocabulary; use correct grammar (e.g. she needs to change 'do any different...'); avoid expressive punctuation, e.g. informal use of brackets.

Lesson 4 Form

Resources required

Student book pages 64–69

Audio 4.1: Boat at sea podcast

Weblink 4.1: Around the world at 3mph

Image 4.1: Dog

Worksheet 4.1: What's wrong with crating? text

Worksheet 4.2: What's wrong with crating? leaflet

Worksheet 4.3: Recycling speech

Worksheet 4.4: Greatest movie sequels

Worksheet 4.5: Forms

Worksheet 4.6: Controlled assessment form

Assessment objectives

English AO3i / English Language AO4i

Write clearly, effectively and imaginatively, using and adapting forms and selecting vocabulary appropriate to task and purpose in ways that engage the reader.

Learning objectives

→ Understand how to use the correct form for your task.

→ Use the form to help you decide what to include and how to write your text.

1 Starter

- Display the unformatted text version of *What's wrong with crating?* (**Worksheet 4.1**) and the image of a crated dog (**Image 4.1**) on the ActiveTeach.

- Ask students to work in pairs to suggest ways in which the text and image should be designed to be an effective leaflet persuading dog owners not to crate their dogs.

- Share ideas as a class.

Worksheet 4.1

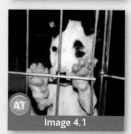

Image 4.1

3 Group work

Ask students to work in groups to complete **Activity 1** on **Worksheet 4.5**, identifying the features which belong to different forms of writing. If the form that their assessment task brief requires is not featured, you could also add an example of that form to the worksheet. The four texts are available on **Worksheets 4.3** and **4.4**, **Weblink 4.1** and **Audio 4.1**.

Worksheet 4.3

Weblink 4.1

2 Whole class work

- Before students open their books, provide them with their own copy of the leaflet *What's wrong with crating?* (**Worksheet 4.2**). Ask them to find and annotate the following features: main heading, subheadings, different font colours, paragraphs, informal language, image.

- Share ideas as a class. When students identify a feature, extend their thinking by asking them to suggest why the writer uses that feature, for example: subheadings to break up the text and make it easier to follow or make it easier to find particular information. This will help students become intentional writers. As students share their ideas, annotate **Worksheet 4.2** on the ActiveTeach.

- Ask students to brainstorm other features that can appear in texts and specify the texts they might appear in, for example: interactive buttons on websites, columns in newspapers, websites and leaflets. You might like to produce a class poster or table to record these ideas.

Worksheet 4.2

Worksheet 4.4

Worksheet 4.5

Additional support

Starter

- **Talk partners:** Pair fluent English speakers with EAL students to establish and revise language to do with presentation and to ensure text types are fully understood. Add the vocabulary to the **word wall** created in previous lessons to use as an *aide memoire*.
- **Active listening:** Ask fluent English speakers to read the texts on pages 64–66 aloud, using expression, pauses, gesture and facial expression to facilitate comprehension.

- **Clarify** difficult words as necessary (e.g. 'bladder', 'incapable', 'security', 'anxiety', 'plywood', 'propel', 'Puss. In. Boots', 'nuts', 'catnip', 'straight men', 'sidekick', 'cameos' and names of actors).

Group work

- Ensure groups include both strong English speakers and EAL students.
- Use **ICT tools** to take a simple text and re-present it in different ways to match different audiences, making text changes as well as presentational ones.

---

4 Independent work

- Ask students to complete **Activity 2** independently, considering the features of a blog and writing the first two paragraphs of the blog.
- Ask volunteers to read their paragraphs to the class. Encourage students to feed back on what features of blog are included.

---

5 Independent work

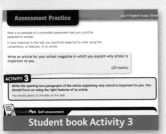
Student book Activity 3

- Ask students to look at the task on page 67 and complete the example controlled assessment task in **Activity 3**. Students should then assess their own work using the criteria given in the ResultsPlus Maximise your marks section.
- Students should work in pairs to complete the **Putting it into practice** activity on page 69.

---

6 Plenary

- Write each of the different text types covered in the lesson on a separate slip of paper, for example: podcast, online review, formal speech. Fold the slips and put them in a container.
- Students work in groups. As you draw out one of the slips, students compete to be the first group to list all the features that type of text might include. The first group shares their list of features and you scribe them on the board. Award a point for each correct feature and deduct a point for an incorrect feature.
- Other groups should cross off the features from their list as they are called out. They can score further points by correctly adding other features to the list, or challenging a 'wrong' feature that is suggested by another group.

---

7 Further work

Ask students to find further examples of the form they will have to write in for their controlled assessment task. They should make notes on the features included in each text and explain whether or not they will include them in their own response. Students can record their ideas on **Worksheet 4.6**.

Worksheet 4.6

Suggested answers

Student book Activity 1

Text A Speech. Features: direct address, opinions, questions.

Text B Webpage. Features: heading, paragraphs, formal language, facts, image.

Text C Podcast script. Features: direct address, sound effects, informal language, facts, opinions.

Text D Online review. Features: informal language, facts, opinions, heading, subheadings, image, paragraphs.

Lesson 5 Generating ideas

Resources required

Student book pages 70–71
Worksheet 5.1: Writing task chart
Worksheet 5.2: Spider diagram
Worksheet 5.3: Research ideas

Learning objectives

→ Create appropriate and engaging ideas for your writing.

→ Make sure you have enough to write about.

Assessment objectives

English AO3i / English Language AO4i
Write clearly, effectively and imaginatively, using and adapting forms and selecting vocabulary appropriate to task and purpose in ways that engage the reader.

1 Starter

• Ask students to suggest different ways they generate and record ideas when they are planning a piece of writing, for example: list, chart, spider diagram. Record these on the board.

• Discuss the pros and cons of each one. For example, listing ideas can make it hard to see new links between them – this is easier with a spider diagram. To make effective use of charts you need to work out carefully what the columns should record.

2 Whole class work

• Explain to students that before they start generating ideas they must have a clear sense of what they need to write about (content), who they are writing for (audience), why they are writing (purpose) and how they will write it (form). Using the following brief: *Write a script for a podcast for a children's website in which you describe your favourite film*, demonstrate how to work this out. Encourage students to provide detailed answers to the what, who, why and how questions. For example, students should think carefully about what they know about the audience (they are children, they use websites, they are interested in films).

• Explain how looking at all the brief's requirements helps you weed out unsuitable or irrelevant ideas. For example, if they chose *Slumdog Millionaire* (Certificate 15) then this would not be suitable for the audience, who are under 12 years of age. Tell students that they should revise their ideas to fit the brief.

3 Independent work

• Ask students to complete **Activity 1** independently, making notes on the content, audience, purpose and form of their controlled assessment task. Students can record their ideas on **Worksheet 5.1**.

Worksheet 5.1

• Ask students to swap their chart with a partner and give each other feedback. Have they thought carefully about the audience and the purpose?

4 Whole class work

• Model constructing a spider diagram using the film review podcast task on page 70 of the student book. Begin with generating 'main points' (categories of information). Tell students that they should include any main points that are suggested in the task, but can also add more of their own.

Student book page 70

• Then show how students should generate detailed ideas from each main point and link them to that main point to form the next layer of spider diagram 'legs'.

• As you add information, keep checking that it will fit the brief. If possible add, and then cross out, a suggestion that won't fit, such as: *Cubby Broccoli original producer, now it's his daughter* or *Pierce Brosnan used to be Bond, most recent film was Mamma Mia*. Encourage students to comment on what they think, and don't think, is relevant.

Additional support

Starter
- Clarify 'pros and cons' using **message abundancy**.

Whole class work
- Note: EAL students sometimes lack the first-hand experiences or prior knowledge which would help them generate ideas. **Pairing**

an EAL learner with a fluent English speaker could provide support for writing about events they have not personally experienced. **Discussion in first language** may also be appropriate for some students.
- The names of actors and films may be unknown to EAL learners so it may be necessary to **clarify** as the **modelling** progresses.
- Add to the **word wall**: what (content), who (audience), why (purpose) and how (form).

 5 Independent work

Ask students to work independently to complete **Activity 2** question 1, generating their own spider diagram with ideas for the text they are writing for their controlled assessment task. Students can record their ideas on **Worksheet 5.2**.

Worksheet 5.2

 6 Peer assessment

Ask students to swap their work with a partner and check that each other's ideas will fit in with the brief (they can tick these).

 7 Independent work

- Ask students to study their spider diagrams and highlight any information they need to research, as set out in **Activity 2** question 2.

Student book page 71

- Ask volunteers to share some of their ideas with the class and help them generate more specific questions to research. Explain that it helps to have clear questions in mind before students start their research as it will help them find the information they need more quickly.

- Students should then work on their own spider diagram plans to generate a list of their own research questions on the left-hand side of a page.

- Brainstorm different sources of information as a class (e.g. internet, books, people, newspapers) for **Activity 2** question 3. Then discuss as a class how to find out different kinds of information. Ask students to share some of their questions and encourage the class to suggest where they might find this information. Discuss the pros and cons of each source, including reliability and accuracy.

- Encourage students to note down possible sources of information for each question. They can record their ideas on **Worksheet 5.3**.

- Students can begin their research in class.

Worksheet 5.3

8 Plenary

As a class, generate a flow diagram that shows how to plan ideas for a text. This should include questioning the brief, the questions they need to ask about the content, audience, purpose and form, how to generate and refine ideas and how to plan research.

9 Further work

Using **Worksheet 5.3**, ask students to continue their research for the controlled assessment task.

Lesson 6 Organising and linking paragraphs

Resources required

Student book pages 72–73
Worksheet 6.1: What's wrong with crating? text
Worksheet 6.2: Paragraph chart
Worksheet 6.3: Ordering paragraphs
Worksheet 6.4: Connective challenge

Learning objectives

→ Organise your ideas within paragraphs.
→ Make links between your paragraphs.

Assessment objectives

English AO3ii / English Language AO4ii
Organise information and ideas into structured and sequenced sentences, paragraphs and whole texts, using a variety of linguistic and structural features to support cohesion and overall coherence.

1 Starter

- Give students the unformatted text *What's wrong with crating?* on **Worksheet 6.1**. It is useful to use a text they already understand for this exercise. Ask students to share what they already know about a) when to begin a new paragraph; b) how paragraphs should be organised; and c) how to set them out on the page. List correct contributions on the board.

Worksheet 6.1

- Ask students to work in pairs and place the mark // on the *What's wrong with crating?* text to show where each new paragraph should begin. Students should annotate the text with their reason for beginning each new paragraph, for example: a change in idea, person, place or time.

- Display the original text on page 64 of the ActiveTeach. Compare this text with students' answers. Discuss why the author chose to break up the paragraphs as they are.

Student book page 64

- Use the original leaflet's paragraphs to discuss how a text is organised into paragraphs that follow a logical sequence for readers to follow.

- You might like to cut and paste the paragraphs of the text to produce an alternative, illogical, version of the text. Display this second version and ask students whether it is as easy to follow the writer's ideas, and if not, why. Then ask students to compare it with the original text and ask: *How does the writer's order of paragraphs help them achieve their purpose better?*

2 Whole class work

- Model how to produce a paragraph plan which will ensure students write their points in a logical sequence for readers to follow, using the process outlined on page 72 of the student book. Use the sample task: *Write an article arguing in favour of school uniform.* Write the following points on the board as a spider diagram and show students how to put them into logical order: *School uniform makes all pupils equal. Students can't compete over clothes. Uniform doesn't take away individuality – it's what you do, not what you wear, that is important. Uniform is better value for parents. Uniform helps create a school spirit and sense of community. You can be proud of your school uniform.*

- Then show how you transfer ideas from the spider diagram into a paragraph plan. Begin by identifying the main points and linking them to related minor points or details. Now number the main points in a logical order using numbers. Explain to students that it is a good idea to start with the most important point. You could ask students to help you put the points in order. Tell students that they should check the order of their ideas again and change it if necessary.

Worksheet 6.2

- Once you are happy with the order in which you will write your points you can transfer them into a chart like the one on **Worksheet 6.2**.

EAL Additional support

Starter/Whole class work

- **Talk partners:** Pair an EAL learner with a fluent English speaker and **activate prior knowledge** by reminding students about topic sentences as a clue to starting a new paragraph.
- Note: EAL students often find logical sequencing difficult so the cut and paste exercise and the modelling of a paragraph plan are very helpful.

Independent work Activity 1

- EAL learners often benefit from hearing their work read out so it may be helpful to ask **talk partners** to assess together the plans of one partner, then the other, and discuss suggestions for improvement.

Whole class work

- **Card sort activity:** Write example sentences for each connective in the chart on page 73 and ask students to identify the connectives, then group them by purpose, referring to the first column in the chart.
- A **substitution table** could be used to demonstrate grammatical constraints on use of certain connectives (e.g. 'although', 'however') and how others can be substituted.
- Worksheet 6.4 is an exemplar **writing frame**. Further exemplar texts could be turned into short **dictogloss** or **cloze activities** to reinforce good use of connectives.

3 Independent work

- Ask students to complete **Activity 1** independently, completing their paragraph plan for the controlled assessment task. Students can record their ideas on **Worksheet 6.2**.
- Students should then swap their plan with a partner and check each other's plan follows a logical sequence. In pencil, students should tick points that logically follow on from each other, underline any points that do not make sense and add any questions or suggestions they have which would improve the plan or content.
- Refer students to the ResultsPlus box on page 73.

4 Whole class work

- Discuss a selection of the connectives in the chart on page 73 of the student book. Ask volunteers to give examples of connectives they could use in their paragraphs.
- Ask students to work in pairs to look at the purposes list and decide which types of connective they will need to use in their paragraphs.
- Feed back as a class and make a list of the connective groups selected. Now ask students to identify the connectives in these groups that they a) use all the time; b) recognise but don't often use; c) never use and may not recognise. Ask students for their c) group connectives and list them on the board.
- Ask students who have used the connectives you have listed on the board to give a sentence using that connective. You could fix the subject of all the sentences as a sentence that would be part of the text you planned with them earlier. After sharing their expertise, ask all the students to use that connective to compose a sentence orally. Share examples.
- Repeat with other connectives, asking students to compose sentences, then share them with a partner to check they make sense. Share some examples with the class.
- Ask students to complete **Activity 2**, adding the connectives they need to use to their paragraph plan, making sure they use at least some of the connectives they placed in group c).

5 Independent work

Students write a paragraph plan for the task discussed earlier: *Write an article arguing in favour of school uniform*, remembering to include connectives they can use in their writing.

6 Plenary

As a class, study **Worksheet 6.3**. Ask students to put the paragraphs into a logical order and to justify their choices.

Worksheet 6.3

7 Further work

Ask students to complete **Worksheet 6.4**. They should fill in the blanks with suitable connectives. Encourage students to read the whole text before adding in the connectives. Depending on level, you might want to give students a list of connectives to choose from.

Worksheet 6.4

Suggested answers

Worksheet 6.3: Ordering paragraphs

- *BADCE or BCADE*

Lesson 7 Organising your writing

Resources required

Student book pages 74–75
Worksheet 7.1: Effective openings 1
Worksheet 7.2: Effective openings 2
Worksheet 7.3: Different openings

Assessment objectives

English AO3ii / English Language AO4ii
Organise information and ideas into structured and sequenced sentences, paragraphs and whole texts, using a variety of linguistic and structural features to support cohesion and overall coherence.

Learning objectives

→ Structure your writing with a clear and effective beginning, middle and end.

→ Choose the best order to write about your points.

1 Starter

- Hand out copies of **Worksheet 7.1**, an exercise on writing openings, before students open their books. Ask them to tick the statements they agree with that describe what an opening should do.

- Ask students to read the opening on **Worksheet 7.1** and grade it against the criteria they have set.

- Share ideas and ask students to justify their decisions. Ask students what they can tell about the text from the opening, for example: it will be humorous; it will be about Christmas; it will be truthful; it will focus on how the writer's mother transforms Christmas.

Worksheet 7.1

- Discuss and explain further reasons why the opening is effective. For example, the writer creates a relationship with the reader in the opening two sentences using direct address ('you') and asking a personal question. His list of Christmas disappointments identifies his audience clearly as parents and shows he understands the audience. The writer surprises the reader by saying that Christmas can be awful.

2 Pair work

- Ask students to work in pairs to complete **Activity 1**. Students should suggest that 'Smoking causes many problems' is the key point as it sums up the main idea of the argument.

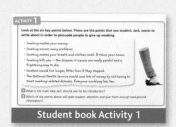

Student book Activity 1

- Discuss different ways that an opening point can grab the reader's attention, for example: by using a question, a startling statement, humour or an anecdote. Model some examples of these strategies on the board, using the opening point 'Smoking has many problems'. For example:

  - *Smoking is cool. Of course it is! Lung cancer, smelly clothes, an empty wallet and brown teeth are all the rage this year.*

  - *Smoking kills. But before it does, it will burn a hole in your wallet, make you stink and ruin your health. Yet every year millions of teenagers take up the habit.*

  - *You wouldn't pay someone to make your house smell, take your money and make you ill. So why would you smoke?*

- Ask students to work in groups to come up with some different openings using one of the techniques discussed. Share responses as a class. Discuss each opening in the context of the criteria on **Worksheet 7.1**.

Additional support

Starter
- **Brainstorm** ways of grabbing the reader's attention as a class. This will help students when they complete Worksheet 7.1 and will help with the sequencing of sentences and paragraphs in later work.
- **Clarify** cultural and idiomatic vocabulary in the 'opening' such as 'glued to', 'Big Christmas Film'.

Independent work Activity 2
- EAL learners often benefit from hearing their work read out so it may be helpful to ask **talk partners** to assess together the plans of one partner, then the other, and discuss suggestions for improvement.

Whole class work
- Find a good example of a concluding paragraph and create a **dictogloss** or **cloze activity**. Use exemplars that link the conclusion to the rest of the piece.

---

3 Independent work

- Students should work independently to complete **Activity 2**, finding the main ideas and writing an introduction to the task given. They can complete their answers on **Worksheet 7.2**.

- Ask students to swap their introduction with a partner and peer assess each other's work using the checklist on **Worksheet 7.1**.

Worksheet 7.2

4 Whole class work

Discuss the order of the points given on page 75 of the student book. Explain that the conclusion should make a strong ending to the text. For example, you might keep a strong point until last then sum up the content covered. You could also demonstrate how repeating a phrase from the opening can be used to create a satisfying ending.

5 Independent work

- Students work independently to complete **Activity 3** question 1. They should refer to their paragraph plan from Lesson 6 or to the list of key points made earlier in this lesson.

- Now ask students to complete **Activity 3**. They should compose the middle and final paragraphs of their text. Encourage students to conclude their draft using one of the techniques you modelled earlier.

6 Pair work

- Working in pairs, students take turns to justify their choice of ending technique and peer assess their partner's conclusion. Encourage students to pinpoint whether/how the conclusion rounds off or sums up the subject being written about, helps the text achieve its purpose and/or links back to the opening. Students should comment on what makes the conclusion memorable.

- Students then redraft their paragraphs, taking account of the feedback given.

7 Plenary

- Ask volunteers to share their opening and closing paragraphs with the class. Ask other students to comment constructively on each other's work. Students should explain the choices they have made and how the opening and conclusion achieve all that they should.

- Refer students to the ResultsPlus tip on page 75.

8 Further work

Ask students to find three effective openings to a text. Suggest that students look in books, magazines, newspapers, podcasts and web articles. Ask students to copy the openings onto **Worksheet 7.3** and comment on why they think they are effective.

Worksheet 7.3

Lesson 8 Crafting vocabulary

Learning objectives

→ Make appropriate and effective vocabulary choices.

Resources required
Student book pages 76–77
Worksheet 8.1: Target audience
Worksheet 8.2: Writing for an audience
Worksheet 8.3: Vocabulary choices
Worksheet 8.4: Impersonal language
Worksheet 8.5: Award citation

Assessment objectives

English AO3i / English Language AO4i
Write clearly, effectively and imaginatively, using and adapting forms and selecting vocabulary appropriate to task and purpose in ways that engage the reader.

English AO3ii / English Language AO4ii
Organise information and ideas into structured and sequenced sentences, paragraphs and whole texts, using a variety of linguistic and structural features to support cohesion and overall coherence.

1 Starter

- Hand out copies of **Worksheet 8.1** before students open their books. Ask them to work in groups to decide which text appeals to experts or non-experts and to annotate the vocabulary to justify their decisions.

- Get feedback, then display Texts A and B on the ActiveTeach. As a class, pinpoint how their different vocabulary choices are appropriate for different audiences.

- Ask students to suggest a topic that they know a lot about and to discuss what specialist vocabulary they know that relates to the topic. If students find this difficult, suggest they consider technical sporting vocabulary (e.g. *cut*, *drive*, *leg side* for cricket). Ask students if they might use different words when explaining the sport to someone who had never seen it.

Worksheet 8.1

2 Group work

- Students work together to attempt **Activity 1**, using a thesaurus and dictionary to rewrite the texts for different audiences. Students can record their new versions on **Worksheet 8.2**.

Student book page 76

- Encourage groups to share their work with another group and discuss how effective their vocabulary choices are in creating their intended effects.

Worksheet 8.2

3 Pair work

- Ask students to choose a topic about which they are expert, for example: using Facebook, a game, sport or other activity. Working in expert pairs, students should write two mini texts giving tips about their topic. The first mini text should be written for other experts and the second should be written for non-experts.

- Ask pairs to swap texts with another pair who are not experts in their topic. Students take it in turns to peer assess each other's writing, pinpointing how clearly the writers have communicated by underlining any vocabulary or terms they cannot understand.

- Ask pairs to redraft their texts based on the feedback they have received.

4 Whole class work

- Display Texts C and D on the ActiveTeach or from **Worksheet 8.3**. Ask students which advice they would rather be given, and why.

- Discuss the value of precise, detailed vocabulary and why it is helpful.

Worksheet 8.3

66

(EAL) Additional support

Starter

- **Ensure** that all students understand the meaning of 'appropriate' and 'effective' in the lesson objective.
- **Active listening**: Read the two texts on page 76 aloud and elicit comments from the students about the quality of the vocabulary (perhaps ask them to count the syllables), e.g. simple, slang, colloquial, sophisticated, polysyllabic, specialist technical. Do they understand it? Would they use it?
- **Clarify** words as appropriate using **message abundancy** (e.g. 'relevant', 'political message', 'naff').
- **Washing line**: Arrange the types of vocabulary from page 76 on a washing line arranged from the most informal to the most formal.

- Create **cloze** exercises where a mix of everyday and 'slang' vocabulary choices is offered, but where context demands one or the other to maintain the tone of the sentence.

Group work

- **Collaborative work**: Always ensure groups include strong **L1** English students as support for EAL learners.
- Use **e-dictionaries** and **thesauruses** or **bilingual dictionaries** to look up the highlighted words in Texts A and/or B.
- In addition, it may be appropriate to do some basic **dictionary** and **thesaurus** work as even the most advanced bilingual learners find difficulty in selecting the most appropriate word for the context when faced with the choices in dictionary definitions and nuances of meaning in a thesaurus.
- **Jigsaw reading**: Ask different groups to work on the different texts then write their edited texts on an **OHT** (or large sheet of paper) to feed back to the class.

5 Independent work

Ask students to work independently to complete **Activity 2**, working on the task they wrote in Lesson 7. Students should read through their blogs, paying particular attention to vocabulary. Students may use a thesaurus and dictionary again to try to find better words.

6 Whole class work

Explain the difference between personal and impersonal writing: personal writing may address the reader directly, or refer to the writer (e.g. 'I think', 'I believe'). Share the following example: *I think you should move on to free the prisoners first before paying the evil king back but you can do either.* In an impersonal text there is no reference to 'I 'or 'you', for example: *It is best to move on to free the prisoners before taking revenge on the king, but it is possible to pay back the king first if preferred.*

7 Pair/Independent work

- Using **Worksheet 8.4**, ask students to work in pairs or independently to complete **Activity 3**, rewriting the text to make it impersonal.
- Share responses. As an extension, challenge students to write an impersonal response to argue that the canteen should remain open and the canteen staff keep their jobs.

Worksheet 8.4

8 Plenary

As a class, discuss when it is appropriate to write in an impersonal or personal way. Compile two lists on the board. Have students look at their controlled assessment writing task and determine whether they need to write in an impersonal or personal way.

9 Further work

Ask students to write a one-paragraph citation awarding a prize to someone they know for something good that they do, for example: best comedian; award for super-mum for cooking, cleaning and caring; award for a youth worker for running the local youth club. The paragraph should be written in impersonal English suited to a general audience. It should be written in standard English. **Worksheet 8.5** supports this activity.

Worksheet 8.5

Lesson 9 Crafting sentences

Resources required

Student book pages 78–79
Worksheet 9.1: Sentence errors
Worksheet 9.2: Connectives
Worksheet 9.3: Complex sentences

Assessment objectives

English AO3iii / English Language AO4iii
Use a range of sentence structures for clarity, purpose and effect, with accurate punctuation and spelling.
At least a third of the AO3 weighting relates to bullet 3 (iii).

Learning objectives

→ Understand the range of sentence types and structures you can use in your writing.

→ Use a variety of sentences to suit the purpose of your text.

1 Starter

- Ask students what they know about writing in sentences already. Ask students to share all the rules they know.

- Display **Worksheet 9.1**, which gives examples of incomplete or incorrect sentences.

- Ask students to be the 'sentence mechanics' and identify the problem and rectify it. Record the correct sentences on the board.

Worksheet 9.1

2 Whole class work

- Model how to compose and check a sentence using the examples and the annotation tool on the ActiveTeach, or working on page 78 of the student book.

- Compose a class paragraph describing what film actors do. Encourage students to suggest longer sentences that include connectives such as 'because', 'which' and 'when'. When students offer a sentence, ask them to listen to it and decide whether it makes sense. Appeal to other students to act as 'sentence mechanics' to fix the sentences that don't make sense.

3 Independent work

- Ask students to work independently to complete **Activity 1**. Write the sequence, Compose – Check – Improve – Write, as a flow chart on the board. Then ask students to follow that sequence as they compose, check and then perfect their sentence before writing it down.

- Ask students to swap their sentences with a partner and check they have followed the three rules on page 78 of the student book.

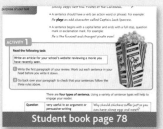

- Students should identify which rule they need to work at most to improve their sentence writing.

Student book page 78

4 Whole class work

- Discuss the sentence types on page 78 of the student book (question, statement, command, exclamation). Ask students to suggest examples of each sentence type to write on the board.

- Share the following paragraph with the class. Ask students to identify the sentences types used.
Battery chickens are kept in very overcrowded conditions. They live in tiny cages and can hardly move. Their cages are almost never cleaned. This is not fair. It is cruel. Free range chickens live in the open air and can roam around. They live happier lives. It is better to buy free range eggs.

- Students should note that all the sentences are statements. Ask volunteers to suggest how they could use different sentence types to make the text more interesting. Rewrite the text as a class.

Additional support

Starter

- **Talk partners:** Pairing EAL students with fluent English speakers to revise sentence types (see also Unit 1a Lesson 12).

- It may be appropriate for students who share the same **first language** to **discuss** sentence types in their first language to establish the different concepts.

- Make a **word wall** of sentence types for ready reference throughout the lesson.

Whole class work (4)

- **Clarify** as appropriate: 'complex' and 'compound', 'dependent clause', 'independent', 'connectives'. You may need to give more than one example when discussing the definitions of different sentence types.

- **Collaboration:** Divide students into groups of three or four to use **substitution tables** for the three kinds of sentence structure and four sentence types.

- **Competition:** How many sentences can your group make?

- Consider creating a short **dictogloss** activity which includes all types of sentence for the students to identify.

Pair work/Group work/Activities 2 and 3

- Use **envoys** to share ideas with other groups and pairs.

5 Pair work

- Ask students to work in pairs or independently to complete **Activity 2**. They should then share their writing with another pair and peer assess each other's work by marking each other's sentences for accuracy. They should look for variety and award a point for each different type of sentence used.

- Refer students to the ResultsPlus tip on page 79.

6 Whole class work

- Model simple, compound and complex sentences using the examples on page 79 of the student book. Ensure students understand that the two halves of a compound sentence make sense on their own, for example: *Bournemouth is on the coast. It has a sandy beach.* Challenge students to suggest some examples of each sentence type.

- Display the connectives chart from Lesson 6, page 73, on the ActiveTeach, which is also available on **Worksheet 9.2**, and demonstrate how to select the best connectives to write a complex sentence. Challenge students to suggest examples using a variety of connectives.

Worksheet 9.2

7 Group work

- Display the connectives chart on the ActiveTeach while students attempt **Activity 3** in small groups. They should use the information in the paragraph provided but rewrite it so that a variety of types of sentence are used.

- Ask students to share their results with the class. The class should identify where different types of sentence have been used and how this adds to the impact of the text. If appropriate, discuss how different effects can be created by inserting a short simple sentence after long complex or compound sentences.

8 Plenary

- Give students three minutes to list five ways they can vary their sentences and to give examples. Share responses.

- Then ask students what they will look for when checking their sentences. As a class compose a checklist that can be displayed.

9 Further work

Using one of the controlled assessment tasks on page 85, challenge students to select five connectives they would use to write complex sentences. They should write five complex sentences and check that they are correct. **Worksheet 9.3** supports this activity.

Worksheet 9.3

Suggested answers

Worksheet 9.1

A no verb; B run-on sentence; C no capital, no full stop; D no punctuation; E no capital; F no capital, fragment.

Lesson 10
Crafting punctuation

Learning objectives

→ Use a range of punctuation to suit your purpose.

Resources required

Student book pages 80–81
Worksheet 10.1: Punctuation quiz
Worksheet 10.2: Punctuation exercise
Worksheet 10.3: Effective punctuation
Worksheet 10.4: Punctuation
Answer sheet 10.1: Suggested answers

Assessment objectives

English AO3iii / English Language AO4iii
Use a range of sentence structures for clarity, purpose and effect, with accurate punctuation and spelling.
At least a third of the AO3 weighting relates to bullet 3 (iii).

1 Starter

- Put students into pairs or groups to complete the quiz on **Worksheet 10.1**. Set a time limit.

- Ask groups to swap sheets, then mark the quiz as a class, asking students to tell you the answers.

- Students should look at their answers and discuss what their strengths and weaknesses are.

- Discuss the punctuation issues the quiz raises, for example: use of capital letters, apostrophes and commas, and encourage students to recognise that knowing the rules or being able to correct punctuation mistakes is a step towards being able to write with good punctuation.

- Focus on any rules that students find difficult. Explain the rules, give an example, then ask students to give further examples.

- You might like to create a class punctuation rules and examples chart for display.

Worksheet 10.1

2 Independent work

- Ask students to use **Worksheet 10.2** to punctuate the text about computer games in **Activity 1**.

- Ask students to swap their work with a partner and discuss any differences.

Worksheet 10.2

3 Group work

- Display **Activity 2** on the ActiveTeach. Ask students to work together to attempt **Activity 2** questions 1 and 2, reading the two versions of the text on **Worksheet 10.3** and then discussing how the change in punctuation affects the meaning.

- Discuss their findings as a class, marking the texts using the annotation tool on the ActiveTeach. Focus the discussion on how and why removing commas or adding inverted commas changes the meaning of the text. For example, in Text A there is a hot dog that is huge whereas in Text B it is a dog that is huge and hot. In Text B the commas separate the descriptors. Without inverted commas in A the keeper is speaking but in B the inverted commas make it clear that the monkey is speaking.

Worksheet 10.3

4 Independent work/ Peer assessment

- Ask students to complete question 3 of **Activity 2** independently. They should review the writing task they completed in Lesson 9. Students may rewrite areas where necessary, focusing on using punctuation to create the meaning they want their reader to understand. Tell students to check the punctuation when they have finished the paragraph.

- Ask students to swap their work with a partner and peer assess each other's paragraph. They should tell each other what they think the paragraph is saying to check that the punctuation has created the intended meaning.

Additional support

Starter

- **Talk partners** may be a useful strategy at each stage of the lesson, both EAL learners paired with fluent English speakers to check punctuation terms are understood, and EAL students with the same L1 to discuss how punctuation is used in that language.

- The **punctuation triangle** should be displayed around the classroom to show how punctuation becomes increasingly advanced.

- Put the information on page 80 onto the **word wall** then ask for volunteers to read the table of punctuation and exemplar sentences, pointing to each punctuation mark in turn.

Independent work Activity 1

- **Read** the passage in Activity 1 aloud, trying not to pause where punctuation should be. Allow EAL learners **sufficient time** to complete the activity (they may work more slowly).

Group work

- Ask two students to read Text A and Text B about the monkey and the keeper aloud. Choose strong readers who will make the meaning of each text clear.

- **Be aware** that even higher achieving EAL students often find difficulty with capital letters for the names of places, days, etc. – even when writing their own names, and sometimes in the middle of words. They may find difficulty identifying and understanding proper nouns/names because of cultural and social differences (and could lose marks unnecessarily for inaccuracy).

Further work

- Be aware that some students may not have a television and may not watch films.

---

5 Independent work

- Ask students to look at the task on page 81 and complete the example controlled assessment task in **Activity 3**. Students should then assess their own work using the criteria given in the ResultsPlus Maximise your marks section.

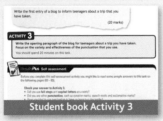

Student book Activity 3

- Students should work in pairs to complete the **Putting it into practice** activity on page 83.

6 Plenary

Ask students to work in pairs. They have to explain to each other how they can use punctuation to change the meaning of the following sentence:
The driver says the pedestrian should never have stopped there.

7 Further work

Students should use **Worksheet 10.4** to write two paragraphs reviewing a film or programme they have watched this week. Their focus is on using punctuation, especially full stops, question marks, capital letters, commas and apostrophes to make their meaning clear to their reader.

Worksheet 10.4

8 Controlled assessment practice

- On pages 84–85 of the student book, practice controlled assessment writing tasks are provided. You could work through these with students as they practice before they sit their assessment.

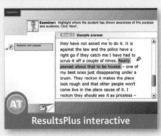

ResultsPlus interactive

- On the ActiveTeach there are accompanying ResultsPlus grade improvement activities which help students understand how to improve their answer.

Suggested answers

Worksheet 10.1 – See Answer sheet 10.1

Lesson 1 Purpose

Learning objectives

→ Understand *what* and *how* to write for different purposes.

Resources required

Student book pages 88-91
Worksheet 1.1: Features of text types
Worksheet 1.2: Writing tasks
Worksheet 1.3: Explain
Worksheet 1.4: Persuade
Worksheet 1.5: Argue
Worksheet 1.6: Comment
Worksheet 1.7: Purpose and features
Answer sheet 1.1: Suggested answers

Assessment objectives

English AO3i / English Language AO4i
Write clearly, effectively and imaginatively, using and adapting forms and selecting vocabulary appropriate to task and purpose in ways that engage the reader.

1 Starter

- Before students open their books, hand out **Worksheet 1.1**, which contains features lists for different text types. Ask students to decide which text types go with which features.

- Discuss the features of a discussion (similar to argument, but always gives both sides) and explain that a review is similar to a comment piece.

Worksheet 1.1

2 Whole class work

- Display the task: *Write a magazine article arguing for or against the following statement: 'Mobile phones should be banned in schools.'* Then model how to pinpoint the key words which will tell you the purpose of the text you have to write, underlining the word *arguing*.

- Complete part of **Activity 1** as a class. Display **Activity 1** on the ActiveTeach, or use **Worksheet 1.2**. Using the annotation tool on the ActiveTeach, ask volunteers to underline the key words in tasks A and B that show what the reader will get from the text and discuss each text's purpose as a class. Students should record their responses on **Worksheet 1.2**.

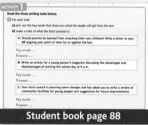

Student book page 88

Worksheet 1.2

3 Independent work

- Ask students to underline the words and identify the purpose of task C independently.

- Share responses.

4 Whole class work

- Focus students' attention on **Activity 2**. Display the flu text on the ActiveTeach and, using Text A and the chart showing the features of an explanation on **Worksheet 1.3**, model how to find examples of these features in the text.

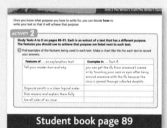

Student book page 89

- Pinpoint each explanation (how and why) in Text A. Demonstrate that the order of the points is logical: it describes the spread of flu in sequence, from the original carrier to the newly infected person, then goes on to explain how it takes hold in the new carrier's body.

Worksheet 1.3

- Ask the class what sort of a text they think it is. Challenge them to explain why, drawing on the features you have pinpointed to support their ideas.

- Point out that each reason is explained in detail. To help students understand this, you might want to show what the text might look like if the points were not fully explained (e.g. *You can catch flu from being near someone who sneezes. You can catch flu from touching your nose or eyes. The virus then spreads through your body*).

Additional support

Starter/Whole class work/Activity 1

- Use **message abundancy** to **clarify** difficult words on Worksheet 1.1 as necessary (e.g. 'logical', 'issue', 'sway', 'emotive').
- **Talk partners:** Pair EAL students with the same first language to **discuss** the 'purpose' verbs in their first language then use a thesaurus to find synonyms for each.
- **Talk partners:** Always use groups which include fluent English speakers and EAL learners to ensure the idea being discussed (e.g. 'key words') is properly understood.

- Create a **word wall** of language and purpose which can be added to during this and succeeding lessons. If the words are fastened with sticky tack, they can be selected as appropriate for many lessons.

Activity 2

- **Active listening:** Read around the class the extracts on pages 89–91, taking the opportunity to clarify any problem words (e.g. 'tube', 'droplets', 'illegal', 'hefty', 'slop'). Ensure EAL students understand how the language links to the purpose of the text.
- It may be appropriate to suggest **sentence starters** as a **scaffold** for justifying student responses.

5 Group work

- Ask students to work together to complete the rest of **Activity 2**, filling in the charts with examples of each feature in Texts B–D. You could give different groups different texts to work on or each group can work on all the texts. Students can annotate copies of each text – see **Worksheets 1.4–1.6**.

Worksheet 1.4

- Ask groups to swap their charts and check each other's work. Discuss any differences as a class, and annotate a class copy of each text using the annotation tool on the ActiveTeach.

6 Pair/Independent work

- Ask students to attempt the first part of **Activity 3** in pairs, working out the purpose of each text and suggesting the features that could be included.
- Share responses as a class. Challenge students to give concrete examples, for example: points for or against using size 0 models.
- Now ask students to work in pairs to consider what was wrong with the sample student's response. Students should understand that his argument lacks evidence or well-developed reasons – he needs to be more specific.
- Students should now brainstorm ways to improve the writing and agree what needs to be done, for example: separating the points into different paragraphs with evidence and detailed reasons.
- Challenge students to work independently to rewrite their text, making the agreed improvements.
- Working in different pairs, students should peer assess, evaluating and reflecting on whether their changes have improved the text. Remind students to use the argument checklist when assessing each other's work.
- Share responses.

7 Independent work

Students should work independently to write a paragraph responding to task A, including appropriate features for a discussion.

8 Plenary

- Share some of the paragraphs on size 0 models and discuss the features. Ask students to suggest improvements.
- Broaden the discussion, asking students to suggest a structure for the whole piece, for example: a point making one side of the argument followed by a point making the other side and a concluding paragraph at the end.

9 Further work

Ask students to identify the purpose of a text they have been asked to write in another subject (e.g. a write-up of a science experiment, an essay for history). They should make a list of the features the text has to contain (e.g. a description of the experiment, a conclusion explaining the results). Students can record their responses on **Worksheet 1.7**.

Worksheet 1.7

Suggested answers

Worksheet 1.1: Features of text types

1 C, 2 D, 3 E, 4 A, 5 B

Student book Activity 1

1.b) A <u>argue</u> for or against banning parents from smacking their children

   B <u>discuss</u> the advantages and disadvantages of starting the school day at 8 am

   C <u>review</u> community facilities for young people and suggest ways of improving them

Student book Activity 2 – See Answer sheet 1.1

Lesson 2 Audience

Resources required
Student book pages 92–93
Worksheet 2.1: Different audiences
Worksheet 2.2: Darren's response
Worksheet 2.3: Audience and formality

Assessment objectives
English AO3i / English Language AO4i
Write clearly, effectively and imaginatively, using and adapting forms and selecting vocabulary appropriate to task and purpose in ways that engage the reader.

Learning objectives

→ Understand how knowing the audience can tell a writer *what* and *how* to write.

1 Starter

- With the class, brainstorm a list of places to visit and things to do in your local area, for example: library, museum, cinema, leisure centre. Record suggestions on the board.

Worksheet 2.1

- Organise students into groups. Give students these four different audiences: elderly; young adults; mums and toddlers; unemployed. Ask them to brainstorm what would be important to each audience when considering what to do with their spare time and their likely interests. Students can record their ideas on **Worksheet 2.1**.

- You might like to ask lower attainers to focus on one or two of the audiences and higher attainers to work on all of the audiences.

- Ask students to suggest which of the places to visit and things to do listed on the board will suit each audience based on the profiles they have drawn up. Students should give reasons for their choices.

2 Whole class work

- Share the task on page 92 of the student book: *Write a speech for the end-of-year student awards discussing whether the age that students can leave education should be lowered to 14.*

- Ask students to identify the audience; then ask students to suggest what aspects of the topic might interest the different groups in the audience (teenagers, parents and teachers). You might like to share the examples on page 92 of the student book.

- With this in mind, ask students to decide what areas of information and ideas they should include in the text, for example: information on the kinds of job students can get at 14, and examples of jobs they could get with higher qualifications.

3 Pair work

- Write the following strategy on the board:
  - Read the task.
  - Decide what content you are asked to write about.
  - Identify the audience and work out the audience's profile, for example: interests, needs, attitudes.
  - Decide what content will suit your audience.

- Ask students to work in pairs and follow the strategy to complete **Activity 1**. Remind students that in the exam they should take a mature approach to the topic in hand. Sometimes, to suit the brief, they may need to make points or argue for things that they personally disagree with.

4 Whole class work

- As a class, brainstorm the difference between formal and informal writing to check prior understanding. Ask students to suggest the features of formal and informal writing and draw up a list on the board, referring to the examples on page 93 of the student book as necessary.

Student book page 93

- Share the examples of formal and informal writing on page 93 of the student book. Ask students to suggest additional sentences in each register on the same subjects.

- Then demonstrate how to change the formal into informal and vice versa. Use the examples on page 93 of the student book and the annotation tool on the ActiveTeach. Change the first sentence to suit an audience of teenagers on a website. Change the second to suit a formal letter to the local council.

- Tell students they are more likely to be asked to write formally in the exam, and even if they have to write for a teenage audience it will still need to be in standard English. Students should understand that they must never use text-speak abbreviations or incorrect grammar in an exam.

Additional support

Starter
- Use a **mind map** or spider diagram to organise the information about audiences on page 92 and then adapt it for Activity 1.
- **Talk partners:** Pair EAL students with fluent English speakers to work together to complete Worksheet 2.1 as a **model** before doing later tasks.

Whole class work/Pair work/Activity 1
- **Active listening:** Read the notes on page 92 of the student book using expression and pauses to aid understanding.
- **Clarify** any difficult words as necessary using **message abundancy**, (e.g. 'contribute', 'disruption', 'concentrate').
- Read the task in Activity 1 to students. **Be aware** that some EAL learners may have no experience of films and games and rating certificates.

Pair/Independent work/Activity 2
- Pairs of EAL students who share a first language could **discuss** terms such as register, formality and slang and find examples from their **first language** to share with the class.
- **Clarify** colloquial/informal terms in the text in Activity 2 (e.g. 'stuff', 'shouldn't', 'for a laugh') ensuring that students understand why these are informal.
- For a more kinaesthetic activity a **washing line** could be made of the words and phrases, ranging from very informal to very formal.
- **Jigsaw reading:** Find two texts (one formal, one informal) on the same topic. Cut the texts up sentence by sentence and then mix them. Students could then reassemble the sentences into coherent texts with a consistent level of formality.
- **Sentence starters** could be given to emphasise conventions of formal letter writing.

5 Pair/Independent work
- Students should work in pairs to attempt **Activity 2**, deciding on the appropriate level of formality for a task.
- Give students **Worksheet 2.2**, a paragraph Darren wrote in response to the task. Students should identify why it is not suitable for the audience. They should discuss their decisions with another pair, explaining their reasoning before sharing as a class. Students should understand that it is too informal – he has included:

Worksheet 2.2

slang ('cool', 'stuff,' 'for a laugh'), expressive punctuation ('AMAZING!'), contractions ('There's') and the overall tone is too chatty for a general audience.
- Ask students to work independently to write a better version of his text and then peer assess to evaluate the success of the new paragraphs.

6 Plenary
- Ask students to work in pairs to write a revision card of key points reminding them how they can tell a) what audience they need to write for b) how to make sure the text will suit the audience c) the key differences between formal and informal writing.
- Share ideas with the class.

7 Further work
Hand out **Worksheet 2.3**. Students need to consider the audience and level of formality for the writing task and then write a letter about work experience.

Worksheet 2.3

Suggested answers
Student book Activity 1
1. *The audience is teenagers.*

Student book Activity 2
1. *The guide should be formal.*

Lesson 3 Understanding form

Learning objectives

→ Understand the typical features used in different forms of writing.

1 Starter

- Display a variety of texts. You may wish to display the texts from **Weblinks 3.1–3.4** as examples, or you can hand out newspaper articles, magazine articles, etc.

- Ask students to identify what forms the texts are written in. How did they know what the forms were?

- Explain that students will need to recognise the features typical of different forms of writing and include these in their own writing.

2 Whole class work

Display Text F using the zoom function on the ActiveTeach, or display **Worksheet 3.7**. Model how to identify features of a form of writing. For example, ask students what the purpose of the first sentence is (to introduce the topic of the blog).

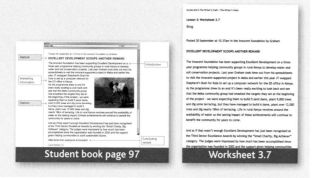

Student book page 97   Worksheet 3.7

3 Pair work

- Ask students to work in groups of three to attempt question 1 of **Activity 1**, using the texts on Student book pages 95–97 or on **Worksheets 3.1–3.7** and **Video 3.1**, recording their ideas on **Worksheet 3.8**.

Resources required

Student book pages 94–97
Video 3.1: Obama speech
Weblink 3.1: Formal report
Weblink 3.2: Review
Weblink 3.3: Leaflet
Weblink 3.4: Blog
Resource 3.1: Texts A–F
Worksheet 3.1: Similarities and differences
Worksheet 3.2: Review
Worksheet 3.3: Formal report
Worksheet 3.4: Speech
Worksheet 3.5: Leaflet
Worksheet 3.6: Formal letter
Worksheet 3.7: Blog
Worksheet 3.8: Features table
Answer sheet 3.1: Features checklist

Assessment objectives

English AO3i / English Language AO4i
Write clearly, effectively and imaginatively, using and adapting forms and selecting vocabulary appropriate to task and purpose in ways that engage the reader.

English AO3ii / English Language AO4ii
Organise information and ideas into structured and sequenced sentences, paragraphs and whole texts, using a variety of linguistic and structural features to support cohesion and overall coherence.

NB: Lessons 3 and 4 cover the same objectives, providing students with ample practice in a vital skill and allowing them to become familiar with a wide range of forms.

Worksheet 3.1   Worksheet 3.8

- Share ideas as a class, asking volunteers to point out the features in the different texts. The rest of the class should check their chart and add any necessary corrections so that by the end of this activity everyone has a checklist of features for each form (also provided on **Answer sheet 3.1**). This can be used for revision.

- You may want to display **Resource 3.1**, a PowerPoint slide displaying each text with its features, while going through the texts.

Resource 3.1

Starter/Activity 1

- **Active listening**: Read the introduction to Activity 1 and **revise** words as necessary.
- Use the **word wall** to **recap** prior knowledge of the text types and conventions.

Activity 1

- **Talk partners**: All group and pair work should include both EAL learners and fluent English speakers to establish and revise language connected with form. Ensure that cultural differences between all the forms/types of texts are understood.
- Create **spider diagrams** for each of the form/feature combinations using the Suggested answers.

4 Group work

- Divide the class into groups. Give each group a different pair of forms to compare as set out in **Activity 1** question 2. Students mark their answers on **Worksheet 3.8**.

- Now create new groups where each student work on a different text. Each student has to act as expert and present their findings to the rest of the group.

Access Unit 2 The Writer's Craft / The Writer's Voice

Lesson 3: Worksheet 3.8

Features table

Study Texts A–F, which are written in different forms.

Complete this table to show what features are included in each of the different forms.

Form	Features
Review	
Formal report	
Speech	
Leaflet	

Worksheet 3.8

Suggested answers

Student book Activity 1

1. See Answer sheet 3.1.

2. a) *Magazine and leaflet. Similarities: headings, introductions, subheadings, conclusions, logical order to delivering ideas. Differences: magazine will tend to entertain and engage more, using devices such as personal stories, an ending that links back to the beginning.*

   b) *Letter and speech. Similarities: both address audience/reader, introduce topic, cover points in a logical order and conclude in a memorable way. Differences: use of different greetings and closures in a letter. Speech is more likely to contain rhetorical devices and be designed to resonate with a wider audience.*

   c) *Blog and letter. Similarities: logical organisation; devices used to engage reader. Both offer opportunities for the reader to respond, but in different ways (comment on blog, email, or return letter). Differences: letter is written to a specific person rather than an unknown reader; letters must directly address reader through greeting; formats of letter and blog are very different.*

   d) *Report and review. Similarities: both give information, are organised in logical order, both draw conclusions. Differences: reports should be impersonal, reviews give personal opinions; reports based on evidence, reviews based on personal judgement.*

5 Plenary

- Students play 'speed-dating'. Arrange students in two rows, A and B, so that A will keep moving along the row to a different partner each time. Row A must face the whiteboard; row B must be unable to see it. You write a form on the board. Each student in row A has to describe the features of the form to their current partner in row B, who has to guess the form. Before each new form is written down, the A row moves one space along to work with a new partner in row B.

- After a few rounds, have the rows swap places so that row B faces the board and has to describe the form's features, while row A has to guess it correctly.

6 Further work

Ask students to find two examples of different forms, highlight their key features, and bring their examples into class. Suggest sources for these texts, such as the local library, junk mail, charity shops, doctors' surgeries, etc. Alternatively, provide examples of leaflets, junk mail promotional letters, reports, etc. for students to annotate.

Lesson 4 Form in action

Learning objectives

→ Understand how to write in the correct form.

Resources required
Student book pages 98–99
Worksheet 4.1: Writing tasks
Worksheet 4.2: School leaflet 1
Worksheet 4.3: School leaflet 2
Worksheet 4.4: Television review
Answer sheet 4.1: Features checklist

Assessment objectives
English AO3i / English Language AO4i
Write clearly, effectively and imaginatively, using and adapting forms and selecting vocabulary appropriate to task and purpose in ways that engage the reader.

English AO3ii / English Language AO4ii
Organise information and ideas into structured and sequenced sentences, paragraphs and whole texts, using a variety of linguistic and structural features to support cohesion and overall coherence.
NB: Lessons 3 and 4 cover the same objectives, providing students with ample practice in a vital skill.

1 Starter activity

Play 'Just a minute'. Have the list of different forms students have already learned written on individual slips of paper and placed in a pot. Students take it in turns to pull out a form and describe its features, without naming the form. The rest of the class have to guess the form correctly. Splitting the class into two teams can add to the fun and motivation.

2 Whole class work

• Explain how knowing what form your text has to be written in helps you plan what to include. For example, if you are writing a magazine article you know it will have a headline, subheadings, paragraphs and quotes. A review will always include a description of the thing being reviewed and a personal opinion about it.

• Take students through the worked example about the magazine article on page 98 of the student book to demonstrate this.

3 Pair/Independent work

• Ask students to work in pairs or independently to complete **Activity 1**, writing two paragraphs of the magazine article while following the plan on page 98 of the student book. Remind students to think about their audience as well as the form when they write.

Student book page 98

• Share responses as a class. Ask students to give feedback on each other's responses, commenting on how appropriate it is for the audience and form.

4 Independent work

Ask students to work independently to attempt **Activity 2**. Using their completed charts from **Activity 1** in Lesson 3, or **Answer sheet 4.1**, students should decide what features they need to include in their writing for tasks A–C. They may record their ideas on **Worksheet 4.1**.

Worksheet 4.1

Additional support

Activity 3

- Use **message abundancy** as appropriate to **clarify** cultural, idiomatic and other difficult language used in the exemplar plan on page 98.

- You could create a **cloze** or **dictogloss** passage to model/scaffold the task.

5 Independent work

- Students consolidate their learning by attempting **Activity 3** questions 1 and 2, using **Worksheet 4.2**. Students should work independently to identify the form in which they have to write, list the features they should include, and then use this list to generate their plan.

- Then ask students to attempt the rest of **Activity 3**. Students should study the brief and the notes before deciding what form the text needs to be written in, listing its features and using these to generate a plan. Tell students that they can add their own ideas to William's, which are available on **Worksheet 4.3**.

- Students write their responses on **Worksheet 4.3** and share them with a partner. Ask partners to give each other feedback, ticking each feature that is correctly used in their partner's writing and listing any features that are missing.

Worksheet 4.2

Worksheet 4.3

6 Plenary

Ask students to close their books. Shout out a text form and ask students to brainstorm its features. You might like to do this in groups and turn it into a competition.

7 Further work

Ask students to use their plan from **Activity 3** and what they have learned about form to write a review of their favourite television programme. They should complete **Worksheet 4.4** for support.

Worksheet 4.4

Suggested answers

Student book Activity 2

A) *speech*, B) *report*, C) *letter*.

Features checklist – See Answer sheet 4.1

Lesson 5 Producing ideas

Learning objectives

→ Understand the writing task you are set.

→ Come up with ideas to include in your writing.

Resources required

Student book pages 100–101
Resource 5.1: Sample writing task
Worksheet 5.1: Sample writing task
Worksheet 5.2: Writing task
Worksheet 5.3: List of points
Worksheet 5.4: Spider diagram
Worksheet 5.5: Practice plan

Assessment objectives

English AO3i / English Language AO4i
Write clearly, effectively and imaginatively, using and adapting forms and selecting vocabulary appropriate to task and purpose in ways that engage the reader.

English AO3ii / English Language AO4ii
Organise information and ideas into structured and sequenced sentences, paragraphs and whole texts, using a variety of linguistic and structural features to support cohesion and overall coherence.

1 Starter

Ask students to suggest different ways they know to record ideas they want to use in a text, such as lists, planning frames or mind maps. Ask students to describe or demonstrate each technique.

2 Whole class work

- Ask students what four pieces of information they need to find out from the writing task before they start planning their answer (the form, content, audience and purpose). Tell students that they can find out this information by reading the task and asking themselves what (content), who (audience), why (purpose) and how (form).

Worksheet 5.1

- Display page 100 on the ActiveTeach, and demonstrate this using the worked example there, or on **Worksheet 5.1**. Display only the task and challenge students to answer the what, who, why and how questions, asking them to underline the key words and ideas in the task. Alternatively, you could use **Resource 5.1** to display the task and questions.

Resource 5.1

3 Independent work

Ask students to work independently to complete **Activity 1**, identifying the form, purpose, audience and content of a task. Students can record their ideas on **Worksheet 5.2**.

Worksheet 5.2

4 Whole class work

- Using the information on page 101 of the student book, or from **Worksheets 5.3** and **5.4**, model how to plan ideas. Start by modelling a list, then model the same ideas as a spider diagram.

- Emphasise that students should check all the ideas they have added to their diagram are relevant to the task's requirements and cross out any that are not.

- Then show students how to number their ideas in the best order in which they should be written about.

- If students need further support, create a class list and class spider diagram to generate ideas for the mobile phone task given on page 100 of the student book. Ask volunteers to come to the board and write their ideas.

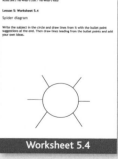

Worksheet 5.3

Worksheet 5.4

EAL Additional support

Whole class work/Activity 1

- **Active listening**: Ask students to take turns to read small chunks of the explanatory text on page 100. **Clarify** key words as necessary using **message abundancy**.

- EAL learners may have difficulty appreciating the implication of 'argue for or against'. It may be helpful to encourage students who share a **first language** to **discuss** the introductory text on page 100 and then share their understanding (or difficulty) with the teacher.

- Create a sample answer to the what/who/why/how questions (for a different writing task). Use this to create a **matching activity** in which students match the questions to the analysis.

- Alternatively, use the **word wall** to match: who (audience), what (content), why (purpose) and how (form).

Independent work/Activity 2

- EAL students sometimes lack the first-hand experiences or prior knowledge which would help them to generate ideas so you might like to create groups that have a **mixture** of EAL learners and fluent English speakers who could provide support by sharing experiences and ideas. EAL students are often unsure about using their own unique experiences to 'think outside the box' so **discussion in first language** or **talk partners** may also be appropriate for some students.

- Before the students work independently, the teacher could **model** how to **highlight** and **annotate** the **key words** in the task, asking student volunteers to help. It may be appropriate to also **model** how to change the note form on a spider diagram, list or mind map into full sentences – perhaps for alternative audiences.

5 Independent work

- Ask students to complete **Activity 2** independently. They should recap on the content, audience, purpose and form before using the bullet points given to generate ideas. Ensure that all students complete two plans: one list and one spider diagram. Give students ten minutes to answer the questions and complete their first plan. This will help them get used to the time limit in the exam.

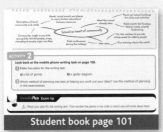

Student book page 101

- Ask students to swap their plans with a partner. Partners should give each other feedback on the ideas. *Are they relevant to the task? Will they suit the audience?* Students can revise their plans following this feedback.

- Now challenge students to write the first two paragraphs in response to the task, using the ideas from their plan.

- Afterwards, encourage students to decide which idea-recording method works best for them, and which method they should plan to use in the exam. Remind them that the ideas have to be turned into a piece of writing so they need to look at both a) which method they found easiest to use to record their ideas, and b) which method from which they can extract their ideas easily when they turn it into a detailed plan.

7 Further work

Ask students to practise their preferred method of recording ideas by coming up with at least five ideas they could use in a magazine article about their favourite hobby. **Worksheet 5.5** supports this activity.

Worksheet 5.5

Suggested answers

Student book Activity 1

- *What: suggestions for how the school can play a key role in the community*
- *Who: school council*
- *Why: to inform the school council what the school already does for the local community and to suggest ways to improve this*
- *How: report format – headings, bullet points, etc.*

6 Plenary

As a class, discuss which method of recording their ideas students will use in the exam. Encourage them to explain how to do it and why it works best for them.

Lesson 6 Planning

Resources required
Student book pages 102–103
Worksheet 6.1: Practice plan
Worksheet 6.2: Flow chart

Learning objectives

→ Organise your ideas into a clear and effective structure.

Assessment objectives
English AO3ii / English Language AO4ii
Organise information and ideas into structured and
sequenced sentences, paragraphs and whole texts, using
a variety of linguistic and structural features to support
cohesion and overall coherence.

1 Starter

In order to be able to plan paragraphs students need to
know how to identify what the task requires in terms of
form, audience and purpose, and how to generate suitable
ideas to write about. Encourage students to recap these
skills by compiling a list of bullet points showing how they
will work out what they have to do. Begin the list with
asking the what, who, why and how questions and work
through to generating ideas in a list or mind map.

2 Whole class work

• Display the task from page
102 of the student book on
the ActiveTeach. Work through
the annotations as a class,
demonstrating how the key
words reveal the form, purpose
and audience for the task.

Student book page 102

• On the right-hand side of the
board, write the heading 'form'
and list what features the form
suggests the writer needs to
include, and the structure their text needs. Then write the
heading 'purpose' and list what features their text should
include to achieve its purpose.

• Now ask students why it is important to consider the
audience before they start writing. Discuss briefly, then
ask students to complete **Activity 1** in pairs, completing
the sentences to say how they should write for the
given audience.

• Share responses.

3 Whole class work

• Read through the information on pages 102–103 of the
student book, asking students to recall what they have
already learned about producing ideas in Lesson 5.

• Ask students to work in pairs
to generate ideas for the
second bullet point of the exam
question (information that
students could be given) as set
out in **Activity 2**.

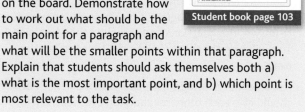

• Share ideas as a class, and
produce a class mind map or list
on the board. Demonstrate how
to work out what should be the
main point for a paragraph and

Student book page 103

what will be the smaller points within that paragraph.
Explain that students should ask themselves both a)
what is the most important point, and b) which point is
most relevant to the task.

4 Pair work

• Ask students to complete **Activity 2** in pairs, making
notes on what they could include for each point and
adding these to the paragraph plan.

• Share ideas as a class. Encourage students to justify
their decisions.

Additional support

Note: The strong correlation between the quality of the planning and the quality of the response to the task cannot be emphasised enough.

Starter
- **Talk partners:** Pair EAL learners with fluent English speakers to quickly revise what they already know about preparing to write a task (e.g. identifying the audience, purpose, form, level of formality, etc.).

Whole class work/Activity 2
- It may be appropriate in some classes for EAL students with a common first language to **discuss** what a paragraph is like and how to develop the paragraph map from the choices suggested.

Independent work/Activity 3
- Display the previous work on who/what/why/how prominently as a reference.
- Use the **word wall** built up during previous lessons to select examples of useful language to describe, argue, persuade and explain.
- Briefly revise the typical features of a review. It may be appropriate to use **talk partners**.

5 Whole class work

Show students how to plan what should go into the introductory and concluding paragraphs of the text. This skill is developed more fully in Lesson 7, so for the moment keep it simple, explaining that the introduction engages the reader, introduces the topic and may reveal the purpose to the reader; the conclusion sums up or rounds off the topic and recaps on the main argument or point of the text.

6 Independent work

Give students ten minutes to complete **Activity 3. Worksheet 6.1** is provided for this task.

Worksheet 6.1

7 Peer assessment

- Ask students to swap their work with a partner. Students should give each other feedback on the following points:
  - The quality and relevance of the ideas
  - The order of the paragraphs
  - The order of the points within the paragraphs
- Ask students to discuss any disagreements with you. Students should then amend their plan in light of feedback given.

8 Plenary

Ask volunteers to share their plans with the class. They should comment on the feedback they received and justify their ideas and structure.

9 Further work

Ask students to make a flow chart they can use for revision, showing what they have to do in the exam to make sure they can write well, and within the time limit. Students can record their ideas on **Worksheet 6.2**.

Worksheet 6.2

Suggested answers

Student book Activity 1
1. a) *head teacher; formal standard English*
   b) *correct grammar and punctuation and higher level vocabulary; not contractions or slang*

Lesson 7 Writing openings

Resources required

Student book pages 104–105
BBC Video: Writing effective openings
Worksheet 7.1: Opening options
Worksheet 7.2: Example openings
Worksheet 7.3: Different openings
Worksheet 7.4: Improving openings

Learning objectives

→ Begin your writing clearly and effectively.

Assessment objectives

English AO3i / English Language AO4i
Write clearly, effectively and imaginatively, using and adapting forms and selecting vocabulary appropriate to task and purpose in ways that engage the reader.

English AO3ii / English Language AO4ii
Organise information and ideas into structured and sequenced sentences, paragraphs and whole texts, using a variety of linguistic and structural features to support cohesion and overall coherence.

1 Starter

- Before they open their books, give students the task: *Write an article for your school magazine explaining how to make good use of the internet.* Ask students to identify the task's purpose, content, audience and form.

- Ask students to work in pairs for five minutes to compose several interesting ways to begin that article.

- Each pair should choose their best opening and share it with another pair, justifying why their opening will grab the reader's attention.

- Ask each group to decide which opening worked best and why and then share it with the rest of the class. Then have students vote for the best opening.

- While listening to students' openings, make a note on the board of the range of techniques people tried.

2 Whole class work

- Ask students to generate a list of things an ideal introduction should do: e.g. engage the reader; introduce the topic; possibly reveal the purpose to the reader; get the reader's attention. Record this checklist under the heading 'What makes a good opening' on the board or as an A3 poster to refer back to later in the lesson.

BBC Video: Writing effective openings

- Play the **BBC Video: Writing effective openings** on the ActiveTeach. Students should make notes on what the video instructs about good openings in writing. Take feedback from students about any differences between the video and the list they generated as a class.

Worksheet 7.1

- Display student book page 104 on the ActiveTeach, and introduce the options for openings for the example task. This information is also available on **Worksheet 7.1**. Discuss and exemplify what each suggestion means and how to write it. You may be able to draw on examples students have already produced in the starter activity.

3 Group work

- Ask students to work in small groups to attempt **Activity 1**, demonstrating their understanding by identifying which type of opening has been used and commenting on which example would suit the task best. They can record their answers on **Worksheet 7.2**.

Worksheet 7.2

- Ask students to share their ideas about which opening would work best for the task. Encourage debate and ask students to justify their ideas.

4 Pair work

- Ask students to work in pairs to attempt part 1 of **Activity 2**, completing the chart and crafting their own openings for the suggested task. Students should record their ideas on **Worksheet 7.3**. *NB*: To do the next part of the activity each student in the pair will need to have recorded all their openings.

Worksheet 7.3

- Ask students to find a new partner. They should share their ideas for openings and attempt part 2 of **Activity 2**. Students should decide which openings are most effective.

- Ask students to share their best openings with the class. Write their ideas on the board and discuss the merits of the different openings students have composed. Refer back to the criteria 'What makes a good opening' that you created earlier.

Additional support

Starter
- **Talk partners**: Pair EAL learners with fluent English speakers to work through the starter activity.

Whole class work
- **Active listening**: Ask fluent readers to read the introduction and openings on page 104 and ensure that 'rhetorical question', 'humorous' and 'blunt statement' are understood.
- It may be difficult for EAL students to find the right tone for 'humorous' and 'blunt' openings. It may be beneficial for some EAL students with a common first language to **discuss** comparable strategies in their **first language** then share their ideas with the class.
- After hearing the BBC clip, **talk partners** (pairing EAL students and fluent English speakers) could discuss ways of grabbing the reader's attention.
- Options for openings and an example of each could be added to the **word wall**.

Pair work/Activity 1
- A **substitution table** could help EAL students to create new sentences.
- Use a **collaborative activity**: groups of three or four students could make up a short **role-play** to illustrate humorous or controversial conversations about the events of the past year. Facial expression and tone of voice would enable greater understanding.
- **Card sort**: Write two or three sentences to make up an effective opening. Cut them up and ask students to **sequence** them. Alternatively, you could include enough sentences for a variety of openings and ask students to create the best one from the sentences given.

Independent work
- Before Activity 3, it may be necessary to **clarify** 'Churchill Academy'.
- **Writing frames/sentence starters**: A **cloze** or **dictogloss** activity could be used to provide further examples and practice of different strategies.

5 Whole class work

- Display the 'What makes a good opening' criteria you collated earlier in the lesson.
- Ensure students have their books closed. Write the example of a poor opening from the student book on the board: *A bad day can feel like it goes on and on for ever and ever. A good day at Churchill Academy can last a lifetime.*
- Ask students to use the checklist to identify what might be wrong with the opening.
- Ask students the following questions:
  - *Can you make the meaning clearer?*
  - *Are there words you can remove or change to give it more impact?*
  - *Should you change the order of ideas or words to give them more impact?*
- Model how to improve the opening, taking suggestions from students as appropriate.
- Ask students to share examples of openings that students composed which they didn't feel worked as well as their best and redraft them as a class.

6 Independent work

- Ask students to attempt **Activity 3** independently, selecting the best opening and improving it. Then students could work at improving an opening they developed in **Activity 2**.
- Share responses as a class.

7 Plenary

- Without looking at the student book, ask students to write a revision card on which they list four things an effective opening should do, four different types of opening they can use when writing a text, and three questions they need to ask to check if an opening is effective.
- Check that their lists are complete. They can use the cards for revision prior to the assessment.

8 Further work

Give students the task on **Worksheet 7.4** and ask them to write three different openings. They should then select their most effective opening and attempt to improve it, using the strategies they have learned this lesson.

Worksheet 7.4

Suggested answers
Student book Activity 1
1. *A rhetorical question*
   B opinion
   C blunt statement
   D fact (and blunt statement)

Lesson 8 Linking paragraphs

Learning objectives

→ Make your writing flow from one paragraph to the next.

Resources required

Student book pages 106–109
BBC Video: Analysing a newspaper
Worksheet 8.1: Connectives chart
Worksheet 8.2: Text A
Worksheet 8.3: Text B
Worksheet 8.4: Using connectives
Worksheet 8.5: Writing feedback
Worksheet 8.6: Five connectives

Assessment objectives

English AO3ii / English Language AO4ii
Organise information and ideas into structured and sequenced sentences, paragraphs and whole texts, using a variety of linguistic and structural features to support cohesion and overall coherence.

English AO3iii / English Language AO4iii
Use a range of sentence structures for clarity, purpose and effect, with accurate punctuation and spelling.
At least a third of the AO3 weighting relates to bullet 3 (iii).

1 Starter

- Hand out **Worksheet 8.1**. Ask students to study the connectives chart and highlight in different colours a) connectives they know and use regularly; b) those they recognise but don't often use; and c) those they don't use.

- Ask volunteers to share some of the connectives they put in group c).

- Where some students are expert in using a connective that others are not, they should explain how the connective is used and give example sentences using the connective. For connectives which no one is confident in using, you will need to explain their meaning and model how they are used.

Worksheet 8.1

2 Group work

- Display the two texts on page 106 on the ActiveTeach and read the texts with the class (also provided on **Worksheets 8.2** and **8.3**). Ask students to suggest which they think is easier to read.

- Ask students to work in groups to attempt **Activity 1**, listing the connectives in Text B and then explaining how each links ideas to add to the clarity of the text.

- Ask groups to feed back their ideas to the class. Have students highlight and annotate the connectives using the annotation tool on the ActiveTeach.

Worksheet 8.2

Worksheet 8.3

3 Independent work/ Peer assessment

- Ask students to attempt **Activity 2** independently, improving Andrew's text by using connectives. Challenge students to use connectives that they don't normally use. **Worksheet 8.4** supports this activity.

- Ask students to swap their text with a partner. They should highlight the connectives each other has added, ticking ones that improve the sense of the text and underlining any that do not. Students should give each other feedback, explaining why they did not think the connectives they underlined made sense.

- Share ideas and construct a whole class version of Andrew's text.

Worksheet 8.4

4 Whole class work

- Watch the **BBC Video: Analysing a newspaper**. Discuss as a class and ask students to suggest why topic sentences are important.

BBC Video: Analysing a newspaper

- Explain that the topic sentence should be followed by sentences that explain the point further, giving details, examples and reasons as necessary. The paragraph should end with a final sentence which links

Additional support

Starter

• EAL students who share a **first language** could **discuss** connectives in their first language to consolidate understanding and enable them to use the categories of connectives on Worksheet 8.1.

• Create a set of **cards** with the categories of connectives from Worksheet 8.1 and make other cards with one connective on each. Students would **sort** the connectives into the correct categories.

Group work

• Ensure each group has a mix of EAL learners and fluent English speakers.

• **Jigsaw reading**: Make copies of Texts A and B. Cut up and jumble the sentences. Students can work in pairs to **sequence** the sentences. This will help them organise the ideas and recognise the connectives and reinforcement devices where they are present. Students can share their findings with the other pair in their group.

Independent work/Activity 2

• Clarify 'flat', 'proms' and 'posh'.

Whole class work/Activity 3

• The notes for paragraph 3 on page 108 could be presented as a **dictogloss** activity as a preparation for the task in Activity 4.

---

what has been said either to the main subject of the text or to the idea that will be in the following paragraph.

• You could discuss the similarity of this method of writing paragraphs with the Point Evidence Explanation pattern students might be used to using when writing about texts.

5 Whole class work

Complete **Activity 3** as a class. Ask students to identify both topic sentences and comment on what they tell the reader. If appropriate, you might like to share further examples of topic sentences from other texts in the student book.

6 Independent work

• Ask students to work through **Activity 4** independently, writing Andrew's third paragraph, then two paragraphs for each of the two tasks on page 108 of the student book. Students can refer to the connectives chart on **Worksheet 8.1**. Remind them to attempt to use connectives that they don't normally use, from the chart.

• Encourage students to read through their work and make any improvements necessary. They should then swap one of the paragraphs they wrote and give each other feedback by answering the following questions, available on **Worksheet 8.5**:

– Are the topic sentences relevant? Do they introduce the main idea in the paragraph?

– Do the connectives help to link ideas? Have they all been used correctly?

– Do the paragraphs link together successfully?

Worksheet 8.5

7 Independent work

• Ask students to read the example examination question on page 109 and work through **Activity 5** independently, writing two paragraphs of a letter to students, focusing on how well they link the paragraphs together. They should spend about ten minutes on this task.

• Students should then assess their own work using the criteria given in the ResultsPlus Maximise your marks sections.

• Students should work in pairs to complete the **Putting it into practice** activity on page 111.

8 Plenary

• Ask students to consider what they have learned in the lesson. Ask them to write down one thing they have done well and one aspect that they need to improve, for example: using connectives or writing topic sentences.

• Ask some students to share their targets for improvement. Ask students to share their 'top tips' for writing and linking paragraphs.

9 Further work

Ask students to pick five connectives that they are less familiar with and to write five sentences using them correctly. **Worksheet 8.6** supports this activity.

Worksheet 8.6

Lesson 9 Choosing

Resources required

Student book pages 112-113
Dictionaries
Thesauruses
Worksheet 9.1: Precise language
Worksheet 9.2: Peer assessment
Worksheet 9.3: Persuasive writing
Worksheet 9.4: Powerful vocabulary

Learning objectives

→ Select appropriate vocabulary that makes your writing clear and effective.

Assessment objectives

English AO3i / English Language AO4i
Write clearly, effectively and imaginatively, using and adapting forms and selecting vocabulary appropriate to task and purpose in ways that engage the reader.

English AO3ii / English Language AO4ii
Organise information and ideas into structured and sequenced sentences, paragraphs and whole texts, using a variety of linguistic and structural features to support cohesion and overall coherence.

English AO3iii / English Language AO4iii
Use a range of sentence structures for clarity, purpose and effect, with accurate punctuation and spelling.
At least a third of the AO3 weighting relates to bullet 3 (iii).

1 Starter

- Choose an object or picture in the classroom then ask volunteers to describe it. Write a list of what they say on the board, including vague and general descriptions, for example: 'this bit', 'that thing', 'the blue part', etc.

- Using the list of words and phrases you have compiled, explain to students that some of them are fine for describing something when they can actually see and point to the object but are too vague or generalised for a written text where the reader cannot see what they are talking about. Give a few examples, then ask students to classify the words and phrases on the board as either suitable or unsuitable for a written text.

- To emphasise the point, you might use the general terms to describe something else that the students cannot see and demonstrate how difficult it is to know what you are talking about.

- Ask students to suggest how they would change the vague words and phrases to make them suitable for a written text.

- You might like to write some instructions using vague and imprecise vocabulary, for example: 'Turn that thing over and fold it and then fold it again and again and then pop it over there.' Demonstrate that this could equally be a TV chef talking about cooking, for example: flipping and filling a pancake.

2 Whole class work

- Display the examples on page 112 of the student book on the ActiveTeach, and use them to model how to use precise vocabulary to describe or explain how someone can improve their football skills.

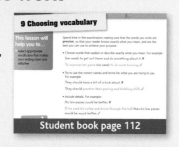

Student book page 112

- Ask one student to make a paper plane in front of the class. The rest of the class must give the plane maker instructions in precise, detailed language using the correct terms. If a student gives a vague instruction, then other students should challenge them, explaining why their instruction is not suitable and suggesting a better alternative.

3 Independent work/ Peer assessment

- Students should work independently to complete **Activity 1**, writing two paragraphs of a review using precise language. Students can record their ideas on **Worksheet 9.1**.

- Ask students to swap their work with a partner and peer assess each other's vocabulary choices, making suggestions for improvement on **Worksheet 9.2**.

Worksheet 9.1   Worksheet 9.2

Additional support

Starter

- **Talk partners:** Pair EAL students with fluent English speakers to help establish the concept of 'precise' vocabulary. Briefly discuss general/vague and 'specific/exact' vocabulary using the words students have used to describe their object in the starter.
- Arrange this vocabulary on a **washing line** from general to specific.
- **Remind** the students what 'appropriate' and 'effective' mean in the lesson objective.
- **Active listening:** Read the vague and specific sentences on page 112 aloud. Elicit comments from the students about the quality of the vocabulary in the two sentences. Emphasise the more specific vocabulary and clarify terms such as 'passing' and 'dribbling' in this context.

Pair work/Activity 2

- **Collaborative work:** Pair EAL learners with fluent English speakers. It may be appropriate for students to use a **dictionary**, **thesaurus**, or **bilingual dictionary**. Be prepared to clarify words as even the most advanced bilingual learners find difficulty in selecting the most appropriate word for the context when faced with the choices in dictionary definitions and nuances of meaning in a thesaurus.
- You could start with a **matching activity**: prepare cards of synonyms for the verbs, adjectives and adverbs, with generic/ordinary words on red cards and more precise/emotive synonyms on blue cards.
- It is important to stress that adjectives can be overused. EAL students often do overuse features such as similes to show that they have understood them.
- Set up **substitution tables** for Activity 2 so that students can see typical substitutions for verbs, adjectives and adverbs. This will be useful preparation for Activity 3.

4 Whole class work

- Model how to make writing more powerful using the examples on page 113 of the student book, adding carefully chosen verbs, adjectives and adverbs.

Student book page 113

- As an extension, rewrite the following section from a charity appeal as a class:

Every year after Christmas thousands of animals are abandoned by their owners. Often they are left on the streets without food or shelter. You can help by giving one of these animals a home.

5 Pair work

- Ask students to work in pairs to complete **Activity 2**, improving the vocabulary used in a student's persuasive writing. Students can use **Worksheet 9.3** to help them complete this activity.

Worksheet 9.3

- Share responses. You might like to compose a class version of the paragraph using the best ideas.

6 Independent work

- Students should work independently to complete **Activity 3**, consolidating all the vocabulary skills they are developing while writing a persuasive leaflet of their own. Students should have access to a dictionary and a thesaurus for this activity.
- Share some responses as a class and comment on successful vocabulary.

7 Plenary

As a class, produce a list of Top Tips for Excellent Vocabulary, drawing on what students have learned in the lesson. Students can then work in groups to turn this into a poster for display in class.

8 Further work

Ask students to find a marketing letter, leaflet or advertisement and pick out six examples of powerful vocabulary which they can make use of in their own persuasive writing. Students can record their findings on **Worksheet 9.4**. Alternatively, you might like to provide students with a letter, leaflet or advertisement.

Worksheet 9.4

Lesson 10 Using effective punctuation and sentences

Resources required

Student book pages 114-115
Worksheet 10.1: Punctuating sentences 1
Worksheet 10.2: Punctuating sentences 2
Worksheet 10.3: Types of sentence
Worksheet 10.4: Using different sentence types
Worksheet 10.5: Persuasive writing
Worksheet 10.6: Connectives chart
Worksheet 10.7: Effective writing

Learning objectives

→ Select appropriate punctuation that makes your writing clear and effective.

→ Use different kinds of sentences in your writing.

Assessment objectives

English AO3ii / English Language AO4ii
Organise information and ideas into structured and sequenced sentences, paragraphs and whole texts, using a variety of linguistic and structural features to support cohesion and overall coherence.

English AO3iii / English Language AO4iii
Use a range of sentence structures for clarity, purpose and effect, with accurate punctuation and spelling. *At least a third of the AO3 weighting relates to bullet 3 (iii).*

1 Starter

- Ask students how they remember when to use different punctuation marks, such as capital letters, full stops, commas, question marks, exclamation marks, apostrophes and inverted commas. Ask students to recap their strategies for writing in complete sentences and checking the accuracy of their work.

- Record ideas on the board.

- Ask each person to identify an aspect of punctuation or writing sentences that they need to improve and write this down as a target for improvement.

2 Whole class work

- Choose a topic your students will be motivated to write about. Model how to compose a sentence, check and write it.

- Ask students to give their own examples, encouraging the class to check each other's sentences as expressed orally before a student writes it on the whiteboard.

3 Independent work

- Ask students to complete part 1 of **Activity 1** independently, composing seven sentences, using each punctuation mark at least once. They can record their answers on **Worksheet 10.1**.

- Ask students to swap with a partner and check each other's sentences for accurate punctuation.

Worksheet 10.1

- Share some examples as a class.

- Students should then attempt part 2 of **Activity 1**, writing an accurately punctuated paragraph for a website article. They should use **Worksheet 10.2** and check their own punctuation before swapping work with a partner to check accuracy.

Worksheet 10.2

4 Whole class work

- Model how to write the four different types of sentence: question, statement, order and exclamation, using the examples on page 114 of the student book (also provided on **Worksheet 10.3**). Choose a topic that will interest your students or one of the sample tasks from the student book and ask them to suggest questions, statements, orders and exclamations related to the topic. Record ideas on the board.

Worksheet 10.3

- Use students' suggestions to compose a class paragraph that uses all four kinds of sentence.

Additional support

Starter/Whole class work

- **Visual presentation:** Write each punctuation mark on a different piece of card to distribute among the students. Read the introduction on page 114 to the class and emphasise the suggested strategies. Write some unpunctuated sentences on the board and invite students with the appropriate punctuation to raise their card as you read each sentence.

- **Talk partners** may be a useful strategy at each stage of the lesson – both EAL students paired with fluent English speakers, to check punctuation terms are understood, and EAL students with the same first language, to discuss how punctuation is used in that language.

Whole class work/Pair work/Activity 2

- Read the introduction to Activity 2 aloud and **clarify** difficult

words as appropriate. **Emphasise** the difference between 'explanation' and 'exclamation' and link them to the words 'explain' and 'exclaim'. EAL learners often confuse or misuse these words. Suggest that <u>one</u> exclamation mark is enough.

- Allow EAL learners **sufficient time** to complete the activity (they may work more slowly).

Independent work/Activity 3

- Read the introduction to Activity 3 aloud and **clarify** vocabulary such as 'rhetorical question', 'logic' and 'connectives'.

- **Revise** features of texts to 'persuade' and 'inform' and ask for suggestions of 'powerful emotions'.

- It could be helpful to read the text aloud before the task and clarify words/names as appropriate such as: 'steroids', 'give them the edge', 'vomit', 'pass blood', and 'ulcers'.

Further work

- **Revise** terms such as 'adverbs', 'adjectives', 'verbs', 'persuasive'.

---

5 Pair work

- Ask students to work in pairs to attempt part 1 of **Activity 2**, rewriting the statement as a question, order and exclamation. They can record their answers on **Worksheet 10.4.** You may like to give students further examples to adapt, for example: *It's your turn to make dinner.*

Worksheet 10.4

- Share and check responses before students complete part 2 of **Activity 2** on the same worksheet, which involves writing a paragraph for the speech that includes each type of sentence.

- Ask a few volunteers to share their paragraphs with the class and comment on how effective the sentences are in one another's writing.

6 Whole class work

- Discuss the different strategies for effective writing on pages 114 and 115 of the student book (varying sentence length, using connectives and different ways of crafting sentences).

- Ask students to share some of the paragraphs they wrote for **Activity 2** and demonstrate how to vary the length of sentences for effect or how to put the important points at the beginning of a sentence.

- You may like to repeat the exercise, sharing a paragraph and asking students for suggestions.

7 Independent work

Ask students to attempt **Activity 3** independently, practising the sentence-writing skills you have demonstrated as they rewrite a text. You may wish to give them copies of the connectives chart from Lesson 7 (**Worksheet 10.6**) or display it on the board. **Worksheet 10.5** supports this activity.

Worksheet 10.5   Worksheet 10.6

8 Plenary

Ask volunteers to share their paragraphs and discuss the effectiveness of the changes they made. Encourage other students to give feedback.

9 Further work

Ask students to rewrite the paragraph on **Worksheet 10.7,** varying the sentence length and type, adding connectives and changing verbs, adverbs and adjectives to make it more persuasive. This will help consolidate their new writing skills.

Worksheet 10.7

Lesson 11 Checking and editing your writing

Learning objectives

→ Check that your work is accurate and effective.

Resources required

Student book pages 116–119
Weblink 11.1: Homophones practice
Worksheet 11.1: Checking/editing checklist
Worksheet 11.2: Editing texts
Worksheet 11.3: Common mistakes

Assessment objectives

English AO3iii / English Language AO4iii
Use a range of sentence structures for clarity, purpose and effect, with accurate punctuation and spelling.
At least a third of the AO3 weighting relates to bullet 3 (iii).

1 Starter

- Ask students to work in groups to complete their own list of rules for checking and editing a text.

- Share responses, compiling a class checklist. Refer students to the checklist on page 116 of the student book to make sure they haven't missed anything (also provided on **Worksheet 11.1**).

Worksheet 11.1

2 Whole class work

- Display the first paragraph on **Worksheet 11.2** on the ActiveTeach and use the annotation tools to model how to apply the checklist to the writing and amend the writing accordingly. Read the text out to students and ask them to make suggestions and spot mistakes.

Worksheet 11.2

- Students can then correct the second paragraph on **Worksheet 11.2** in pairs.

- Share responses as a class.

- Work with the class to develop a mnemonic that will help students remember what to check after they have written their text, for example: *P.S. Voldemort Stinks!* (Punctuation, Spelling, Vocabulary, Sentences).

3 Independent work

- Students should work independently to complete **Activity 1**, which asks them to find the meaning of, and practise using, common homophones. Students should record their answers on **Worksheet 11.3**.

Worksheet 11.3

- Students can get additional practice at this skill by using the BBC website (**Weblink 11.1: Homophones practice**).

4 Independent work

- Ask students to read the example examination question on page 117 and work through **Activity 2** independently, writing a paragraph of a letter to students, focusing on how well they check and edit their work. They should spend about ten minutes on this task.

Student book page 117

- Students should then assess their own work using the criteria given in the ResultsPlus Maximise your marks sections.

- Students should work in pairs to complete the **Putting it into practice** activity on page 119.

Additional support

Starter

• Teacher should read the introduction on page 116 and ask for suggestions from the class to **clarify** the meaning of 'brief', 'purpose and form'.

• As the checklist is read out, remind students about listening to the sentences in their head as they read to ensure that all their sentences say what they intended.

Whole class/Worksheet 11.2

• **Active listening:** Ask students to correct any errors they see/hear as you read as preparation for the whole class correcting activity.

• A **dictogloss** activity could be constructed using the work (anonymously) of a good student who makes several errors which are common to EAL learners, for example: adventurous words misspelt, incorrect homophones, omitted articles and punctuation. These errors could form the basis for further teaching to correct them.

• Similarly, a **substitution table** could be made to improve choices of vocabulary, verbs and punctuation, using common errors observed whilst marking students' work.

5 Plenary

Ask students to share their mnemonics and record card rules with the class.

6 Further work

Ask students to use the checklist (**Worksheet 11.1**) to correct a piece of writing they have done for another subject or in an earlier writing task.

Worksheet 11.1

7 Examination practice

• On pages 120–121 of the student book, a practice examination paper for the Foundation Tier of GCSE English Language Unit 2 and GCSE English Unit 2 is provided. You could work through this with students as a revision exercise before sitting their examination.

ResultsPlus interactive

• On the ActiveTeach there are accompanying ResultsPlus grade improvement activities which help students understand how to improve their answer.

Lesson 1
Generating ideas

Resources required

Student book pages 124–125
Audio 1.1: Guardian podcast
BBC Video: *Big Cat Diary*
Video Weblink 1.1: Lincoln flash mob dance
Image 1.1: Argument
Image 1.2: Student illustration
Worksheet 1.1: Ideas from an image

Assessment objectives

English AO3i
Write clearly, effectively and imaginatively, using and adapting forms and selecting vocabulary appropriate to task and purpose in ways that engage the reader.

Learning objectives

→ Respond to an image, a video or a podcast.
→ Develop appropriate and engaging ideas to include in your writing.

1 Starter

- Explain to students that they will be asked to write a response to a stimulus for their creative writing task. Tell them that this stimulus could be an image, a video or a podcast.

- Launch **Video Weblink 1.1** on the ActiveTeach and play the Lincoln flash mob dance video. Give students two minutes to write down ideas in response to the video.

- Share some ideas as a class. Now ask students how they generated their ideas. What did they focus on first? What kinds of question did they ask themselves? Did they speculate about what might be happening in the video?

2 Whole class work

- Display **Image 1.1** and tell students that you are going to generate some ideas in response to the image and create a mind map to record these ideas.

- Model how to generate ideas using the questions on page 124 of the student book. Ask yourself the questions aloud and record your ideas as a mind map on the board. As students will have completely different responses to the image, it makes sense to record your own ideas for the basic information (where it is, what emotion you feel when you look at the picture, what just happened). You can then ask students for their suggestions, making sure they are consistent with your own.

- Ask students whether they thought the questions you asked yourself were helpful. Were there any questions they had not thought of when they generated their own ideas in the starter activity?

3 Pair work

- Ask students to work in pairs to complete **Activity 1**, generating ideas about the image. Explain there are no right or wrong answers but they need to be clearly drawn from the image.

- Ask each pair to present their ideas to another pair.

4 Whole class work

- Play the **BBC Video:** *Big Cat Diary* on the ActiveTeach. Then discuss why you might ask different questions to help you generate ideas if a video clip is the stimulus. Students should understand that more information is provided in a video clip – for example, sound and movement.

BBC Video: *Big Cat Diary*

- Discuss the questions on page 125 of the student book and generate some ideas as a class for the first four questions. Emphasise the need to focus on a particular person's experience or viewpoint to produce good writing rather than producing a vague general overview of the events. Discuss how questions 5–11 can help you achieve this.

EAL Additional support

Starter
- **Talk partners**: pair an EAL learner with a fluent English speaker to discuss **te**xt differences between narrative, description, dialogue and monologue.
- **Clarify** words such as: 'stimulus', 'podcast', 'response', 'empathise', 'speculate'...
- **Activate prior knowledge**: During the feedback from groups, students should be encouraged to share stories of their own experiences of a place like that in the picture – e.g. seen on TV or in films? in magazines or books? – as well as/instead of actual experiences.

Whole class work
- **Active listening**: Fluent readers should read the text on page 124 aloud before attempting the **mind map**. Nodes should be labelled who, what, where, why.

- Consider using an OHT instead of a large sheet of paper.

Pair work/Activity 1
- Use **talk partners**.
- **Visual presentation**: A **flow chart** could be used to sequence the ideas that will link together to form the writing as preparation for the next stage.

Whole class/Independent work
- Add who/what/where/why...hear/see/experience/think/feel onto the **word wall**.
- In **Activity 2**: Clarify 'doodle'. It may be useful to **model** how to take notes whilst watching a video/podcast/film, on the board, a large sheet of paper or OHT. Ask open-ended questions to collect suggestions about thoughts and feelings of different characters. Students could fill in thought clouds on a **key visual**.
- **Hot seating**: Ask class members to justify their decisions.

5 Independent work

- Play the **BBC Video**: *Big Cat Diary* again and ask students to complete **Activity 2** independently, using the questions to generate ideas and recording them as a mind map on a blank piece of paper.

Student book page 125

- Play the video clip several times. You may wish to pause the film occasionally and ask students questions, giving them time to jot down ideas. At this stage, emphasise there are no right or wrong ideas, but remind students that they must be linked to the stimulus.

- Give students time to review their ideas, highlighting the ideas which they would use for a piece of creative writing.

- Ask students to present their ideas to a partner. Students should give each other feedback, offering advice on which ideas they think are most engaging. If time allows, students could present their ideas to small groups.

6 Independent work

- Explain that students are going to listen to a podcast and complete **Activity 3**. Tell students that they should jot down words, thoughts and images that occur to them as they listen. Explain that they should use whatever method they feel most comfortable with – for example, they do not have to draw images if they find this difficult.

- Remind students that there are no right or wrong ideas, but they must be linked to the stimulus.

- Play **Audio 1.1**, and while students work on their own doodles, you should doodle your own ideas on an A3 blank piece of paper. Make them large enough to be visible when you share them later with students.

- Give students time to add notes to their doodles, developing their ideas further.

- Share your doodles with the class, and explain how you generated your ideas. Alternatively, you might like to demonstrate how to add notes to your doodles and thoughts to develop your ideas further. Ask students to give you feedback on which ideas they think work best.

- You may also want to display **Image 1.2**, the illustration in the book of a drawing to go with the podcast reading. Discuss how each drawing may be different, but many different ideas linked to the podcast are appropriate.

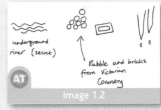

Image 1.2

- Students should share their ideas with a partner and can discuss which ideas they think would work best in a piece of engaging creative writing.

7 Plenary

- Ask students to work in pairs and share which stimulus they found most easy to generate ideas from, and why.

- Briefly discuss as a class. Encourage students to share their expertise, offering tips for generating ideas from their preferred stimulus.

8 Further work

Hand out **Worksheet 1.1**. Ask students to find a powerful image and attach it to their worksheet. They should then use the six questions to generate ideas for an engaging piece of creative writing, practising the techniques used in the lesson.

Worksheet 1.1

Lesson 2
Writing a narrative

Learning objectives

→ Work out the plot for your story.

→ Plan different features of your story.

Resources required

Student book pages 126–129
Image 2.1: Boy playing football
Image 2.2: Road
Image 2.3: Door
Worksheet 2.1: Planning grid (completed)
Worksheet 2.2: Planning grid (blank)
Worksheet 2.3: Character profiles
Worksheet 2.4: The crater's edge text

Assessment objectives

English AO3i

Write clearly, effectively and imaginatively, using and adapting forms and selecting vocabulary appropriate to task and purpose in ways that engage the reader.

1 Starter

NB: Depending on your students' ability, you might need to spend more time on each section. This lesson can be split into several lessons, each focusing on a different aspect of writing a story: plot ideas, character, setting and atmosphere. Students learn more about writing different parts of a narrative in later lessons (description in Lesson 3; character in Lesson 6; effective vocabulary in Lesson 8).

Ask students to work in groups and list the key components of a narrative. Students might suggest some of the following: an exciting opening or an opening that sets the scene; background information on characters and scenario; a developing plot (e.g. different events, deepening knowledge of the characters, something unexpected); a final resolution in which all the loose ends are tied up.

2 Whole class work

- Show students the image of the teenage boy playing football (**Image 2.1**) and ask them to use the techniques from Lesson 1 to generate ideas for a piece of creative writing.

Image 2.1

Worksheet 2.1

- Use the planning grid on page 126 of the student book or **Worksheet 2.1** to demonstrate how to move from the ideas generated from a stimulus to writing a narrative.

- Explain that it is helpful if students use a real event that they can write about convincingly for their story, for example: car washing, and that it is all right to change details as the narrative doesn't have to be 'true'. Also explain that the story has to be a maximum of 1000 words so a simple 'one-problem plot' is needed.

3 Group work

- Display **Image 2.2**. Spend some time brainstorming ideas using the techniques learned in Lesson 1 before attempting **Activity 1**.

- Remind students a) to use a real event where possible, and b) that they only need to come up with a 'one-problem plot'.

- Encourage students to work together to discuss their ideas and to complete the blank version of the chart on **Worksheet 2.2**. Each student must then complete their own individual planning chart for their own story.

Worksheet 2.2

4 Pair/Independent work

Working in pairs, students should test their plot ideas on each other. List these questions on the board to help them get started: *Does the plot make sense? Is there just one problem for the main character to overcome? Has the writer decided why the problem really matters to the main character? Is the ending satisfying?*

5 Whole class work

- Display **Image 2.1**, and model how to build a character profile for the main character. Using the questions on page 127 of the student book, go through each stage of your story plan and ask, for each character: *What do they look like? How do they react? What do they think? What do they say?*

- Record your ideas in the grid on **Worksheet 2.3**.

- Prepare the character profile for the gang leader with the class. Ask students to work in groups to complete the profile for the car owner.

EAL Additional support

Starter
- Use **message abundancy** to **clarify** terms such as 'scenario', 'resolution', 'loose ends'…

Whole class/Group work
- **Active listening:** Read around the class points in the table on page 126 (and page 127-28) so that difficult words such as: 'goal' in two contexts, 'gang', 'tense', 'mugged', 'cauldron', 'compass needles', 'threatening', 'atmosphere', 'mood', 'vivid'… can be clarified. Worksheets 2.1 and 2.2 provide **writing frames** for scaffolding the students' own plots and narratives later in the lesson.
- **Talk partners:** EAL students may find it easier in the first instance to contribute ideas to plots initiated by fluent English students. Care in organising groups will help everybody to contribute to the best of their ability.

- Alternatively, it could be appropriate to pair students who share the same first language to work out plots in their **first language** at the initial stage. EAL students can participate. **Activity 1** gives important advice.
- **Activate prior knowledge:** It may be useful for teachers to recount a few small events in their own lives as suggestions of the kind of event which is suitable.
- Example features of narrative could be added to the **word wall** and used as revision before independent work.

Activity 2
- Construct simple texts that demonstrate the structure of narrative. Cut up the texts into sentences and ask the students to label: background/character 1/place, etc. then **sequence** the sentences into full text.

Activities 3 and 4
- Use an **online thesaurus** to build vivid vocabulary for use in the narrative (see earlier note about EAL students' difficulty in choosing the most appropriate words from dictionaries and thesauruses).

---

6 Independent work

- Ask students to attempt **Activity 2**, completing their own character profiles by answering the questions and filling in the grid on another copy of **Worksheet 2.3**.

Worksheet 2.3

- As a class, brainstorm a checklist students can use to peer assess each other's ideas, for example: *Are the characters responding in believable ways in the plot? Can you picture this character? Are the character's feelings likely?*

7 Whole class work

- Model how to develop the idea of the setting for each event of the story using the plot ideas in the student book, for example: the car park, the chase.
- Ask where and when the event takes place, what you want the reader to notice in order to be able to a) picture it, and b) have the right feeling about the place. For example, if you want to make the scene happy, pick out things that give it a jolly feel such as children laughing and playing, and/or the sunshine bouncing off the cars.

8 Pair/Independent work

- Attempting **Activity 3**, students think about how to vividly describe the setting for each of the main events in their story. They could quickly sketch and annotate the scene of each event or just make rough notes.
- Emphasise that students choosing to sketch their scenes will need to come up with effective vocabulary in their writing, so focus on the annotations, not the quality of the sketch.

9 Whole class work

- Model how to choose vocabulary that will create an atmosphere or feeling, using the example text on page 128 of the student book or on **Worksheet 2.4**.
- Ask students to attempt **Activity 4** to come up with ideas of vocabulary and imagery they may want to use in their stories.

10 Independent work

- Ask students to look at **Image 2.3** and read the example controlled assessment task on page 129. Students should then complete **Activity 5** and assess their own work using the criteria given in the ResultsPlus Maximise your marks section.
- Students should then work in pairs to complete the **Putting it into practice** activity on page 131.

11 Plenary

Ask students to make a flow chart showing each step they take from generating ideas for a story from the stimulus material to a) knowing what will happen in the story; b) knowing the important characters; c) knowing the setting for each event; and d) creating atmosphere.

12 Further work

Students should consolidate their learning in one of the areas by choosing another minor character to profile for their storyline using **Worksheet 2.3**.

Lesson 3
Writing a description

Learning objectives

→ Create interesting and realistic descriptions.

→ Use a variety of techniques to build descriptions.

Resources required

Student book pages 132–135
Image 3.1: Woman in shop
Image 3.2: People in busy street
Image 3.3: Fireworks night
Image 3.4: Men and fire
Image 3.5: Trees in desert
Image 3.6: Elephants in desert
Image 3.7: Trees in wind
Worksheet 3.1: Similes and metaphors
Worksheet 3.2: Organising information

Assessment objectives

English AO3i

Write clearly, effectively and imaginatively, using and adapting forms and selecting vocabulary appropriate to task and purpose in ways that engage the reader.

1 Starter

Ask students how a description differs from a narrative. Students should understand that a narrative tells the reader what happened whereas a description tells the reader what something or someone is (or was) like. Narratives always include descriptions, but they also include action, a developing plot and a resolution in the end.

2 Whole class work

- Display Image A (**Image 3.1**) on the ActiveTeach. Model how to write a description of this woman. Go through the whole image, noting details such as age, clothes and facial expression. Demonstrate how these can give clues to the person's mood, circumstances, personality and interests.

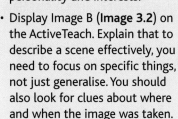
Image 3.1

- Display Image B (**Image 3.2**) on the ActiveTeach. Explain that to describe a scene effectively, you need to focus on specific things, not just generalise. You should also look for clues about where and when the image was taken.

Image 3.2

- Put students into small teams and challenge them to spend three minutes searching the image for clues to help them give a detailed account of what **Image 3.3** is showing. They should make a list of important details they could describe.

Image 3.3

- Students should share their ideas, explaining what the details suggested to them. Other teams can challenge their ideas if they do not make sense. Make a list of the details you could describe in this image on the board.

- Now ask students to imagine being inside the picture. Ask them what they would see first, hear and smell if they were in the picture. What might they taste? What might they feel if they touched something in the picture?

3 Pair work

- Display **Image 3.2** (Image B). Ask students to use the same skills as they attempt **Activity 1**, finding specific details in Image B. Remind students to imagine being in the picture and note what their five senses would pick out.

- Ask students to share the details they have picked out and list these. Use the annotation tool on the ActiveTeach to annotate Image B with student responses.

- Explain that you can choose adjectives and imagery to describe the details in your list. Demonstrate by adding adjectives to some of the nouns. Challenge students to suggest some of their own.

4 Pair work

- Ask students to work in pairs to complete **Activity 2**, picking out details from **Image 3.4**, choosing the impression they would like to give and selecting adjectives accordingly.

Image 3.4

- Ask students to swap the adjectives and details they have written with another pair, without telling each other what impression they are trying to create. Students should read each other's lists and say what impression they think will be created with these adjectives. Did the details and adjectives give the right impression? Would they change any adjectives in the light of feedback?

Additional support

Starter/Whole class work

- At each stage of the lesson it is important for the teacher or fluent English speakers to read the explanation texts on pages 132–5 so that any difficult words can be **clarified** by **message abundancy**.
- **Talk partners**: Pair EAL learners with fluent English speakers. One student chooses a noun to describe a **person** and an adjective to go with it. He/she then tells the other student the noun and asks the other to guess the adjective. Reverse roles. Think up another adjective to describe each noun. Repeat with **scene** and **event**.

Pair work/Activity 1

- Share the nouns as a group. Sort them like a **washing line** from the most basic to the most adventurous, then select the best five. Justify choices.

Whole class work/Activities 2 and 3

- EAL students who share the same **first language** could consider the five senses (sight, smell, touch, sound, taste) and think of typical examples from their own culture for each. These could be shared with the whole class as a good way of helping English-speaking students to see non-cliché opportunities for similes and metaphors.
- Clarify the understanding of metaphors and similes. Ask students to identify and highlight similes and metaphors in the texts.
- N.B. Before the independent work it is important to stress that adjectives, similes and metaphors can be overused in descriptive writing. EAL students often do overuse these features to show that they have understood them.

Independent work/Activities 3 and 4

- **Clarify** the students' understanding of third person and past tense – including irregular verbs, which could be on a **word wall**.
- An online thesaurus could be useful (with care) for building vivid vocabulary for the narrative.

5 Whole class work

- Display **Images 3.5** and **3.6**, explaining the metaphor and simile provided on page 134 of the student book. Ask students to explain the difference between metaphors and similes. You might like to challenge students to create some of their own metaphors and similes to check understanding.

Image 3.5

- Display **Image 3.2** and pick details that you could describe effectively using a metaphor or simile, and model writing metaphors and similes, for example: 'clothes as bright as a rainbow' or describing the streets as 'a rabbit warren'.

Image 3.6

- Explain that successful metaphors and similes help build up the overall impression of a piece of writing. For example, if you are writing a sad story, your imagery should reflect that.

6 Independent work

Challenge students to complete **Activity 3** on page 134 of the student book independently. They should fill in the chart provided on **Worksheet 3.1** to create similes and metaphors related to **Image 3.7**.

Image 3.7

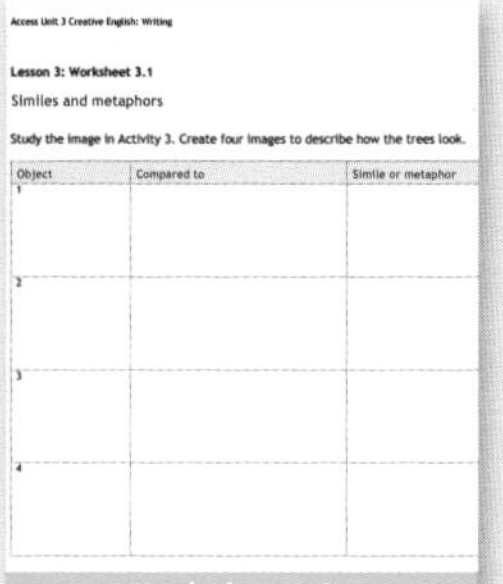

Worksheet 3.1

Access Unit 3 Creative English: Writing

Lesson 3: Worksheet 3.1
Similes and metaphors

Study the Image in Activity 3. Create four images to describe how the trees look.

Object	Compared to	Simile or metaphor
1		
2		
3		
4		

7 Independent work

- Display the texts on page 135, and read them as a class (**Worksheet 3.2**). Point out how the author creates effective descriptions, for example: how he sets the scene in the first extract, and uses vivid verbs and contrast between the world inside and outside the estate in the second.

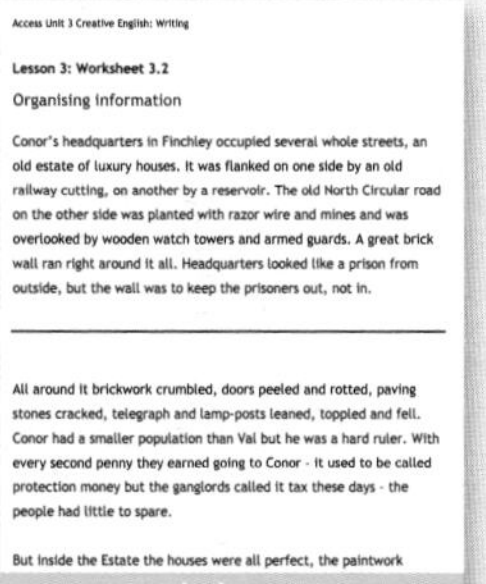

Access Unit 3 Creative English: Writing

Lesson 3: Worksheet 3.2
Organising information

Conor's headquarters in Finchley occupied several whole streets, an old estate of luxury houses. It was flanked on one side by an old railway cutting, on another by a reservoir. The old North Circular road on the other side was planted with razor wire and mines and was overlooked by wooden watch towers and armed guards. A great brick wall ran right around it all. Headquarters looked like a prison from outside, but the wall was to keep the prisoners out, not in.

All around it brickwork crumbled, doors peeled and rotted, paving stones cracked, telegraph and lamp-posts rusted, toppled and fell. Conor had a smaller population than Vai but he was a hard ruler. With every second penny they earned going to Conor - it used to be called protection money but the ganglords called it tax these days - the people had little to spare.

But inside the Estate the houses were all perfect, the paintwork

Worksheet 3.2

- Now ask students to complete **Activity 4** independently, revisiting the preparation work they did in **Activity 2** and writing a description of the scene. Remind students to think about the impression they want to give. Students can then write a second paragraph, contrasting the person with their surroundings.

8 Plenary

As a class, compile a checklist of things to remember when writing a description for the controlled assessment task.

9 Further work

Students should learn their checklist for writing descriptions, then apply them to writing a description of an image which you give them, or which they choose themselves.

Lesson 4
Writing a script

Learning objectives

→ Write in the form of a script.

→ Reveal character and plot through what people say.

Resources required
Student Book pages 136–137
Image 4.1: Ethan
Image 4.2: Mark
Worksheet 4.1: Character overview: Ethan
Worksheet 4.2: Character overview: Mark
Worksheet 4.3: Plot overview
Worksheet 4.4: Further scenes

Assessment objectives
English AO3i
Write clearly, effectively and imaginatively, using and adapting forms and selecting vocabulary appropriate to task and purpose in ways that engage the reader.

1 Starter

- Ask students to work in groups. Ask students to draw on their experiences of watching television, films and plays and come up with a checklist of what is important when writing a script.

- Take feedback and compile a whole class checklist. Look for responses which emphasise the importance of plot (for example, problems to be resolved, climax and resolution), character (for example, interesting or contrasting characters who react in realistic ways) and dialogue (for example, characters sound real, dialogue helps give a sense of what the character is like). Students may also mention the importance of stage directions.

2 Whole class work

- Using the examples in the student book, model how to develop contrasting characters for a script. Read the character profile for Ethan in the student book or on **Worksheet 4.1**.

- Display the image of Mark and complete **Activity 1** as a class, deciding what Mark is going to be like by completing the chart on **Worksheet 4.2**. Encourage students to come up with a character that contrasts with Ethan.

- Discuss how making sure Mark contrasts strongly with Ethan provides opportunities for plot developments as they struggle against each other.

Worksheet 4.1

Worksheet 4.2

3 Pair work

- Display the plot idea on page 136 (above **Activity 2**) of the student book or on **Worksheet 4.3**.

- Ask students to work in pairs to attempt **Activity 2**, coming up with ideas about Mark's actions and Ethan's reaction. Students can record their ideas on **Worksheet 4.3**.

- Then ask pairs to improvise a scene in which Mark practises answering questions for the interview with his brother or sister and tries to speak 'posh'.

- Ask students to study the example of how to lay out a script on page 137 of the student book. Then ask one pair of students to perform their role-play, and model how to write down their speech as a script. Continue by sharing the writing of this scene as a class.

Worksheet 4.3

4 Group work

- Ask students to work in groups of three. They should attempt **Activity 3** by first improvising and then writing a short scene in which Mark, the boss and Ethan meet.

- As students write their script, check they are using the correct layout for a script.

- Ask groups to swap their work and peer assess each other's scripts, checking that they are laid out correctly and that they make sense.

Student book page 137

(EAL) Additional support

Starter
- **Collaborative activity:** The brainstorm and question prompts will be very helpful for EAL students as they discuss the idea of scripts. Throughout the lesson, ensure all groups and pairs include both EAL learners and fluent English speakers.
- Create a **word wall** of the class checklist for future reference.

Whole class work/Activity 1
- **Active listening:** The teacher could read the questions on Worksheet 4.1 and different students could read the responses. Use **message abundancy** to **clarify** cultural and idiomatic vocabulary such as 'laid back', 'snaps', 'council estate', 'polite standard English'.
- Use **talk partners** or pair EAL learners who share a **first language** to discuss possible contrasting characteristics for Mark.

Pair work/Activity 2
- **Activate prior knowledge** of the suggested scenario, lifeguards, interviews and reactions. EAL students may have problems thinking up their own dialogue for Worksheet 4.3 so it may be useful to use the ideas of a **stronger** student as a **dictogloss** or **cloze activity**. Compare different versions that may be created.

Group work/Activity 3
- **Ensure** students understand 'set the scene', 'how the set looks'.
- **Visual presentation:** Draw a plan of a stage to facilitate a short discussion of literal 'stage directions' and stage sets.
- **Active listening:** Use fluent readers to improvise the dialogue as an exemplar for EAL learners, using expression, pauses, gestures and facial expression to aid understanding and pronunciation.

Pair/Independent work/Activity 4
- **Envoys** could be used to answer questions 3, 4 and 5 to provide choices before the independent work.

Peer Assessment
- **Clarify** vocabulary in the assessment criteria such as 'realistic', 'appropriate' and 'constructive'.

5 Whole class work

- Ask volunteers to share their plot ideas from **Activity 2**.
- Choose one and ask students to improvise the scene where Ethan reacts to Mark's action, focusing on the different ways each would speak.
- Ask a volunteer to perform their improvisation. As a class, discuss how well the students have captured the way each character spoke.
- Use the improvisation to model how to write different voices for different characters, for example: using apostrophes and phonetic spelling to show different pronunciation.
- Discuss questions 1 and 2 of **Activity 4** as a class.

6 Pair/Independent work

- Ask students to work in pairs or independently to write four or five lines of dialogue in response to either question 3, 4 or 5 of **Activity 4** (the conversation between Mark and the boss, Mark speaking to Ethan or the boss speaking to his wife). Ensure that all three scenarios are covered across the class.
- Remind students to focus on recreating the way these characters would speak in the given situation.

7 Peer assessment

- Ask students to swap their dialogue with a partner or another pair. Ask students to give feedback on each other's work, focusing on the following criteria:
  - *Does the dialogue sound realistic? Would the character speak this way in this situation?*
  - *Has the writer used appropriate vocabulary and spelling to recreate the character's voice?*
- Remind students to give constructive feedback. They should try to comment on at least one thing their partner has done well and suggest one area for improvement.

8 Plenary

Ask volunteers to share their scripts with the class and share the results of the peer assessment. Do the class agree with the comments in the peer assessment?

9 Further work

- Ask students to write a scene in response to one of the following tasks:
  - *Write a scene from earlier in the play that shows the difference between the way Ethan normally speaks and how he talks to the boss.*
  - *Write a scene in which Mark and Ethan travel to the interview on the same bus, but are unaware of each other. Write dialogue to show Mark and Ethan talking to the bus driver or other passengers there (but not to each other).*
- **Worksheet 4.4** supports this activity.

Access Unit 3 Creative English: Writing

Lesson 4: Worksheet 4.4
Further scenes

Write a ONE of the following scenes from earlier in the play about Mark and Ethan.

1 Write a scene that shows the difference between the way Ethan normally speaks and how he talks to the boss.

2 Write a scene in which Mark and Ethan travel to the interview on the same bus, but are unaware of each other. Write dialogue to show Mark and Ethan talking to the bus driver or other passengers there (but not each other).

Remember to lay out your script like this:

Bus driver: Where to, son?

Mark: Leisure centre please, mate. (digs in his pocket for change)

Worksheet 4.4

Lesson 5
Writing a monologue

Learning objectives

→ Write interesting and imaginative monologues.

Resources required
Student book pages 138–139
Video 5.1: *A Cream Cracker under the Settee*
Image 5.1: Teenage boy
Worksheet 5.1: *A Cream Cracker under the Settee*
Worksheet 5.2: Character's voice

Assessment objectives
English AO3i
Write clearly, effectively and imaginatively, using and adapting forms and selecting vocabulary appropriate to task and purpose in ways that engage the reader.

1 Starter

- Organise students into groups and ask if they know, or can work out, what a monologue is – write clues on the board if necessary, for example: *A similar word is* <u>dialogue</u>*; think about the meaning of other words beginning with mono, e.g. monocycle, monochrome.*

Video 5.1: *A Cream Cracker under the Settee*

- Play students **Video 5.1**, a clip from Alan Bennett's *A Cream Cracker under the Settee*, available on the ActiveTeach. The script of the extract is provided on **Worksheet 5.1**.

- Explain what a monologue is: one character speaking directly to the audience.

Worksheet 5.1

2 Whole class work

- Display the three-sentence plot of *A Cream Cracker under the Settee*. Explain that a monologue has a story to tell, but it needs to be very simple and focused on the experience of the character whose monologue you are writing.

- Show **Image 5.1** of the teenage boy playing football from Lesson 2. Then model how to write a three-sentence storyline. Sentence 1 should describe the character with a goal or problem (e.g. boy needs to earn

Image 5.1

money to pay for football boots); sentence 2 is how the character tries to overcome that problem (e.g. by washing cars); sentence 3 is the result of their efforts (e.g. boy is mugged while washing cars, meets a talent scout who buys him boots and watches him play).

3 Group work

- Ask students to work in groups of three. They should choose an image from anywhere in the student book and practise writing three-sentence storylines.

- Ask groups to share their best efforts with the class, justifying why their plot is engaging but simple.

4 Independent work

- Explain to students that to create a really successful monologue they must 'get inside the head' of their main character. You should understand what they are like: what makes them happy, what worries them and what they think about.

- Ask students to attempt **Activity 1** independently, answering the questions to develop a character for the monologue task given. They should then produce a three-sentence plot for the monologue.

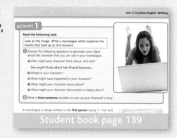
Student book page 139

EAL Additional support

Whole class work
- **Active reading**: Give students copies of the text of the script. The script should be read aloud by the teacher with expression, pauses, facial expression and gestures. Students should **highlight** any phrases and words which are outside their experience.
- **Clarify** unknown details as a class.

Group work
- **Talk partners/groups** with a mix of EAL and fluent English students should use the suggested questions to interrogate the monologue script to 'get inside the head' of the speaker. Cultural references could be **clarified** here too.

Independent work/Activity 2
- **Clarify** any words which need to be revised such as 'dialect', 'slang', 'jargon', 'authentic' ...
- It would be helpful to draw attention to features of the monologue such as sentence starters, the different lengths of sentences, punctuation, verb tense... as models for EAL students to use.
- Ask students to rehearse responses like thoughts in their own heads, making sure they sound like the phrases and sentences in the monologue or how they have heard peers, teachers, TV characters... speak.
- N.B. It is important that EAL students hear a wide variety of English speech used in different situations, from newsreaders to children's TV and soap operas. Bear in mind that in some cultures the students may not be allowed to watch programmes other than in their own language or cartoons, so it could be useful to build up a bank of exemplars to use as whole class experiences.

5 Whole class work

- Return to the plot you modelled for the boy playing football. Write the following sentences on the board:
  - *This job is beginning to do my head in. I swear, sometimes I think I'm going to pass out it's so boring.*
  - *I do not really enjoy washing cars. I find it a rather boring job.*
- Ask students which sentence they think sounds most like the boy in the picture.
- Explain that when writing monologues it is important to consider how the person might speak. Emphasise the need to 'hear' the character speaking (in your head in the actual assessment) and to write in the first person (using 'I', 'me', 'mine', etc.).
- Model a few more sentences and ask students to suggest further sentences in the voice of your character.

6 Independent work

- Ask students to return to the character they created in **Activity 1**. Tell students to spend a few minutes thinking about how the character might speak and to try to hear the voice in their head. If students find this difficult, suggest they ask themselves the following questions: *How old is my character? Where are they from? What sort of accent do they have? Do I know anyone who speaks like them?*
- Encourage students to note down words and phrases that their character might use.
- Students should then complete **Activity 2**, writing the monologue for the task from **Activity 1**.

7 Plenary

Ask students to swap their work and peer assess each other's monologues. Does it sound like the character speaking? Which of his thoughts and feelings about events/the situation are most believable? Have they remembered to use the first person throughout?

8 Further work

- Students should spend time improvising speaking as their character to gain a sense of 'voice'. If possible, students could record their efforts on their mobile phone or an mp3 player. They can then show this to a partner next lesson and give each other feedback. If this technology is not available, ask students to note down words, phrases and sayings that their character might use.
- Alternatively, ask students to write 'in character' to describe an event that is not part of the monologue for the controlled assessment task. It could be something as straightforward as going to the shops. This will help them feel more comfortable writing in the voice of their character. **Worksheet 5.2** supports this activity.

Suggested answers

Starter

A monologue is a speech given by one character whereas a story can contain dialogue from lots of characters as well as narration. A monologue gives one character's thoughts, feelings, viewpoint and must be in the first person. A narrative can give different characters' thoughts and feelings and be in the third person or first person. A monologue does not include speech marks as it is all spoken. Dialogue in a narrative should include speech marks.

Lesson 6
Creating characters

Learning objectives

→ Create interesting characters.

→ Use different techniques to show what characters are like.

Resources required

Student book pages 140–141
Worksheet 6.1: Text A
Worksheet 6.2: Character profile
Worksheet 6.3: Controlled assessment character
Worksheet 6.4: Text B
Worksheet 6.5: Creating a character

Assessment objectives

English AO3i

Write clearly, effectively and imaginatively, using and adapting forms and selecting vocabulary appropriate to task and purpose in ways that engage the reader.

1 Starter

• Students work in groups. Each student should talk about a character they remember from a film, book, soap, TV programme or book which they find memorable or interesting and explain what made the character engaging.

• Drawing on their experiences students should come up with a list of what makes an interesting character.

• Share ideas as a class and write a class list on the board.

2 Whole class work

• Explain that it is important to show what a character is like rather than directly telling the reader. Read the character profile for the narrator on page 140 of the student book. Then display page 140 on the ActiveTeach, or use **Worksheet 6.1**. Use the annotations to demonstrate what the text reveals about the narrator.

Worksheet 6.1

• Now ask students to describe Danielle's character. Ask them to point out the parts of the text that show them this. Remind students that character can be revealed through appearance, behaviour and speech.

• Challenge the class to suggest ways the writer could use appearance, behaviour and speech to show how a teacher reacts when he sees the two girls chatting.

3 Group work

• Ask students to work in groups to write another paragraph in the story, showing what the narrator's teacher is like through his appearance, behaviour and speech. Tell students they do not have to use the ideas already discussed and can make up a different character for the teacher. Students can record their ideas on **Worksheet 6.2**.

Worksheet 6.2

• Ask groups to swap their work and peer assess each other's writing. Students should tick the parts that <u>show</u> what the character is like and underline any parts that just <u>tell</u>.

4 Independent work

Ask students to attempt **Activity 1** independently. They should focus on one character they will include in their response to the controlled assessment task or a sample task from page 153 and work out how to show rather than tell what the character is like using appearance, behaviour and speech. Students can record their ideas in the first part of the table on **Worksheet 6.3**.

Worksheet 6.3

Additional support

Starter/Whole class work

- **Visual presentation:** Before reading the extract, use a photographic portrait from a newspaper and **brainstorm** with the class what the person looks like and what the person might do for a living. Record the suggestions in two columns on the board: what is fact and what is inference.

- **Talk partners:** Pair an EAL student and fluent English speaker to **discuss** what 'SHOW don't TELL' means on page 140.

- **Active listening:** The teacher should read the original extract with expression, pauses, facial expression and gestures to aid understanding before asking students to suggest what can be assumed from the passage.

Group work/Activity 1

- **Ensure** that groups include EAL and fluent English speakers.

- Whilst reading and annotating the character description on page 140, teachers could take the opportunity to **clarify** unusual words by **message abundancy** AND reinforce how to comment on texts with **sentence starters/writing frames,** such as 'which suggests that...', 'which makes the reader assume that...', which help to scaffold responses.

- N.B. Stressing that readers do not always make the same assumptions or the ones which the writer intended in the **envoys** activity (Worksheet 6.1) is also excellent preparation for more original individual responses to any reading activity.

- It may be useful for **Activities 1 and 2** to make a **washing line** of words which show characters, appearance, behaviour and speech.

5 Whole class work

- Display page 141 on the ActiveTeach and read the text as a class (see **Worksheet 6.4**). Pinpoint how the writer has revealed the narrator's character through thoughts, feelings and attitudes.

- Explain and show that the narrator also reveals further aspects of Danielle's character in this section.

Worksheet 6.4

- Now ask students to imagine the story is being narrated by the boss. Ask students to suggest ways the writer could use thoughts, feelings and attitudes to show what the teacher is like when he walks away from the two girls.

- Compose a paragraph as a class.

6 Pair work

Ask students to write a paragraph from Danielle's perspective giving her reaction after the teacher has gone. Students must show her character through thoughts, feelings and attitudes.

7 Independent work

- Ask students to work independently to complete **Activity 2**, working out how to show rather than tell what the characters are like in their controlled assessment tasks through their thoughts, feelings and attitudes. Students can record their ideas on the second part of the table in **Worksheet 6.3**.

- They should then complete **Activity 3**, writing a paragraph about the first time that the narrator and Danielle meet. They should read through their paragraph and make sure they are always showing what is happening.

8 Plenary

- Ask students to close their books. Challenge them to recall the six ways they can show readers what a character is like (appearance, behaviour, speech, thoughts, feelings and attitudes).

- Compose a class mnemonic to help them remember this. Alternatively, produce a class poster for display.

9 Further work

Ask students to create a new character. They might like to invent a character for a television show or book they particularly enjoy. Students should complete the table then attempt to write a paragraph that shows the reader what the character is like. **Worksheet 6.5** supports this activity.

Worksheet 6.5

Lesson 7 Writing from different perspectives

Resources required
Student book pages 142–143
Image 7.1: Parent and child
Image 7.2: Boys fighting
Worksheet 7.1: Narrative viewpoints
Worksheet 7.2: Two perspectives

Assessment objectives
English AO3i
Write clearly, effectively and imaginatively, using and adapting forms and selecting vocabulary appropriate to task and purpose in ways that engage the reader.

Learning objectives

→ Write from different perspectives.
→ Create different voices.

1 Starter

- Divide the class into pairs and label each pair A or B. Give each pair two plain sheets of paper.
- Display **Image 7.1** showing the parent and child. Ask A pairs to prepare a thought bubble giving the parent's thoughts about what might have happened, for example: *You must have…* Ask B pairs to prepare a thought bubble giving the child's thoughts about what might have happened, for example: *I was only… when…* Both students should keep a copy of their thought bubble.

Image 7.1

- Ask students to form new groups with one A and one B pair. Groups should take turns expressing their thoughts of the different characters.
- Ask students to discuss why the character's thoughts are so different, and which perspective or viewpoint would make the most engaging story for a reader.
- Introduce the idea that different characters in the same story will have different views (perspectives) on what happens. Discuss this with reference to a novel or story the class has read recently.

2 Whole class work

- Display the chart on page 142 of the student book (also available on **Worksheet 7.1**) outlining the differences between first person and third person narrators. Read through the chart and discuss each point. Challenge students to draw on texts they have read to give examples.

Worksheet 7.1

- Complete **Activity 1** as a class, asking students how you can tell which person the examples are written in. Be sure students understand why each example is first or third person.
- Ask students to suggest which kind of narration would work best for their controlled assessment task, giving reasons for their choice.

3 Group work

- Display the picture of the fight from the student book (**Image 7.2**) and ask students to comment on what they see.
- Divide the class into groups of four. Ask students to work together to pick two characters involved in the fight and brainstorm what they think they are like, how they speak and the part they played in the events as set out in **Activity 2** part 1.
- Ask each group to improvise a role-play: two members of the group can be two characters involved in the fight while the other members of the group play police officers who take it in turns to interview each character to establish what happened.

EAL Additional support

Starter/Whole class work
- Use **talk partners**, pairing an EAL student and fluent English speaker to revise the different kinds of text on page 142.
- **Visual presentation:** 1) Use visuals to teach root meaning of perspective, moving point of view to show perspective changes 2) Use Venn diagram to show how a common set of events can be interpreted quite differently.

- **Active listening:** Teacher and fluent readers should read the chart aloud using expression and pauses, highlighting features of first/third person and **clarifying** any difficult words such as: 'shorn', 'stubble', 'squinted' ...

Independent work
- A short **dictogloss** could be created from the stimulus or a good response. Ask students to write it as a narrative, monologue or description.
- **Sentence starters** or **writing frames** could be useful to scaffold first attempts at each type of independent writing for EAL students who are newer to English.

4 Independent work

- Ask students to complete questions 2 and 3 of **Activity 2** independently, writing an account of the fight in the first person from the perspectives of the two characters they role-played, then in the third person from another character's perspective. Encourage them to use dialogue in their writing.
- Ask students to read over their work, checking they have consistently used the first or third person. When writing in the first person, have they captured the character's voice? Students may wish to share their work with a partner and seek feedback.

5 Independent work

Students attempt **Activity 3**, writing a narrative in response to the task given in **Activity 2** both in the first person and then in the third person.

6 Plenary

- Ask students to comment on whether they preferred writing in the first or third person and describe the challenges and advantages of both.
- Ask students whether they will use the third or first person in their controlled assessment task and ask them to justify their decision.

7 Further work

- Students should choose an event that happened to them when they were younger which involved another person.
- Ask them to write two accounts of the event. The first account should be written from their perspective but in the third person. The second should be written from the other person's perspective in the first person.
- Remind students that they should still include the thoughts and feelings of characters when writing in the third person. **Worksheet 7.2** supports this activity. You might also like to give them a copy of the table on **Worksheet 7.1** for reference.

Worksheet 7.2

Lesson 8 Choosing the best vocabulary

Resources required

Student book pages 144–145
Image 8.1: Interesting person
Image 8.2: Wedding photo
Worksheet 8.1: Character description
Worksheet 8.2: Extract
Worksheet 8.3: Description of a bride
Worksheet 8.4: Precise description

Assessment objectives

English AO3ii

Organise information and ideas into structured and sequenced sentences, paragraphs and whole texts, using a variety of linguistic and structural features to support cohesion and overall coherence.

Learning objectives

→ Choose the best words to express ideas.
→ Use vivid and varied vocabulary.

1 Starter activity

- Display **Image 8.1**. Ask students to work on their own, brainstorming ten words or phrases to describe the person and noting them down.

Image 8.1

- Draw a continuum on the board with the left-hand end labelled 'general' and the right-hand end labelled 'precise'. Add some sample descriptions to each end of the scale, for example: brown hair (quite general), chestnut-coloured hair (precise).

- Put the students in groups. Give the groups three minutes to find five words out of all their suggestions that they could place at the general end of the scale and five at the precise end.

- Take feedback and ask groups to position their words on the scale on the board. Other groups should agree or challenge the positioning of the words, gradually taking up more of the scale as they decide whether some words are more general or precise than others.

2 Whole class work

- Display the example text on page 144, which describes a character (**Worksheet 8.1**).

- Work with students to identify describing words and classify them as precise or general, discussing possible replacements that would be more or less precise.

Worksheet 8.1

3 Pair work

- Ask students to complete **Activity 1** in pairs, deciding where vocabulary from the extract (available on **Worksheet 8.2**) would fit on a precise/general continuum.

- In their same pairs, ask students to complete **Activity 2**, adding or changing adjectives in the extract to make the description more precise.

Worksheet 8.2

- Share ideas as a class and encourage students to comment on how effective the adjectives were.

4 Whole class work

- Write a version of the example text on the board with 100% precise facts, for example:
She was 23 years, four months, three days, six hours, two minutes and forty-three seconds old . She had on blue, Miss Sixty jeans purchased in January 2009 by her mother for £95, and a pair of shiny black peep-toe Christian Louboutin 2008 five-inch heels, with the red soles slightly worn just at the balls of the feet and a scuff mark on the left heel. Her jet black hair, cropped fashionably at the chin, bounced up and down as she strutted down the yellow hallway with its cream and black tiled floor and crumpled bits of paper in the back corners.

- Discuss the effect this has on the reader. Students should understand that this level of detail would make their writing difficult to read and boring.

- Explain that you don't need to use as many adjectives as possible; carefully chosen adjectives, adverbs and verbs are more effective. Read the example sentences on page 145 of the student book to demonstrate this.

EAL Additional support

Starter
- **Talk partners:** Pair EAL students with fluent English speakers to **discuss** 'general' and 'specific' vocabulary – perhaps starting with 'stuff' and thinking what it can refer to. **Remind** students what 'vivid' and 'varied' mean in the lesson objective.

Activity 1
- Arrange the vocabulary on a **washing line** from the most general to the most precise.

Whole class work
- It may be appropriate to use a **dictionary, thesaurus, bilingual dictionary** because even the most advanced bilingual learners find difficulty in selecting the most appropriate word for the context when faced with the choices in dictionary definitions and nuances of meaning in a thesaurus. **Clarify** 'synonym', 'emotive'…
- Teacher could start with a **matching activity:** prepare cards of synonyms for the verbs, adjectives and adverbs, with generic/ordinary words on red cards, and more precise/emotive synonyms on blue cards.
- **Substitution tables** could be set up for **Activity 3**, with several sentences so that students can see typical substitutions for verbs, adjectives… which will be preparation for **Activity 4**.

Activity 3
- **Active listening:** Read the sentence and edited version aloud and elicit comments from the students about the quality of the vocabulary in the two sentences. The teacher should read the explanation text aloud **emphasising** the synonyms.

- Write the following sentence on the board:
An old woman walked along the road.

- Tell students that the woman in the sentence is extremely old and she doesn't walk very well. Tell them that the 'road' she is walking along is in the countryside, and it is not paved. No cars use it and it runs through a forest. Ask students to suggest more precise verbs and change the sentence on the board.

- Now ask students to add in adjectives and adverbs to build a more vivid description. Advise students as you change the sentence, helping them understand the difference between vivid writing and overkill.

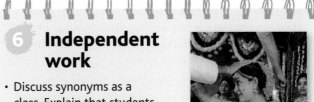

5 Pair work

- Ask students to work in pairs to attempt **Activity 3**, redrafting the sentences with more precise and powerful vocabulary.

- Pairs should form groups of four and peer assess each other's choices. Each group should come up with an improved list of sentences, using the best vocabulary choices.

- Share ideas as a class.

Student book page 145

6 Independent work

Image 8.2

Worksheet 8.3

- Discuss synonyms as a class. Explain that students should try to use synonyms rather than repeat the same words. Brainstorm a list of synonyms for 'angry' to check understanding.

- Display **Image 8.2** on the ActiveTeach. Ask students to attempt **Activity 4** independently, redrafting the text with precise, varied and powerful vocabulary. Students can record their answers on **Worksheet 8.3**

7 Plenary

As a class, work together to compose a 'best possible' version of the text in **Activity 4**. Ask students to justify their new vocabulary choices.

8 Further work

Worksheet 8.4

- Ask students to find an interesting image in a magazine, newspaper or online. Alternatively, you could provide them with an image. They should keep a copy and attach it to **Worksheet 8.4**.

- Ask students to write a short description of the image, focusing on using precise nouns and verbs, adjectives and adverbs and varying their vocabulary.

Lesson 9
Crafting sentences

Learning objectives

→ Write different types of sentence.
→ Use different sentences to create specific effects.

Resources required

Student book pages 146–147
Image 9.1: Washing cars
Worksheet 9.1: Building tension 1
Worksheet 9.2: Building tension 2
Worksheet 9.3: Creating tension

Assessment objectives

English AO3iii
Use a range of sentence structures for clarity, purpose and effect, with accurate punctuation and spelling.
At least *a third of the AO3 weighting relates to bullet 3 (iii)*.

1 Starter

- Ask students to work in groups and brainstorm what they already know about writing different types of sentence, and what effects they can create with them in a text.
- Share ideas as a class. Students may suggest that including a short sentence after several long sentences will give the last sentence greater impact, or that questions get the reader thinking.

2 Whole class work

- Rewrite the extract from *Double Cross* from page 146 of the student book on the board, joining the last three sentences together so that all the sentences are long (*The prickling of my nape left me in no doubt about that and I looked around nervously – the question was, who was watching me?*)
- Now display the text (available on **Worksheet 9.1**) and ask students to compare the two texts and comment on which is more successful at building tension.

Access Unit 3 Creative English: Writing

Lesson 9: Worksheet 9.1

Building tension 1

Read and compare the two texts below. Comment on which is more successful at building tension.

The prickling of my nape left me in no doubt about that. I looked around nervously. The question was, who was watching me?

The prickling of my nape left me in no doubt about that and I looked around nervously - the question was, who was watching me?

Worksheet 9.1

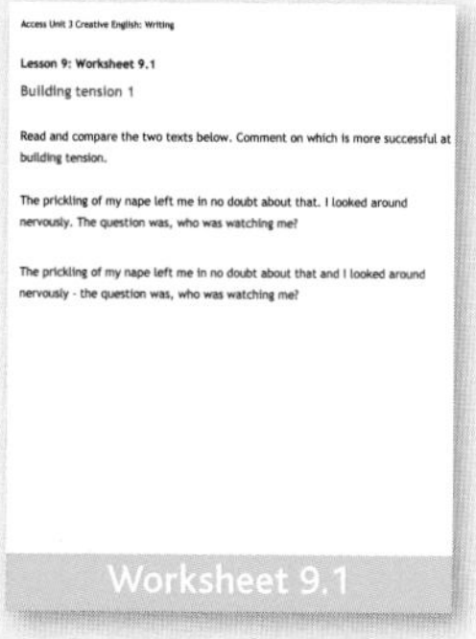

- Ask students to identify the different types of sentence used in the text. As a class, explore and explain what effect they have and why the writer might have chosen to write it like this. Students may suggest that it is a tense moment in the story so using short sentences to build pace and ending with a question helps create a sense of tension; a longer sentence slows it down.

3 Pair work

- Write the following on the board:

  Build tension using:
  – long sentences, followed by several short sentences
  – short direct questions

- Ask students to attempt question 1 of **Activity 1** in pairs, redrafting the sentences in the example paragraph to build tension. **Worksheet 9.2** supports this activity.

Access Unit 3 Creative English: Writing

Lesson 9: Worksheet 9.2

Building tension 2

You can **build tension** using:
- long sentences, followed by a few short sentences
- short, direct questions.

Read the paragraph below. Redraft it so that the sentences build tension.

We were running through the estate, down the long paths then suddenly turning right and hurtling off in another direction. We jumped over low walls, through gardens then leapt back up over and onto another path. All the time we ran we could hear them following us and they were never far behind so we had to keep on going even though we were sweating and our hearts were banging inside us.

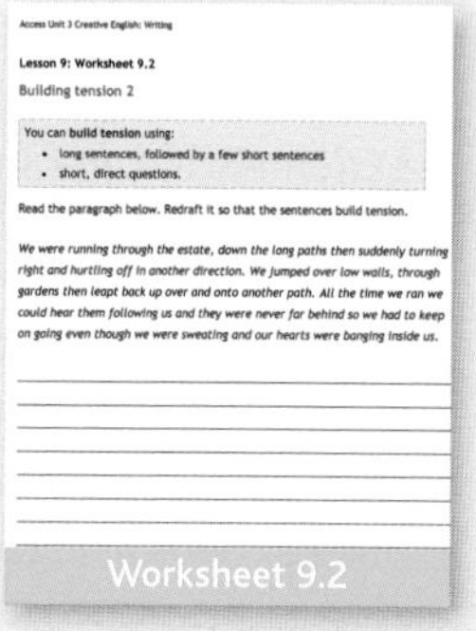

Worksheet 9.2

- Ask pairs to swap their work and peer assess each other's redrafts, commenting on how well the paragraph builds tension. Students can make suggestions for improvement as appropriate.

4 Independent work

Students should work independently to answer question 2 of **Activity 1,** writing the next paragraph of the story. They should concentrate on building tension, using long sentences to describe the situation, then follow the long sentences with a few short sentences to build tension. They should aim to use a question, too.

5 Whole class work

- Using the examples on pages 146 and 147 of the student book, explain how changing the position of information in a sentence can make a reader notice it more or less. Tell students that in creative writing, the most important part of a sentence is the beginning and the most important part of a paragraph is often the end.

Additional support

Starter

- **Talk partners:** Pair EAL student and fluent English speaker to **discuss** the differences in the sentences. They could read the sentences aloud and decide which words should be emphasised if they were being read. **Clarify** 'impact'.

- **Active listening:** The **teacher** should read the extracts pausing at the commas and varying the pace and expression to illustrate the effect of the sentences and aid understanding. Throughout the lesson, **clarify** vocabulary as necessary.

Whole class work

- Ensure there are EAL and fluent English speakers in the groups.

- **Activate prior knowledge:** Have any of the students been chased? How did the experience involve all or some of their senses? Where were they? Who was chasing?... Or ask students to think of a film they have seen of a chase or imagine what a chase would be like.

Independent work

- **Writing frames** could be made to show students how to vary their sentences by starting them with: an adverb, an -ed, an -ing, a subordinate clause, a connective, a prepositional phrase.

- EAL students may need help to think of a topic for their creative writing task.

- A previously written grade C quality paragraph could be used as a **scaffold**, **dictogloss** or **cloze** before their creative work. Text highlighting and annotating could be helpful.

- Write the following two sentences on the board. Ask students who or what they think is the most important thing in each sentence. Students should understand that the first sentence puts the emphasis on the van, whereas the second gives greater prominence to the children.

  - *The ice cream van came speeding round the corner, honking its horn as the children were playing in the street.*

  - *The children were playing in the street as the ice cream van came speeding round the corner, honking its horn.*

- Tell students that when they are writing an exciting, tense or dramatic moment of a story, or planting a clue, they should spend time working out where to place the information in their sentence for maximum effect. For example, in a detective story, red herrings might go at the front of a sentence, while the real clues which the writer must place but doesn't want to be too obvious could go at the end of a sentence mid-paragraph.

6 Independent work

- Display **Image 9.1.** Ask students to attempt the first part of **Activity 2** independently, rewriting the sentences so that the reader will focus on what the character is experiencing rather than on what is happening.

Image 9.1

- Students can swap their work with a partner to check that they have included all the information and that the sentences make sense.

- Students can now edit the sentences to build tension, adding questions or making some of the sentences shorter.

- Ask students to swap their work with a different partner and comment on how well their partner has built tension in the sentences.

7 Plenary

Ask students to share some of the sentences they rewrote for **Activity 2** with the class. Invite students to give feedback on one another's sentences, commenting on the good points as well as making suggestions for improvement.

8 Further work

Ask students to write a tense section of a story using the skills they have learned during the lesson. **Worksheet 9.3** supports this activity.

Worksheet 9.3

Suggested answers

Student book Activity 2

a) *Sweat poured down Nicola's face as she steadily washed car after car while traffic sped by, shoppers popped in and out of stores, and children nagged for ice creams.*

b) *Nicola's heart pounded as the biggest youth sneered and kicked away the car wash bucket and sponges.*

c) *Nicola stood up slowly and carefully as if stiff from crouching, then suddenly sprinted off and pushed the shortest gang member to the ground, taking the gang by surprise.*

d) *Nicola heard them shout 'Get her!' and pounding feet raging towards her as the gang gave chase.*

Lesson 10
Using paragraphs

Learning objectives

→ Show the reader what is new in each paragraph.

1 Starter

- Ask students to work in pairs and list the reasons for beginning a new paragraph. They should note down anything else they remember about writing in paragraphs.

- Share ideas as a class and list the reasons for beginning a new paragraph on the board, for example: a change in time, place, event, idea, person speaking. Discuss how a paragraph break allows a reader to understand that a change is being introduced, and how this helps the reader to follow the writer's ideas.

- Construct a class text, recounting a recent school event. Ask students to suggest when to use a new paragraph.

2 Whole class work

- Display the *Fearless* text on the ActiveTeach or from **Worksheet 10.1**. Ask students to identify both a) why the writer began each paragraph, and b) which words in the paragraph's opening sentence signal to the reader what the change is.

- Discuss the use of connectives and ask students to look over the table on page 148 of the student book (also provided on **Worksheet 10.2**).

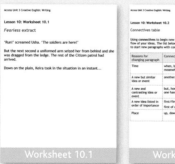

Worksheet 10.1

Worksheet 10.2

Resources required

Student book pages 148–151
Image 10.1: Children at window
Image 10.2: Door
Worksheet 10.1: *Fearless* extract
Worksheet 10.2: Connectives table
Worksheet 10.3: Changing paragraph
Worksheet 10.4: Writing in paragraphs

Assessment objectives

English AO3i
Write clearly, effectively and imaginatively, using and adapting forms and selecting vocabulary appropriate to task and purpose in ways that engage the reader.

English AO3ii
Organise information and ideas into structured and sequenced sentences, paragraphs and whole texts, using a variety of linguistic and structural features to support cohesion and overall coherence.

English AO3iii
Use a range of sentence structures for clarity, purpose and effect, with accurate punctuation and spelling.
At least a third of the AO3 weighting relates to bullet 3 (iii).

3 Pair work

- Hand out **Worksheet 10.3**. Ask students to work in pairs to add paragraphs to the text, marking // to indicate where a new paragraph should begin, and annotating their text to explain why a new paragraph is needed.

- Afterwards students can work with another pair and peer assess each other's corrected work, ticking where paragraphing has been correctly added and placing a star where using a new paragraph would improve understanding of their text further.

Worksheet 10.3

Additional support

Starter
- **Talk partners:** Ensure that the pairs involve an EAL learner and a fluent English speaker (or students who share a **first language**) to consolidate knowledge of paragraphs.

Whole class work
- **Active listening:** Read the extract on page 148 aloud, asking students to **highlight** the connectives and topic sentences.

- Create a set of cards with connectives on them to **match** with the categories of connectives from page 146. Add these on to the **word wall** for reference in the controlled assessment.

Pair work
- It may be useful to read the text on Worksheet 10.3 aloud with expression, pauses, gestures and facial expression to aid understanding. **Clarify** words as necessary such as: 'option', 'downpour', 'mumbled', 'unconvincingly'...and people's names.

---

4 Independent work

Students should look at **Image 10.1** and work on their response to the controlled assessment creative writing task given in **Activity 1**, making sure that they begin each paragraph with a sentence that lets the reader know whether they are being shown a new idea, event, time, place, or speech. Students should use the link words in the connectives chart.

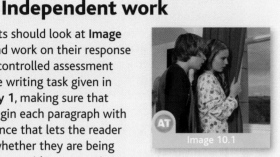
Image 10.1

7 Further work

Students should use what they have learned about paragraphs and the connectives chart to help them write a text describing the unexpected arrival of something new at their home. **Worksheet 10.4** supports this activity.

Worksheet 10.4

---

5 Independent work

- Ask students to look at **Image 10.2** and read the example controlled assessment task on page 149. Students should complete **Activity 2** and assess their own work using the criteria given in the ResultsPlus Maximise your marks section.

Image 10.2

- Students should then work in pairs to complete the **Putting it into practice** activity on page 151.

8 Controlled assessment practice

- On pages 152–155 of the student book, a practice creative writing task is provided. You could work through this with students as they practice before they sit their assessment.

ResultsPlus interactive 3a

- On the ActiveTeach there are accompanying ResultsPlus grade improvement activities which help students understand how to improve their answer.

---

6 Plenary

Ask students how confident they feel in using paragraphs, and to give themselves a rating on a scale of 1–5 with 5 being the most confident. Discuss strategies for improving students' use of paragraphs, for example: paying attention to when and why new paragraphs have been used in texts they are reading.

Lesson 1 Identifying the features of spoken language

Learning objectives

→ Understand how spoken language works.

→ Identify some of the features of spoken language.

→ Understand how spoken language changes depending on the situation.

Resources required

Student book pages 158–161

BBC Video: *Strictly It Takes Two*

Audio 1.1: Conversation about the weather

Audio 1.2: Weather forecast

Weblink 1.1: Examples of formal/informal speech

Worksheet 1.1: Glossary for spoken language

Worksheet 1.2: Analysing a transcript

Worksheet 1.3: Formal and informal spoken language

Worksheet 1.4: Formal and informal situations

Worksheet 1.5: Conversation diary

Answer sheet 1.1: Suggested answers

Assessment objectives

English Language AO2i

Understand variations in spoken language, explaining why language changes in relation to contexts.

English Language AO2ii

Evaluate the impact of spoken language choices in their own and others' use.

1 Starter

- Ask students to complete **Activity 1**, listing five different times they have used spoken language during the day. For each example they should explain where they were speaking, and to whom, and for what purpose.

- Ask students to discuss with a partner how they vary the way they use spoken language to suit different situations.

2 Independent work

- Explain that everyday speech – including the speech students have been using so far in the lesson – is spontaneous (not planned). Explain there is another form of spoken language: scripted speech. Read out examples of spontaneous and scripted speech and ask students to give a thumbs up for spontaneous speech and thumbs down for scripted speech. For example: asking your friend if you can borrow a DVD; a police officer giving a presentation to members of the public about why making copies of DVDs is wrong; a radio advertisement.

- Play the weather forecast **Audio 1.2** and the conversation about the weather **Audio 1.1** to the class in turn. Students should attempt **Activity 2**, comparing spontaneous speech and scripted speech.

- Take feedback. Support students as they list differences such as pauses, hesitation, fillers, false starts, incomplete sentences, etc. Ask students which recording they found easiest to listen to, and why.

- Display the glossary of spoken language terms on **Worksheet 1.1**. Using the examples and explanations on page 159 of the student book, explain and give examples of: pauses, false starts and ellipsis. When discussing ellipsis, ask students what words they think have been left out in the example given. Students should understand that 'not gonna' is incomplete for two reasons – firstly because 'going to' has changed to 'gonna' and also because it leaves the listener to assume the end of the sentence ('not gonna come with you').

3 Pair work

Distribute **Worksheet 1.2**. Ask students to attempt **Activity 3** in pairs, identifying pauses, a false start and an example of ellipsis in the transcript, before giving reasons for each example.

Student book page 160

4 Group work

- Ask pairs to make groups of four to compare and discuss their answers to **Activity 3**. Explain that if an answer is incomplete, students should work in their groups to prepare a more developed answer to share with the class. It may help to brainstorm words and phrases that can be used in explanations, such as 'because...', 'in order to...', 'that's why...'

- Share ideas as a class. Encourage active listening by asking students to assess each other's reasons.

5 Whole class work

- Display **Worksheet 1.3**. Read the explanatory text on page 161 of the student book with the class and discuss the concepts of formal and informal language. Explain that people speak formally or informally depending on situation and the relationship they have with the person they are speaking to. Ask students to give examples of how they speak to a variety of people.

Additional support

Starter

- **Talk partners**: Pair EAL student with a fluent English speaker to **discuss** Activities 1 and 2 and features of the glossary to ensure EAL students are confident in their **understanding** of the terms, can **pronounce** them and feel confident in **using** the terms themselves.

- In some classes it may be appropriate for students who share a first language to **discuss** the conventions in their **L1** and compare them with English.

- **Active listening**: The **teacher** or fluent readers should read the explanations and activities on pages 158–9.

- **Cloze tests** of spontaneous and scripted texts could be created to identify the text types.

Independent work/Activity 2

- EAL students will benefit from **repeated listening** to the audio recordings.

- **Read the prompting questions** after the first hearing to help the students gather ideas and examples that they can use to answer the questions during the second hearing.

- **Spoken Language Glossary** in the panel on page 160 and Worksheet 1.1 will be helpful to EAL students, although some terms may need explanation (e.g. 'ellipsis' and 'false start'). It may be useful to display them on the **word wall**. **e-reference tools** could be used to develop understanding.

Pair work

- Use **talk partners**.

- **Active listening**: Use **message abundancy** to **clarify** any difficult words in the transcript on p.162 as necessary e.g. 't'church', 'monk', 'monastery', 'rectory', 'few and far between' and names. **Use actions** to **clarify** prepositions such as 'beyond'.

Group work

- Ensure groups always include both EAL students and fluent English speakers.

- A **jigsaw reading** or **envoys** activity could be created using four more spontaneous or scripted texts to give more practice in recognising the two text types.

- The role-play activity will be very useful. EAL learners should hear as many examples of spoken English as possible to prepare them for assessments later.

- A listening diary is a novel idea but some students may not hear much English outside school.

6 Independent work

- Ask students to complete **Activity 4** independently, deciding whether they would use formal or informal language in each situation. Students can record their answers on **Worksheet 1.4** and compare their results with a partner's.

Worksheet 1.4

7 Pair work

- Ask students to think of different situations and audiences with different formality requirements, for example: meeting the Queen; discussing *EastEnders* with a friend; talking to a grandparent; at a job interview. Record ideas on the board.

- Ask students to work in pairs to prepare a role-play for one of the situations. Explain that their role-play conversation should include examples of the spoken language features that would appear in them.

- Ask students to perform their role-plays to the class. Ask the other students whether they agree or disagree with the way the speakers chose to use language. Students should explain their reasons, identifying the language features included in the role-play. Draw out the idea that both the audience and the purpose in a conversation affect the level of formality.

8 Plenary

- Play the **BBC Video:** *Strictly It Takes Two*, available on the ActiveTeach.

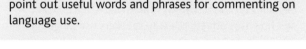
BBC Video: *Strictly It Takes Two*

- Ask students to write a sentence commenting on the use of language in the conversation. Share sentences as a class and compile a class paragraph, taking this opportunity to help students improve their sentences.

- Read the completed paragraph as a class. Ask students to point out useful words and phrases for commenting on language use.

9 Further work

Ask students to keep a listening diary. They should make notes on two conversations, one with a friend and one with a teacher. Using **Worksheet 1.5**, they should record the language features used in each conversation.

Suggested answers

Student book Activity 4 – See Answer sheet 1.1

Lesson 2 Understanding style and context

Resources required
Student book pages 162–167
Image 2.1: Doctor and patient
Image 2.2: Politician and panel
Worksheet 2.1: Context chart
Worksheet 2.2: Transcript A
Worksheet 2.3: How people speak
Worksheet 2.4: Features of conversations
Worksheet 2.5: Transcript B
Worksheet 2.6: Analysing a conversation
Answer sheet 2.1: Suggested answers

Learning objectives

→ Understand how people change the way they speak (the style) depending on the situation.

→ Identify and explain examples of the way context changes the way people speak.

Assessment objectives
English Language AO2i
Understand variations in spoken language, explaining why language changes in relation to contexts.
English Language AO2ii
Evaluate the impact of spoken language choices in their own and others' use.

1 Starter

Image 2.1

• Explain the meaning of 'context' to the class. Read aloud the chart on page 162 of the student book. It is also available on **Worksheet 2.1**.

• Ask students to identify the context (audience, function, situation and topic) for a) a student speaking during this lesson; b) the head teacher addressing students in assembly.

• Show students **Images 2.1** and **2.2** and ask them to identify the context for each.

Image 2.2

3 Group work

• Ask students to close their books. Now ask them to suggest other factors that affect the way people speak and list them on the board.

• Read through the list of factors on page 163 of the student book. Did the class think of all the factors?

Student book page 163

• Ask students to complete **Activity 2** in groups, matching the factor to the example in each case. Take feedback. Ensure students understand the difference between accent and dialect (and specifically standard English and Received Pronunciation).

• Distribute **Worksheet 2.3**, copied onto A3 paper if possible. Ask students to work in groups to suggest their own examples of each feature, recording their examples on the worksheet. This can then be displayed as a poster.

2 Pair work

• Explain that speech always takes place in a context and how this affects the way speakers use language. Ask students to give their own examples of times they have consciously modified the way they speak to suit a specific context. Ask students to speculate on how other people might change the way they speak to suit a specific context and give examples.

• Distribute **Worksheet 2.2**, which contains a copy of the transcript on page 162 of the student book. Ask students to complete **Activity 1** in pairs.

• Share responses as a class. Draw out the idea that the shopkeeper uses more formal language when he asks the man his age. This could show that he wants to appear in control of the situation. Once he realises he is over 18 he is more informal ('Cheers mate').

Worksheet 2.2

4 Whole class work

Complete **Activity 3** as a class, asking students to comment on any times they have modified their language to fit the context. You may wish to give some examples of when you have modified your own language.

Additional support

Starter
- **Collaborative:** The teacher, or fluent English speakers, should **read** the introduction and definitions on pages 162–4 **aloud** to aid understanding. **Clarify** vocabulary as necessary using **message abundancy**, e.g. 'status', 'debating', 'received pronunciation', 'overlaps', 'repairs'.
- The words and definitions could be put on a **word wall** or made into a **matching card sort** activity.

Pair work
- **Oral prediction:** Ask **talk partners** (EAL students and fluent English pairs) to predict how each context might affect the choices of spoken language.

Group work/Activity 2
- **Talk partners:** Ensure that the groups include fluent English speakers and EAL students to discuss greetings. EAL students could swap knowledge from their different **first language** backgrounds as an added dimension to the activity.

- **NB:** Worksheet 2.3 will also allow them to discuss the idea of dialect, slang and accent in their first language. It may be helpful for EAL students to consider talk at home where family members code switch (mix first language and English) in their conversations or think of examples where they pronounce words in a non-standard way – e.g. 'v' pronounced as 'w' or 'r' pronounced as 'l' by speakers of different first languages.

Whole class work/Activity 3
- **Active listening:** EAL students would benefit from hearing the conversation more than once using the **sequence:** listen – follow the words in the transcript – listen again – answer questions.

Activity 4
- As the transcript is performed it may be necessary to **clarify** words such as 'dual carriageway', 'Clifford's Tower', 'mound', 'alongside'.
- **Revise** the terms social, formal, and informal before **Activity 4**.

Further work
- **Clarify** vocabulary in the examiner summaries. Create a short **dictogloss** using the grade C answer.

5 Whole class work

- Display **Worksheet 2.4** on the board. Read the explanatory text about conversational language on page 164 of the student book with the class.

Worksheet 2.4

- Ask three students to hold a conversation about a topical issue in front of the class. The rest of the class act as observers. Observers must actively listen for the features of conversational English on the worksheet.

- Ask students to raise a hand when they hear an example of overlaps, interruptions, repairs or feedback. Pause the conversation at an appropriate point and ask students with their hands raised to explain which feature they recognised. Ask the rest of the class to signal whether they agree (thumbs up) or disagree (thumbs down). Ask anyone who disagrees to explain why. Try not to interrupt the conversation too often or it may become stilted and not include enough features.

6 Pair work

- Ask students to work in pairs to complete **Activity 4**, identifying the different features of conversational language that are recorded in the transcript. They could annotate the transcript, available on **Worksheet 2.5**.

Worksheet 2.5

- Students should try to explain why each conversational feature is used. Remind students that they should focus on why they are used in this specific conversation.

- Share responses to **Activity 4** as a class. Ask students to comment on the function of each language feature in this specific conversation, then ask them to comment on the features more generally. *Why are repairs important? What would it be like to have a conversation without feedback?*

7 Plenary

- Ensure all books are closed. Students work in teams. Call out one of the key concepts from this lesson (e.g. accent, dialect, slang, age, standard English, overlaps, taking turns, interruptions, repairs, feedback). Ask the teams to compete to come up with the clearest definition and example. Encourage active listening by asking the teams who are not giving their definition or example to signal their agreement or disagreement with the answer being suggested, and to offer improvements in order to gain additional points.

8 Further work

- Ask students to make notes on two conversations they have: one with a teacher and one with a friend. Students should answer the questions about context on **Worksheet 2.6** and fill in the table with examples of various language features.

- Students should assess their own work using the criteria given in the ResultsPlus Maximise your marks section.

- Students should complete the **Putting it into practice** activity on page 167.

Suggested answers

Student book Activity 1 – See Answer sheet 2.1

Lesson 3 Writing a script

Resources required

Student book pages 168–171
BBC Video: *EastEnders*
Worksheet 3.1: Factors in scriptwriting
Worksheet 3.2: *Only Darkness* transcript
Worksheet 3.3: *Hobson's Choice* transcript

Learning objectives

→ Understand what a script is.

→ Write your own script.

Assessment objectives

English Language AO4i

Write to communicate clearly, effectively and imaginatively, using and adapting forms and selecting vocabulary appropriate to task and purpose in ways that engage the reader.

English Language AO4ii

Organise information and ideas into structured and sequenced sentences, paragraphs and whole texts, using a variety of linguistic and structural features to support cohesion and overall coherence.

English Language AO4iii

Use a range of sentence structures for clarity, purpose and effect, with accurate punctuation and spelling.

At least a third of the AO4 weighting relates to bullet 3 (iii).

1 Starter

- Ask students to work in pairs and share what they already know about writing scripts, for example: their layout, language features, stage directions, etc.

- Take feedback as a class.

2 Whole class work

- Explain the concepts of audience, function, medium and topic using the table on page 168 of the student book or **Worksheet 3.1.**

- Working as a class, read the two drama scripts on pages 168–169 of the student book. Complete **Activity 1** as a class, asking students to identify the audience, function, medium and topic of each script.

Worksheet 3.1

- Ask students which they think was written for television and which for stage. How did they know?

- Distribute **Worksheets 3.2** and **3.3** which include the scripts on pages 168–169.

- Read aloud the introduction to **Activity 2** on page 170.

- Ask students to work in groups of three to complete **Activity 2** part 1, identifying stage/screen directions and a scene change. They should annotate their copies of **Worksheets 3.2** and **3.3** to show these features.

Worksheet 3.2

Worksheet 3.3

3 Group work

- Watch the **BBC Video: *EastEnders***, available on the ActiveTeach, as a class. Ask students to suggest what information to set the scene might have been included in the script. Watch the video again, stopping now and then. Ask students to suggest what they think the stage directions might have been.

BBC Video: *EastEnders*

4 Pair work

- Explain to students that writers show their audience what characters are feeling and thinking, and what they are like, through:
  - what they say
  - how they say it
  - the character's actions
  - how a character reacts to other characters and events.

- Ask students to work in pairs. Ask them to choose two characters (one from each script) and make notes on what the writer shows the audience about the character based on their speech, actions and reactions.

Additional support

Starter
- **Talk partners:** Throughout the lesson ensure that EAL students are paired with fluent English speakers.

Whole class work/Activity 1
- **Visual presentation:** It may be helpful to **activate prior knowledge** about the theatre by showing a picture of a stage and auditorium when talking about setting the scene.

- **Active listening:** The teacher, or fluent English speakers, should read the stage setting and directions and act out the scripts on pages 168-9 to aid pronunciation and understanding. **Clarify** vocabulary as necessary, such as: 'medium', 'cloakroom', 'gaze', 'aggressive', 'neutral', 'impatient', 'shrugs', 'knitting', 'aprons', ''reviving', 'oblige', 'established solicitor'.

Group work/Activity 2
- Ensure groups have a **mixture** of EAL students and fluent English speakers.
- **Clarify** any difficult words in the introduction on page 170 using **message abundancy**, e.g. 'conventions', 'acts', 'scenes'.

- Share responses as a class and annotate displayed copies of **Worksheets 3.2** and **3.3** with students' ideas.
- Complete the remainder of **Activity 2** as a class, asking students to predict what might happen next between the characters in each script.

5 Pair work

- Read aloud the introduction to **Activity 3** on page 171 of the student book. Students should work with a partner who wants to write the same scene. They should discuss what they want to show their

Student book page 171

audience about each character and their relationships and how they can use their speech, behaviour and reactions to do this. Encourage students to use the questions in **Activity 3** to help them.

- Once students have discussed their ideas, they should improvise their scenes to test their ideas.
- Ask pairs to make groups of four and take it in turns to perform and review each other's scenes. The observers should explain what the scene shows them about events, characters and relationships. The actors should listen to their comments to find out how successful their ideas were.
- Encourage each pair to use the feedback they have been given to improve their ideas.

6 Independent work

Students should work independently to complete **Activity 3**, writing their own script for their chosen scene. They should use their annotated copies of **Worksheet 3.2** or **3.3** to ensure they use the correct layout and style of stage directions.

7 Plenary

As a class, discuss the features of a good script. Use students' ideas to create a class checklist, incorporating ideas on content as well as layout and form. Encourage students to write the checklist in their exercise books.

8 Further work

Students should practise writing a short script. It could be a follow-on from a programme whose characters they know well, for example: a scene from a soap they watch or a film they like. Alternatively, they could develop their own characters and situation.

Suggested answers

Student book Activity 1
1. Text A – mainly teenagers, possibly also adults; Text B – adults
2. Texts A and B – to entertain
3. Text A – television or film; Text B – stage.
4. Text A – modern teenage girls at college talking about their studies and a forthcoming party; Text B – set in last century, the Hobson daughters talking about their father, and someone who is coming to their boot shop

Lesson 4
Writing dialogue

Learning objectives

→ Write dialogue in narratives.

→ Use dialogue to create characters and tell your story.

Resources required

Student book pages 172–177
Worksheet 4.1: *Of Mice and Men* extract
Worksheet 4.2: Girl's conversation
Worksheet 4.3: Making dialogue realistic
Worksheet 4.4: Improving dialogue
Answer sheet 4.1: Suggested answers

Assessment objectives

English Language AO4i
Write to communicate clearly, effectively and imaginatively, using and adapting forms and selecting vocabulary appropriate to task and purpose in ways that engage the reader.

English Language AO4ii
Organise information and ideas into structured and sequenced sentences, paragraphs and whole texts, using a variety of linguistic and structural features to support cohesion and overall coherence.

English Language AO4iii
Use a range of sentence structures for clarity, purpose and effect, with accurate punctuation and spelling.
At least a third of the AO4 weighting relates to bullet 3 (iii).

1 Starter

- Tell students they have to give instructions to a younger student explaining how to punctuate direct speech correctly.

- Display **Worksheet 4.1** which contains the text from *Of Mice and Men*. Ask students to work in pairs to complete **Activity 1** part 1, locating all the examples of speech marks in the extract from *Of Mice and Men*.

- Ask students to share their rules and annotate examples on the displayed text.

- As a class, discuss **Activity 1** part 2. Ask students how the writer makes it clear who has spoken each bit of speech. Annotate the examples on the displayed worksheet.

- As a class, compose a checklist for writing direct speech and display this throughout the lesson.

Worksheet 4.1

2 Whole class work

- Ask students to recap on their learning from the previous lesson, explaining how a character's speech, actions and reactions can reveal their character. Explain that in narrative, dialogue can also help to reveal what a character is like, what they are thinking and their relationship to other characters.

Worksheet 4.2

- You could play a clip from a radio play and ask students what the dialogue reveals about each character and their relationships.

- Display the text about Gemma's dress on the whiteboard. This text is available on **Worksheet 4.2**. Ask students to work out what each speech reveals about each speaker, for example: their age, interests and relationships. Model how to ask yourself questions about dialogue and annotate the details that reveal each point.

3 Pair work

- Ask students to complete **Activity 2** in pairs, annotating the copy of the extract from *Of Mice and Men* on **Worksheet 4.1** with examples of dialogue that reveal key aspects of the setting and characters.

- Ask students to share their work with another pair. Did they all agree? Take feedback as a class and clarify any points of disagreement.

4 Whole class work

- Ask two volunteers to role-play a conversation about a topical issue, for example: whether Facebook is a waste of time; who should win *The X Factor* this year, etc. The rest of the class should listen to the conversation.

- Use the conversation to model writing a piece of authentic dialogue on the whiteboard. Encourage students to contribute to writing the dialogue, asking them how they should write words which are contractions, dialect, accent, slang, etc.

5 Pair work

- Ask students to work in pairs to complete **Activity 3**. They should role-play the dialogue as it is written, then try to role-play it using their own speech patterns so it sounds more realistic.

- Ask students to rewrite the dialogue so it sounds more

Worksheet 4.3

Additional support

Starter

- **Revise** punctuation terms, especially quotation marks, commas, question and exclamation marks (see Lesson 10 in Unit 1 Writing).
- A **word wall** with synonyms for 'said' could be built up.
- **Active listening**: Throughout the lesson, the teacher, or fluent English speakers, should read the introduction and texts – e.g. pages 172–3 – using expression and pauses, and **visual presentation** such as gestures and facial expression to aid pronunciation and understanding.
- **Active listening**: Several readings of the extract from *Of Mice and Men* will help EAL students to understand the non-standard vocabulary such as: 'hell of a lot', 'damn near', 'God awmighty', 'I never seen' and abbreviated talk such as 'em', 'gonna'. Use **message abundancy**.

- **Talk partners** could rewrite the dialogue in standard English as a way to increase understanding before Activities 2 and 3.
- **Acting out** the script will be a good **VAK** activity to aid understanding.
- Alternatively, this could be an **envoys** or **jigsaw** activity. Pairs of students would act out one of the role-plays, then perform it for the other pair. Other scenarios such as teacher/student or teacher/parent on the phone or face to face could be added to extend the theme and be taken to other groups.
- Create a **substitution table** using 'I'm hungry. Can we have lunch?' as a starting point. Use this as a **frame** for other dialogue openers and a selection of alternative words for 'said'.

ResultsPlus and Controlled Assessment Practice

- The tips are always very helpful but **clarify** assessment vocabulary as appropriate. **Emphasise frequently**, by **reminding** during teaching, as well as when looking at tips and exemplar answers, exactly which features make the grade C answer the best.

---

realistic, taking care to punctuate it correctly. Refer students back to the punctuation rules they identified at the beginning of the lesson. Students can record their ideas on **Worksheet 4.3**.

6 Peer assessment

- Ask pairs to swap their work with another pair. They should peer assess each other's work, commenting on how realistic (or otherwise) they found the dialogue. They should also check each other's work for punctuation errors.
- Allow students time to give each other feedback. Following on from this, students can set their own goals for how to improve their writing of dialogue, for example: 'I need to remember to punctuate <u>before</u> closing speech marks.' Ask them to note their goal on **Worksheet 4.4** and then complete the exercise underneath.

7 Independent work

- Students should work independently to attempt **Activity 4** using all that they have learned in this lesson. Give students a few minutes to plan their work, thinking about appropriate language, the purpose of the dialogue and how they can make it realistic. Set a short time limit to maintain pace.
- Students should now write their dialogue and check their punctuation is correct. Explain that the purpose of this exercise is to complete the dialogue and punctuate it correctly.
- Ask students to complete the example controlled assessment task in **Activity 5** on page 175. Students should assess their own work using the criteria given in the ResultsPlus Maximise your marks section.
- Students should then work in pairs to complete the **Putting it into practice** activity on page 177.

8 Plenary

- Ask students to swap their work with a partner, and peer assess each other's work. Was the dialogue realistic? Was it punctuated correctly?

9 Further work

Ask students to complete **Activity 5**, writing a script for a TV soap that contains between 30 seconds and 2 minutes of spoken language. The script should focus on the opening of the first scene. Remind students to follow the conventions of a TV script.

10 Controlled assessment practice

- On pages 178–181 of the student book, practice Spoken Language Study and Writing for the Spoken Language tasks are provided. You could work through these with students as they practice before they sit their assessment.

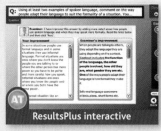

ResultsPlus interactive

- On the ActiveTeach there are accompanying ResultsPlus grade improvement activities which help students understand how to improve their answer.

Suggested answers

Student book Activity 2 – See Answer sheet 4.1

Introduction

This section of the Teacher Guide provides you with guidance on the English Today Controlled Assessment unit, which is common to the Edexcel GCSE English and GCSE English Language specifications. It aims to:

- Familiarise you with the Edexcel specification requirements
- Offer you specific guidance about the type of tasks offered within the Edexcel specification
- Help you consider the choices and challenges involved in planning for the controlled assessment tasks for this unit
- Help you to understand the structure of the mark scheme and its criteria

Non-fiction reading and writing in the Edexcel specifications

This unit is common to both GCSE English and GCSE English Language, which offers increased flexibility for your students. There are two tasks for students to complete in this unit, a reading task and a writing task. The reading tasks are based on themed selections of contemporary non-fiction texts which will be made available before the start of the academic year. Each year there will be two themes to select from, which will both be relevant and meaningful to students. You should choose the theme either **for** or **with** students.

There will be six texts on each theme, three onscreen texts and three paper-based texts.

- Onscreen texts will be drawn from digital technologies, for example digital videos, websites, social networking sites, podcasts, blogs, forums, online newspapers/magazines and advertisements. These texts must be viewed by students on screen.
- Paper-based texts will be drawn from print-based media, for example newspapers, magazines, advertisements, leaflets and brochures.

Students will have to study two texts from this selection.

This unit has been designed to cover the teaching aspects of Functional English in reading and writing. Students will also benefit from the opportunities in this unit to prepare for functional speaking and listening assessment.

Tasks

Students will complete two tasks: one reading task and one writing task. The tasks must be completed by students individually under controlled, supervised conditions. They can prepare for the task by making notes and planning their response, but they must not prepare a draft response in advance of the controlled assessment session.

After preparation, students can have up to two hours for students to complete each task (four hours in total).

They should produce a written response of up to 1000 words for each task.

Task 1 – Reading

Students will be asked to analyse and comment on the language, structure, presentation and layout used by the writers of two texts from the chosen theme. In their response, students must show that they can:

- make comparisons between texts
- select appropriate details from texts to support their ideas
- explore how writers use presentation and language to communicate their ideas and perspectives in the two texts.

Here are two examples of reading tasks:

Theme One: Environment

Your task is to compare the material from **two** texts on the environment.

In your comparison you must:

- explore how the writers communicate their ideas and perspectives
- comment on how the writers use presentation and language
- include examples to illustrate the points you make.

Texts

Guardian podcast: The Lost World Discovered (07/09/2009)
Earth to Humanity video © Blue Man Group
Climate change webpage – Greenpeace UK
Aeroplanes and Global Warming article, Mike Rayner – The British Council
Your Environment magazine cover Issue 18 Feb-April 2008
'You don't need to forsake your fun in the sun to help combat climate change' article, Jane Knight
The Times November 17 2007

Theme Two: Computer Gaming

Your task is to compare the material from two texts on computer gaming.

In your comparison you must:

- explore how the writers communicate their ideas and perspectives
- comment on how the writers use presentation and language
- include examples to illustrate the points you make.

Texts

A podcast with the creators of 'Little Big Planet' from the *Guardian*
A trailer from 'Little Big Planet' computer game
A home page of *The Edge* online gaming magazine
A review of 'Punch-out' from *Games* magazine
'Brain training video games boost children's intelligence' article from *The Telegraph*
The case cover from 'The Sims 2 H&M Fashion Expansion Pack'

Task 2 – Writing

Students will be asked to complete one task from a choice of two. They will be given a brief which asks them to write for a specified purpose and audience. Students need to show that they can express ideas and information clearly. They must:

- make choices in their writing that are appropriate to audience and purpose
- spell, punctuate and use grammatical structures that are accurate and appropriate for purpose and effect.

Here are some examples of writing tasks:

> **Theme One: Environment**
>
> Complete one task from those below.
>
> EITHER
>
> Write an article for a magazine in which you persuade readers about an environmental issue from a specific point of view.
>
> OR
>
> Write the script for a podcast for a website aimed at young people aged 11–14, where you inform them about an environmental issue.

> **Theme Two: Computer Gaming**
>
> Complete one task from those below.
>
> EITHER
>
> Write an article for a computer game magazine in which you describe your ideas for a new computer game.
>
> OR
>
> Write the script for a podcast for a teenagers' website, in which you review your favourite computer game.

From coursework or exam to controlled assessment

Controlled assessment is a different way of internally assessing what teachers and students previously knew as coursework. Controlled assessment is similar to coursework, but the tasks are completed under much more closely defined conditions for **task setting, task taking** and **task marking**.

One of the benefits of controlled assessment is that it ensures a 'level playing field' for students. Since there is a limited amount of time to complete the tasks, and since teachers keep their students' work rather than letting them take it home to work on, there is a real focus on the quality of the content. Controlled assessment is fairer to students as all students complete the same type of task and spend the same amount of time on it. Controlled assessment also enables teachers to authenticate students' work as their own, which was a criticism of coursework in the past. Controlled assessment also reduced the administrative burden on teachers - as the work is done under supervision, teachers do not need to chase lost or missing work!

When students produce a piece of work for controlled assessment, there are controls in place on the task setting, task taking and task marking. You should take note of the controls in place for the unit:

1. **Task setting**: For this unit the task setting for both reading and writing is **High Control**. This means that Edexcel will set the tasks for students to complete.

2. **Task taking**: For this unit the task taking is **High Control**. This means that the completion of the task must be under controlled conditions and that students should be supervised whilst they are completing their responses. This means that there are certain rules in place for the task taking:

   - Students must not prepare a draft response in advance of the controlled assessment. They will be able to write their responses only when supervised.
   - The writing can take place over more than one session, but if this is the case your students' materials must be collected in at the end of each session, stored securely and handed back at the beginning of the next session.
   - When your students are prepared they will have up to two hours to complete the reading task and two hours to complete the writing task. Reading and Writing do not have to be completed at the same time.
   - Your students must write their responses individually, without intervention or assistance from others.

3. **Task marking**: For this unit the task marking is **Medium Control**. This means that teachers mark the controlled assessment task using the assessment criteria provided. You should build on the good practice you already have in coursework assessment and undertake some kind of internal standardisation or moderation to ensure consistency. Edexcel will externally moderate the marking.

Choosing tasks

There is one reading task for each theme which asks students to compare the material from two texts. You need to guide your students to select the most appropriate theme and then the most appropriate texts from the options available. In writing there is a choice of two writing tasks on each theme and students need to complete one.

As a teacher you need to ensure that you have:

- covered all reading and writing skills required
- done robust assessment of skills prior to the controlled assessment
- personalised learning enough so that students are directed to the most appropriate task and texts.

When guiding students to choose tasks you should focus on:

- Theme – one theme may be more attractive and seem to 'speak' to students more
- Texts – some texts may be more attractive or accessible to different groups of students.

Timing

There are different options for you to consider in deciding how long you should spend preparing students and when it is appropriate for them to complete this controlled assessment task. However, it should be noted that the skills developed in this unit are underpinning skills for Units 2 and 3 (and indeed for other GCSEs, hence the opportunities to assess Functional Skills English through this unit). Because of this no preparation is wasted and there is no opportunity for the dreaded question 'is this on the exam?'

The controlled assessment may be taken as soon as students are **suitably prepared**. It is therefore essential that you conduct a robust assessment of skills as your students start the course or use prior attainment as a guide to their reading and writing skills and decide what is best for your groups. The timescale for one group may not be appropriate for another, even in the same centre.

There are two opportunities for internal assessment and external moderation, January and June. Preparation and support therefore need to work towards completion to meet these deadlines. For the majority of teachers the GCSE will be running over two years. For some the course may be offered over a one year period, e.g. in sixth form or further education colleges. A two year course offers four opportunities for moderation, two in Year 10 and two in Year 11 and this should be considered. As a teacher you need to weigh up the options in considering when to start preparation and when to assess, remembering that the themes, texts and tasks are changed every year.

The themes, texts and tasks are replaced every year, and the assessment windows are in January and June. This means that if your candidates take the controlled assessment to be assessed and moderated in January they do have the option to resit the controlled assessment with the same themes, texts and tasks in June. If, however, they first sit the controlled assessment in June and do not do as well as they hope then the themes, texts and tasks will be different for the following January, the next time they can take the assessment. For some groups of students, perhaps those who are performing in the G to C band, there is a benefit in taking the task in January to maximise assessment possibilities. In a two year course it may be appropriate to spend Year 10 on preparation of generic skills, given that these skills underpin the assessment of Unit 2 and Unit 3 in both GCSE English and GCSE English Language. This then could lead into skills being 'sharpened' in specific relation to the themes, texts and tasks in Year 11.

Guidance on carrying out the tasks

As a teacher you may support your students through the preparation process. Students' preparation may be informed by working in groups, but they must provide an individual response to the task. Students should use the range of appropriate resources available in your centre. Students should be made aware of what they can have access to during the controlled assessment

Students may have access to:	Students may not have access to:
Copies of the texts without any annotation	Notes that include continuous phrases or paragraphs
Notes – bullet or numbered points on themes, ideas and linguistic features	A pre-prepared draft of their response
IT equipment	A dictionary or thesaurus
	IT access to the internet, dictionaries, thesaurus, grammar or spell-check and saved pre-prepared materials

There are two main types of preparation you can use with your students for this unit. These are preparation by type of task and preparation by type of text.

Preparation by type of task

This approach encourages you to prepare students for the reading and the writing tasks separately – although there are some key elements that affect both. The advantage of this approach is that it supports lower attaining students by breaking the tasks down into small, clearly identifiable chunks. It also supports the discrete development of skills for the writing task in Unit 2. However, it provides less opportunity for the development of higher order transferable skills.

For reading you should prepare your students through coverage of the following:

Topic	Key Learning Points
1. Audience	how texts are adapted to suit their intended audience
2. Purpose	how the purpose of a text affects its use of language and layout
3. Types of Text	how to identify different types of texts and recognising texts with multiple purposes
4. Subjective and Objective Texts	how to distinguish between fact and opinion in one or more texts
5. Techniques for presenting a point of view	how writers use key techniques to present an argument
6. Techniques for presenting and persuading a point of view	how to identify bias, rhetoric and exaggeration and understanding how they are used to argue and persuade
7. Comparing Texts	how to identify generalisations and counter-arguments and how they convey an argument
8. Layout and Presentation	how layout features such as pictures, captions, headings, bullet points etc are used to impact on the reader
9. Linguistic Devices	how linguistic devices are used, including vocabulary (nouns, verbs, adjectives, adverbs), sentence structure (questions, commands, statements, simple and complex sentences), techniques (alliteration, personification, repetition, emphasis, hyperbole, understatement etc)
10. Controlled Assessment Practice	comparing, contrasting, analysing texts

For writing you should prepare your students through coverage of the following:

Topic	Key Learning Points
1. Analysing material – learning to read	different kinds of reading and the first two stages of reading (for understanding and to establish the provenance of each text): • Who is the writer • The genre of the text • Who is the intended reader • The purpose of the text. • When the text was written
2. Analysing material: choosing categories	learning about stage 3 of reading - reading and categorising texts according to genre
3. Developing summary skills	learning the basic skills involved in making a summary including glossing, paraphrasing and simplifying, an additional technique to use when constructing a new text.
4. Writing Texts: structuring texts	learning about the importance of structure in a text, looking at texts which have given structures and examining and analysing the structures of other texts
5. Writing Texts: coherence in texts	learning about coherence - the way that a text 'hangs together', the importance of structure and coherence in an effective text and the importance of planning the structure as well as the content of the text before writing begins
6. Writing Texts: cohesion in texts	learning how to connect ideas together to form a seamless whole text, looking at grammar: pronouns and syntax, successful transitions, using illustrations and captions and layout strategies
7. Writing Texts: using the right voice	learning the importance of writing using an appropriate voice for audience, learning that an appropriate voice will help the new text achieve cohesion and examining good practice in using different voices.
8. Controlled Assessment Practice	practice in creating texts.

Preparation by Type of Text

This approach encourages you to prepare students for the reading and the writing tasks together by carrying out the types of reading and writing activities given above by type of text. This approach helps to develop higher order transferable skills, supporting higher attaining students, but this approach may be less accessible to D-G candidates.

Your students need to be prepared by becoming aware of some or all of the following types of text, depending on your decisions having followed the guidance on choosing task.

Onscreen texts (taken from digital technologies)	Paper-based texts (taken from print-based media)
Digital videos	Newspapers
Websites	Magazines
Social networking sites	Advertisements
Podcasts	Leaflets
Blogs	Brochures
Forums	
Online newspapers/magazines and advertisements	

The mark scheme

This unit is worth 20% of the total GCSE. There are two overall assessment objectives for this unit:

- English AO2/English Language AO3 – Reading: This counts for 10% of the assessment.
- English AO3/English Language AO4 – Writing: This counts for 10% of the assessment.

Within each assessment objective there are three areas students are assessed on:

English AO2/English Language AO3: Reading

i. Students are assessed on their ability to *read* and *understand* texts. They need to be able to *select* material appropriate to their *purpose, collate* information from different sources and *make comparisons* and cross-references.

ii. Students are assessed on their ability to *develop* and *sustain* their *interpretation* of the *ideas* and *perspectives* of different writers.

iii. Students need to be able to *explain* and *evaluate* how writers use *linguistic, grammatical, structural and presentational features* to achieve an effect and engage and influence the reader.

English AO3/English Language AO4: Writing

i. In writing students need to be able to produce *clear, effective and imaginative writing*, using and adapting *forms* and selecting *vocabulary* appropriate to *task, purpose and audience*.

ii. Students are assessed on their ability to *organise* information and ideas into *structured* and *sequenced* sentences, paragraphs and whole texts. Students need to demonstrate that they can use a variety of *linguistic* and *structural* features to support *cohesion* and overall *coherence*.

iii. Students are assessed on their ability to demonstrate that they can use a *range* of *sentence structures* for *clarity, purpose and effect*, with accurate *punctuation* and *spelling*.

When marking, it is vital that all of your students receive the same treatment. You should apply the mark scheme positively, rewarding students for what they have shown they can do rather than penalising them for what hasn't been done. As examiners do, you should mark according to the mark scheme, not according to your perception of what grades students should achieve. There are 5 bands of marks in both reading and writing and you should use these rather than an idea of grade. Band 3 does not automatically equate to a grade C. You should use all the marks on the mark scheme across the range where appropriate and you should always award full marks if deserved, i.e. if the answer matches the mark scheme. If your students have crossed out work you should mark this unless the student has replaced it with an alternative response.

Interpreting the Bands

In reading you should assess against five bands and mark out of 20, keeping the guidance above in mind. Band 0 (0 marks) is only awarded when there is no material that could be rewarded. The key areas to focus on in reading are identified in the table below.

Assessment Objective: English AO2 (i), (ii) and (iii)/English Language AO3 (i), (ii) and (iii)

Key areas	Band 1 1-4 marks	Band 2 5-8 marks	Band 3 9-12 marks	Band 4 13-16 marks	Band 5 17-20 marks
Comparisons	Limited	Some	Sound	how	how
Exploring Ideas	Limited (on ideas)	Some (on ideas)	Clear (on ideas and perspectives)	Thorough (on ideas and perspectives)	Perceptive (on ideas and perspectives)
Comments on images, presentation and language	Brief and partial	Included but underdeveloped	Sound	Detailed	Perceptive
Selection of examples	Limited or irrelevant	Valid but underdeveloped	Appropriate and some support of points	Detailed, appropriate and support points	Discriminating and fully support points

In writing you should again assess against five bands and mark out of 13. Band 0 (0 marks) is only awarded when there is no material that could be rewarded. The key areas to focus on in writing are identified in the table below.

Assessment Objective: English AO3 (i) and (ii)/English Language AO4 (i) and (ii)

Key areas	Band 1 1-2 marks	Band 2 3-5 marks	Band 3 6-8 marks	Band 4 9-11 marks	Band 5 12-13 marks
Expression of ideas	Basic	Sometimes appropriate	Appropriate and developed	Effective and sustained	Compelling and fully developed
Awareness of purpose and audience	Little	Some	Clear	Secure and sustained	Strong, consistent and sharp
Control and use of vocabulary and sentence structure	Basic	Some	Well chosen vocab and some sense of sentence structure	Apt vocab and well controlled sentence structure	Extensive vocab and varied sentence structure
Organisation	Simple	Some (opening, development and paragraphs)	Sound (opening, development and closure, cohesive devices and controlled paragraphs)	Secure (well judged, effective paragraphing, use of cohesive devices)	Convincing (sophisticated, skilful, sustained paragraphing, effective use of cohesive devices)

Assessment Objective: English AO3 (iii) / English Language AO4 (iii)

Key areas	Band 1 1 marks	Band 2 2-3 marks	Band 3 4-5 marks	Band 4 6 marks	Band 5 7 marks
Accuracy of spelling	Inaccurate at times	Often accurate	Mostly accurate	Almost always accurate	Consistently accurate
Control and use of punctuation to convey intended effects	Basic	Some control	Sound control	Used with precision and supports intended effects	Sophisticated enabling effective intended emphasis
Structure of sentences and control of expression and meaning	Basic	Some	Clearly structured with sound control	Well-structured with effective control	Convincingly structured with sophisticated control

GCSE English Unit 3: Creative English

Introduction

This section of the Teacher Guide provides you with guidance on the Creative English Controlled Assessment unit of Edexcel GCSE English specification. It aims to:

- familiarise you with the Edexcel specification requirements
- offer you specific guidance about the type of tasks offered within the Edexcel specification
- help you consider the choices and challenges involved in planning for the controlled assessment tasks for this unit
- help you to understand the structure of the mark scheme and its criteria.

Creative English in the Edexcel specification

This controlled assessment unit is made up of three parts:

(a) Speaking and Listening

You will be familiar with these tasks from the specification that you are currently working with. Students will engage in a variety of speaking and listening activities. The students will be assessed on three speaking and listening tasks:

- Communicating and Adapting Language
- Interacting and Responding
- Creating and Sustaining Roles.

(b) Poetry (Reading)

Students will study one collection of 15 poems from the Edexcel Poetry Anthology. They will respond to a literary heritage poem, set by Edexcel, from outside the Anthology and two poems of their own choice from the Anthology collection they have studied. Their response could be a traditional written essay, but could alternatively be a response using digital media or a multimodal response.

(c) Creative Writing

Four tasks with accompanying stimuli (e.g. images, podcasts and video clips) will be set, one linked to each of the themes in the Edexcel Poetry Anthology. Students must write a response to one of the tasks. It is not necessary for students to have studied the poems from that collection in order to respond to the task – any theme may be chosen.

All of the tasks set for Unit 3 must be completed under controlled conditions. Controlled assessment replaces coursework, but it is possible for you to prepare students in much the same way.

- You can prepare your students as thoroughly as you wish for controlled assessment tasks. You can provide feedback while students are in the preparation stage and students can work in collaborative groups. However, when students produce their final written response they must work independently, under controlled conditions.
- Students can have access to notes when they are working under controlled conditions, but these notes must not include a pre-prepared draft.
- You should allow up to two hours for students to complete the task, but this time can be spread over one or more sessions.
- You will mark your students' work and it will be externally moderated by Edexcel.

You will need to make a professional decision about how much time you allow the students to prepare for the assessment tasks for Unit 3. It is likely that you will first want to teach the relevant skills and then support the students in their preparation.

Because all of the tasks for Unit 3 will be made available before the start of the academic year, and will be available for both the January and June series of an academic year, you will be able to plan when in a course it would be most appropriate for your students to complete these controlled assessment tasks. For example, you could choose to do one Speaking and Listening task each term. The Poetry task could be completed one term and the creative writing task could be tackled in a different term. The marks for all of the Unit 3 assessment tasks could then be submitted together at the end of the academic year.

When you plan your course you need to be aware that there is a requirement that at least 40% of the students' overall GCSE English assessment must be taken in the examination series in which certification is requested. This means that at least 40% of the students' assessment tasks will be carried out in Year 11. As Unit 3 counts as 40% of GCSE English, it would be possible to satisfy this requirement by carrying out all of the Unit 3 assessments in Year 11.

We will now look at each of the three sections of the unit.

Speaking and Listening

Edexcel will provide exemplar tasks which you can adapt to suit your own assessment purposes. These tasks will be very similar in nature to the three Speaking and Listening tasks that students completed for the pre-2010 specifications. Consequently, you will notice very little difference.

Tasks

The tasks set for Speaking and Listening will be very general, and so you will have a great deal of flexibility to define tasks that will suit your students. The following sample tasks illustrate what is possible.

1. Communicating and adapting language

Students must give an individual presentation. They should choose a topic which will interest their audience and give a talk on a subject of interest or on a problem or challenge. You may choose to develop your own tasks with students. Examples of topics could include:

- A talk to the class on their hobby or interest.
- A speech which argues that school uniform is an outdated concept.
- An account of a week's work experience.

2. Interacting and responding

Students must take part in a group discussion. Students will need to show that they can present their point of view, listen to the ideas of others and help to make suggestions and reach conclusions. You may choose to develop your own tasks with students. Examples of topics could include:

- Discussing ideas for a fundraising event for a local charity.
- Debating a topic such as euthanasia or the keeping of animals in zoos.
- Discussing the relationship between Juliet and her father in Romeo and Juliet.

3. Creating and Sustaining Roles.

For this task students can work individually or in a group. Students must choose a role and take an active role or improvise for part of the activity. The roles which follow are suggestions only; you may choose to develop your own tasks with students.

- Individual: George explaining his feelings about killing Lennie.
- Paired: A celebrity being interviewed on a chat show.
- Group: Mother, father, daughter, and daughter's boyfriend, discussing the daughter's pregnancy.

You can define tasks to satisfy the criteria. It would be possible to base these tasks on the non-fiction material the students have to study for Unit 1, the literature students have to study for Unit 2, or the poetry the students have to study for Unit 3.

Guidance on carrying out the tasks

- The first step should be to share the assessment criteria with the students. For example, students should know that the assessment criteria for "Communicating and Adapting Language" require students to use Standard English. The assessment criteria for "Interacting and Responding" require students to listen closely and attentively, make significant contributions and to engage with others.
- You should then make it clear what is expected from the task that you set. For example, if they are to talk to an audience about an interest or hobby, they should consider how they are going to engage the audience, use non-verbal features of communication and use appropriate vocabulary.

- Students should be given time to prepare for each of the assessments. While this might be obvious for the Communicating and Adapting Language task, and the Creating and Sustaining Roles task, students should also be encouraged to prepare for the Interacting and Responding task.
- Speaking and Listening assessments provide opportunities for self-assessment and peer-assessment. Students should be encouraged to learn from their experiences. The assessment criteria should be shared with the students to encourage them to consider how their performances could have been improved.
- Students will improve their speaking and listening skills with practice. Consequently, they should be given more than one opportunity to meet the assessment criteria.

The mark scheme

It is absolutely essential that you study the assessment criteria for each of the assessment tasks. You will use the assessment criteria to mark your students' work, and the assessment criteria will be used by the moderator when moderating your students' work. This section identifies some of the key features of the assessment criteria, and considers the implications for teaching.

1. Communicating and Adapting Language

- Students need to communicate information, ideas and feelings, promoting issues and points of view. The complexity of the subject matter is rewarded.
- They need to be assessed talking in a variety of situations and audiences, adapting their talk appropriately.
- They should use standard English, a range of well-judged vocabulary and use controlled grammatical structures.

Implications for teaching

Students need to be encouraged to select tasks that allow them to offer feelings and to promote issues and points of view. They should also be directed away from tasks that would not allow them to be credited for the complexity of the material. They need to be given a range of opportunities to communicate information in different situations and to different audiences. They should be clear that under some circumstances Standard English is the most appropriate form of English to use.

2. Interacting and Responding

- Students need to listen attentively and respond perceptively.
- They should make significant contributions that move the discussion forward.
- They should engage with others' ideas and feelings, recognising obvious bias or prejudice.

Implications for teaching:

Students need practise at working collaboratively in groups. Discussion topics need to be interesting enough to encourage students to engage in discussion. Students should be given time to prepare their own responses to group discussion topics before the group discussions take place. The criteria that will be used to assess students' contributions need to be made explicit.

Students need to be taught how to engage appropriately in group discussion.

3. Creating and Sustaining Roles

- Students should use language, gesture and movement to create and sustain characters.
- They should contribute to the development of situations and ideas, demonstrating understanding of the issues and relationships explored while in role.

Implications for teaching
Students should be given opportunities to study how professional actors use speech, gesture and movement to create characters. They should also be given opportunities to explore how actors respond to each other. For students to demonstrate understanding of issues and relationships, the tasks that they undertake should be sufficiently challenging.

Poetry (Reading)

Students should study all fifteen poems from one of the four themed collections in the Edexcel Poetry Anthology: Relationships; Clashes and Collisions; Somewhere, Anywhere; and Taking a Stand. They should be supported to develop interpretations of how poets create meaning and convey ideas.

Tasks

One task and one literary heritage poem (from outside the Anthology) will be set for each of the anthology collections each year. The tasks will be made available before the start of the academic year and will be valid for both the January and June examination series.

Students must respond to one task and one literary heritage poem, drawing on at least two poems from the chosen collection. Students will have to answer the task set for the theme that they have studied from the anthology. However, you will be able to direct students to poems from the theme that are most appropriate for their ability and interest.

Students can prepare their response, with support from yourself and other students. However, they should write up their response in not more than two hours, under controlled conditions. Their response can be:

- A written response of up to 1000 words
- A digital media response which could include a podcast, creation of a website, edit of digital video material presented by the student or a short digital video production
- A multimodal response that combines any of the above options.

Here is an example of a Poetry Reading Task:

Collection B: Clashes and Collisions

Explore the way poets present ideas about conflict.
You should refer to the poem 'Attack' by Siegfried Sassoon and two poems from the Clashes and Collisions collection.

Guidance on carrying out the tasks

The first decision you will need to make is whether the students will respond to the task in a traditional essay, or using digital media. It is important to consider that, whichever form their response takes, students need to demonstrate their appreciation of writing techniques and presentational features.

After sharing the relevant task with students you should ensure that they understand what will be expected from the assignment. You should share the assessment criteria with the students. Revisit the three poems that will be used for the assignment, perhaps drawing on the resources on the Edexcel Poetry Anthology ActiveTeach CD-ROM again.

You should then model how to respond to the task. If students are going to respond in a traditional essay, show them how you would write an essay, illustrating how quotations are used to support the response. If students are going to respond using digital media, provide them with examples of how this could be done. It will be important to keep students focused on the assessment criteria so that digital media responses can still be rewarded using the assessment criteria.

Students should then prepare for the task. At this stage students can work in groups, and they can receive support from yourself. When students complete their final written response under controlled conditions, they will be able to take in notes, but these must not include a pre-prepared draft. Students will need to be shown how to make appropriate and helpful notes.

The mark scheme

It is absolutely essential that you study the assessment criteria for each of the assessment tasks. You will use the assessment criteria to mark your students' work, and the assessment criteria will be used by the moderator when moderating your students' work. This section identifies some of the key features of the assessment criteria, and considers the implications for teaching.

- Students need to explain how writers use literary techniques to create effects.
- They need to demonstrate an understanding of how literary techniques contribute to the effects created.
- They need to make relevant connections between literary techniques and presentational features.
- They should make textual references to support their responses.

Implications for teaching:
There is an expectation that students will have knowledge of literary techniques and how they are used for effect. These need to be taught in the context of the poems that students are going to write about. The students need to be taught how to respond to poetry – this should be modelled for them. It is important that students do not just identify literary techniques; they need to discuss the effects achieved by these literary techniques.

Creative Writing

The requirements for this aspect of Unit 3 are similar to the original writing coursework you may previously have assessed students on, so you are likely to be familiar with preparing students for this style of writing.

Tasks

There will be a choice of four controlled assessment tasks, one based on each of the anthology themes. Stimulus material will be provided on the Edexcel website to support each of the questions, e.g. images, podcasts or video clips. In common with the Poetry Reading task, the tasks will be made available prior to the start of the academic year and will be valid for the January and June examination series.

Students must complete one of the four tasks. It is not necessary for students to have studied the poems from the anthology for the theme chosen for the creative writing task. Students can prepare their response, with support from yourself and other students. However, they should complete their final response in not more than two hours, under controlled conditions.

Here are some examples of Creative Writing tasks:

Choose one theme and complete the task from the choice below. The text may be one of the following:
- Narrative
- Description
- Monologue
- Script.

Theme A: Relationships
Task: Look at the image (Robert Doisneau, Le Baiser de l'Hôtel de Ville, 1950).
Write a text which explores EITHER the events leading up to this moment OR the events which directly follow this moment.

Theme B: Clashes and Collisions
Task: Look at the video clip (Euronews G20 London Protests).
Write a text from the viewpoint of a person in this videoclip.

Theme C: Somewhere, Anywhere
Task: Look at the image (For Sale House sign).
Write a text titled 'A place of my own'.

Theme D: Taking a Stand
Task: Listen to the podcast ('They have been taken hostage' – Paul Watson, Guardian podcast)
Write a text based on the activities of a campaigner.

Guidance on carrying out the tasks

When the task has been chosen, share the corresponding stimulus material provided on the Edexcel website with students along with the task itself. Explore together how students might respond to the stimulus. There will be a wide range of possible responses. For example, the question will enable the students to choose from a list of different genres such as narrative, description, monologue or script.

It might be appropriate for the whole class to write in the same genre. Alternatively, you may wish to give students more choice. The different stylistic expectations of each genre need to be explored.

Students should then prepare their response. At this stage students can work in groups, and they can receive support from yourself. When the students work under controlled conditions to complete their final written response, they will be able to take in notes, but these must not include a pre-prepared draft. Students will need to be shown how to make appropriate and helpful notes.

The mark scheme

It is absolutely essential that you study the assessment criteria for each of the assessment tasks for Unit 3. You will use the assessment criteria to mark your students' work, and the assessment criteria will be used by the moderator when moderating your students' work. This section identifies some of the key features of the assessment criteria, and considers the implications for teaching.

- Students should effectively present appropriate ideas
- They should demonstrate a clear sense of purpose and audience.
- There should be evidence of well-chosen vocabulary and of crafting in the construction of sentences.
- The organisation and structure of their writing should be effective, with the successful use of cohesive devices.
- Their spelling should be accurate, punctuation devices should be used to demonstrate emphasis and effect and sentences should be effectively structured.

Implications for teaching
Students will have some choice of task. They should spend time studying the stylistic devices associated with whichever genre they are going to write in. They should be taught how to structure a narrative, description, monologue or script. They should be encouraged to consider the style of their writing as well as the content. They should also be reminded to check their work for technical accuracy.

GCSE English Language Unit 3: Spoken Language

Introduction

This section of the Teacher Guide provides you with guidance on the Spoken English Controlled Assessment unit of the Edexcel GCSE English Language specification. It aims to:

- familiarise you with the Edexcel specification requirements
- offer you specific guidance about the type of tasks offered within the Edexcel specification
- help you consider the choices and challenges involved in planning for the controlled assessment tasks for this unit
- help you to understand the structure of the mark scheme and its criteria.

Spoken English in the Edexcel specification

This controlled assessment unit is made up of three parts:

(a) Speaking and Listening

You will be familiar with these tasks from the specification that you are currently working with. Students will engage in a variety of speaking and listening activities. The students will be assessed on three speaking and listening tasks:

- Communicating and Adapting Language
- Interacting and Responding
- Creating and Sustaining Roles.

(b) Spoken Language Study

This is a completely new requirement for GCSE. The Spoken Language Study provides students with the opportunity to explore the way spoken language works. Students will submit a response to one of two tasks set by Edexcel, which will require students to analyse two examples of spoken language. In their analysis students will:

- show how spoken language changes depending on the context
- understand some of the choices people make when they are speaking.

(c) Writing for the Spoken Voice

Students will submit a response to one writing task from a choice of three tasks provided by Edexcel. These tasks will include speeches, stories with a focus on dialogue and scripts. In their response to the task students will demonstrate their ability to:

- understand that different media work in different ways
- understand the needs of different audiences and purposes.

All of the tasks set for Unit 3 must be assessed under controlled conditions. Controlled assessment replaces coursework, but it is possible for you to prepare students in much the same way.

- You can prepare your students as thoroughly as you wish for controlled assessment tasks. You can provide feedback while the students are in the preparation stage and students can work in collaborative groups. However, when the students produce their final written response they must work independently, under controlled conditions.
- Students can have access to notes when they are working under controlled conditions, but these notes must not include a pre-prepared draft.
- You should allow up to two hours for students to complete the task, but this time can be spread over one or more sessions.
- You will mark your students' work and it will be externally moderated by Edexcel.

You will need to make a professional decision about how much time you allow the students to prepare for the assessment tasks for Unit 3. It is likely that you will first want to teach the relevant skills and then support students in their preparation.

Because all of the tasks for Unit 3 will be made available before the start of the academic year, and will be available for both the January and June series of an academic year, you will be able to plan when in a course it would be most appropriate for your students to complete these controlled assessment tasks. For example, you could choose to do one Speaking and Listening task each term. The Writing for the Spoken Voice task could be tackled in one term and the Spoken Language Study Task could be tackled in another term. The marks for all of the Unit 3 assessment tasks could then be submitted together at the end of the academic year.

When you plan your course you need to be aware that there is a requirement that at least 40% of students' overall GCSE English Language assessment must be taken in the examination series in which certification is requested. This means that at least 40% of the students' assessment tasks will be carried out in Year 11. As Unit 3 counts as 40% of GCSE Language, it would be possible to satisfy this requirement by carrying out all of the Unit 3 assessments in Year 11.

We will now look at each of the three sections of the unit.

Speaking and Listening

Edexcel will provide exemplar tasks which you can adapt to suit your own assessment purposes. These tasks will be very similar in nature to the three Speaking and Listening tasks that students completed for the pre-2010 specifications. Consequently, you will notice very little difference.

Tasks

The tasks set for Speaking and Listening will be very general, and so you will have a great deal of flexibility to define tasks that will suit your students. The following sample tasks illustrate what is possible.

1. Communicating and adapting language

Students must give an individual presentation. They should choose a topic which will interest their audience and give a talk on a subject of interest or on a problem or challenge. You may choose to develop your own tasks with students. Examples of topics could include:

• A talk to the class on their hobby or interest.
• A speech which argues that school uniform is an outdated concept.
• An account of a week's work experience.

2. Interacting and responding

Students must take part in a group discussion. Students will need to show that they can present their point of view, listen to the ideas of others and help to make suggestions and reach conclusions. You may choose to develop your own tasks with students. Examples of topics could include:

• Discussing ideas for a fundraising event for a local charity.
• Debating a topic such as euthanasia or the keeping of animals in zoos.
• Discussing the relationship between Juliet and her father in Romeo and Juliet.

3. Creating and Sustaining Roles

For this task students can work individually or in a group. Students must choose a role and take an active role or improvise for part of the activity. The roles which follow are suggestions only; you may choose to develop your own tasks with students.

• Individual: George explaining his feelings about killing Lennie.
• Paired: A celebrity being interviewed on a chat show.
• Group: Mother, father, daughter and daughter's boyfriend, discussing the daughter's pregnancy.

Guidance on carrying out the tasks

• The first step should be to share the assessment criteria with the students. For example, students should know that the assessment criteria for "Communicating and Adapting Language" require students to use Standard English. The assessment criteria for "Interacting and Responding" require students to listen closely and attentively, make significant contributions and to engage with others.
• You should then make it clear what is expected from the task that you set. For example, if they are to talk to an audience about an interest or hobby, they should consider how they are going to engage the audience, use non-verbal features of communication and use appropriate vocabulary.
• Students should be given time to prepare for each of the assessments. While this might be obvious for the Communicating and Adapting Language task, and the

Creating and Sustaining Roles task, students should also be encouraged to prepare for the Interacting and Responding task.
• Speaking and Listening assessments provide opportunities for self-assessment and peer-assessment. Students should be encouraged to learn from their experiences. The assessment criteria should be shared with the students to encourage them to consider how their performances could have been improved.
• Students will improve their speaking and listening skills with practice. Consequently, they should be given more than one opportunity to meet the assessment criteria.

The mark scheme

It is absolutely essential that you study the assessment criteria for each of the assessment tasks. You will use the assessment criteria to mark your students' work, and the assessment criteria will be used by the moderator when moderating your students' work. This section identifies some of the key features of the assessment criteria, and considers the implications for teaching.

1. Communicating and Adapting Language

• Students need to communicate information, ideas and feelings, promoting issues and points of view. The complexity of the subject matter is rewarded.
• They need to be assessed talking in a variety of situations and audiences, adapting their talk appropriately.
• They should use standard English, a range of well-judged vocabulary and use controlled grammatical structures.

Implications for teaching

Students need to be encouraged to select tasks that allow them to offer feelings and to promote issues and points of view. They should also be directed away from tasks that would not allow them to be credited for the complexity of the material. They need to be given a range of opportunities to communicate information in different situations and to different audiences. They should be clear that under some circumstances Standard English is the most appropriate form of English to use.

2. Interacting and Responding

• Students need to listen attentively and respond perceptively.
• They should make significant contributions that move the discussion forward.
• They should engage with others' ideas and feelings, recognising obvious bias or prejudice.

Implications for teaching:

Students need practise at working collaboratively in groups. Discussion topics need to be interesting enough to encourage students to engage in discussion. Students should be given time to prepare their own responses to group discussion topics before the group discussions take place. The criteria that will be used to assess students' contributions need to be made explicit. Students need to be taught how to engage appropriately in group discussion.

3. Creating and Sustaining Roles
- Students should use language, gesture and movement to create and sustain characters.
- They should contribute to the development of situations and ideas, demonstrating understanding of the issues and relationships explored while in role.

Implications for teaching

Students should be given opportunities to study how professional actors use speech, gesture and movement to create characters. They should also be given opportunities to explore how actors respond to each other. For students to demonstrate understanding of issues and relationships, the tasks that they undertake should be sufficiently challenging.

Spoken Language Study

This is a completely new form of study for GCSE.

Tasks

Two tasks will be set each year and students must complete one of them. The tasks will be made available before the start of the academic year and will be valid for both the January and June examination series.

Students will be able to choose one of the two set tasks, although in practice it might be that you choose one of the tasks and teach it as a whole class activity. Some resources will be provided by Edexcel, but you could also produce your own resources or students could research their own resources.

Students can prepare their response, with support from yourself and other students. However, they should write up their response in not more than two hours, under controlled conditions. Their response can be up to 1000 words.

Here is an example of a Spoken Language Study Task:

Using two examples of spoken language, comment on the way teenagers adapt their spoken language to suit the situation.

You should comment on:
- How the purpose of the spoken language affects the way it is used
- How language use influences other speakers and listeners
- The level of formality
- The use of slang
- Who speaks most if there is more than one speaker.

Guidance on carrying out the tasks

Many students will not have engaged with formal spoken language study before. Consequently, it is important that they understand what is expected of them and how they will be assessed.

Two key features of the assessment criteria for the Spoken Language Study are:
- the awareness that spoken language changes according to context
- the awareness that someone's use of language may influence other speakers and listeners.

These features will have an impact on the examples of speech that students select for their study. It is important that the students choose two examples that are from different contexts so that they can illustrate how language changes according to context. These features will also have an impact on the focus of students' analysis. Students need to consider not only the use of language, but also the impact it has on other speakers and listeners.

When students have been given the spoken language study task, time should be spent on analysing what might be expected. You will need to consider whether it would be appropriate for students to research their own resources. It might be that students at the Core level will benefit from using the resources that will be provided by Edexcel. This would give you an opportunity to direct students towards appropriate resources of an appropriate length.

You should model how spoken language can be analysed. At this stage it will also be important to consider in detail two different examples of spoken language so that students learn how to compare spoken language from different contexts.

While students prepare their responses to the spoken language task you are able to engage with them. At this stage of their work it might be appropriate to share the assessment criteria and encourage them to consider how they might improve their analysis. For example, Band 3 requires students to offer "sound exemplification" while "thorough exemplification" could move their work into Band 4.

When students work under controlled conditions to complete their final written response, they will be able to take in notes, but these must not include a pre-prepared draft. Students will need to be shown how to make appropriate and helpful notes. These should be organised to reflect the bullet points of the assessment task.

The mark scheme

It is absolutely essential that you study the assessment criteria for each of the assessment tasks. You will use the assessment criteria to mark your students' work, and the assessment criteria will be used by the moderator when moderating your students' work. This section identifies some of the key features of the assessment criteria, and considers the implications for teaching.

- Students need to understand the ways in which spoken language changes according to context.
- They need to support their comments with examples from source material.
- They need to understand the ways in which language use can influence other speakers and listeners.

Implications for teaching:
Spoken language study will be new for most students. You will need to model how to analyse spoken language. The choice of source material will be important – the two extracts will need to illustrate how language changes with context. You will need to model how to use examples from the source material in order to support your analysis.

Writing for the Spoken Voice

The requirements for this aspect of Unit 3 are similar to the original writing coursework you may previously have assessed students on, so you are likely to be familiar with preparing students for this style of writing.

Tasks

In common with the Spoken Language Study, the tasks will be made available before the start of the academic year and will be valid for both the January and June examination series.

Edexcel will provide three controlled assessment tasks. Students must answer one of these tasks. These tasks will be very general and so you will be able to make them relevant to your students' requirements. Students can prepare their response, with support from yourself and other students. However, they should write up their response in not more than two hours, under controlled conditions.

Here are some examples of Writing for the Spoken Voice tasks:

> 1. Write a script that contains between 30 seconds and two minutes of spoken language for:
>   a TV soap **OR**
>   a radio drama **OR**
>   a stage play.
> 2. Write a speech of up to 1000 words in support of a topic of your choice in a debate.
> 3. Write a story of up to 1000 words in which direct speech is a key focus.

Guidance on carrying out the tasks

In their response to this task students need to demonstrate their ability to:

- Understand that different media work in different ways
- Understand the needs of different audiences and purposes.

The first thing that students need to do is to listen to examples of the genre in which they choose to write. For example, if they are writing a TV soap they should study how the characters interact, how they speak and how scenes change.

The students should also study the writing conventions of the genre in which they choose to write. For example, if they choose to write a radio play they will need to know how to set out the play, and how this is different to a conventional stage play. Examples of scripts can be found on the Internet.

The students should also study the conventions of writing for the spoken voice. For example, speakers might interrupt each other, and so not all speech utterances are completed, and ellipsis is common.

While students prepare their responses for the Writing for the Spoken Voice task you are able to engage with them. At this stage of their work it might be appropriate to share the assessment criteria to illustrate how they will be assessed. For example, a sense of purpose and audience is important, as is a sense of structure. The technical accuracy of their work is also important.

When students work under controlled conditions to complete their final written response, they will be able to take in notes, but these must not include a pre-prepared draft. Students will need to be shown how to make appropriate and helpful notes.

The mark scheme

It is absolutely essential that you study the assessment criteria for each of the assessment tasks. You will use the assessment criteria to mark your students' work, and the assessment criteria will be used by the moderator when moderating your students' work. This section identifies some of the key features of the assessment criteria, and considers the implications for teaching.

- Students should demonstrate a clear sense of purpose and audience.
- They should use well chosen vocabulary and show evidence of crafting in the construction of sentences.
- Their writing should be structured effectively, with the successful use of cohesive devices.
- Their spelling should be accurate, and punctuation devices should be used to demonstrate emphasis and effect.

Implications for teaching
Students will have some choice of task. They should spend time studying the stylistic devices associated with whichever genre they are going to write in. They should be taught how to structure a narrative. They should be encouraged to consider the style of their writing as well as the content. They should be encouraged to check their work for technical accuracy.

The CD-ROM that accompanies this Teacher Guide provides fully customisable versions of the lesson plans and associated worksheets.

Important notice

This product is suitable for use on a Windows® PC only. It will not run on Macintosh OS X.

System requirements

- OS: Windows XP* sp2. RAM: 512MB (1GB for Vista) 1GHz processor (2GHz for Vista)
- Microsoft Office 2003*, Adobe Flash Player 9*, Adobe Reader 8*, Internet Explorer 7*/Firefox 3
- Screen display minimum 1024x768 at 32bpp

*or later versions

Playing the product / Standalone Installation

This product may be installed to your computer.

When you insert the disc into your CD/DVD drive, the launcher should start automatically giving you the option to play or install the product.

If it does not, please follow these steps:

– Double-click 'My computer'

– Right-click the CD/DVD drive

– Choose 'Explore'

– Double-click 'Launcher.exe' and follow the on-screen instructions

Network installation

For network installation and RM Networks deployments, please review the relevant section of the Readme.txt file located on the disc.

Note that server-based installations of software powered by ActiveTeach must reside on a mapped network drive.

VLE hosting

The VLE pack(s) that support this product are available for download from:

http://vlepacks.pearson.com

Please review the 'Readme.txt' within the VLE folder on the disc for additional information.